JN 6581 CUL

# Cultural Diversity in Russian Cities

# Space and Place

Bodily, geographic, and architectural sites are embedded with cultural knowledge and social value. The Anthropology of Space and Place series provides ethnographically rich analyses of the cultural organization and meanings of these sites of space, architecture, landscape, and places of the body. Contributions to this series will examine the symbolic meanings of space and place, the cultural and historical processes involved in their construction and contestation, and how they are in dialogue with wider political, religious, social, and economic institutions.

# CULTURAL DIVERSITY IN RUSSIAN CITIES

## The Urban Landscape in the post-Soviet Era

Edited by
**Cordula Gdaniec**

*Berghahn Books*
New York • Oxford

First published in 2010 by

*Berghahn Books*

www.berghahnbooks.com

©2010 Cordula Gdaniec

**Library of Congress Cataloging-in-Publication Data**

Cultural diversity in Russian cities : the urban landscape in the post-Soviet era /
edited by Cordula Gdaniec.
 p. cm.
 Includes bibliographical references and index.
 ISBN 978-1-84545-665-8 (hardback : alk. paper)
 1. Cultural pluralism—Russia (Federation)—History. 2. Imperialism—Social
aspects—Russia (Federation)—History. 3. Rationalization (Psychology)—Political
aspects—Russia (Federation)—History. 4. Language and culture—Russia
(Federation) I. Gdaniec, Cordula.
 JN6581.C85 2010
 304.800947'091732--dc22

2010007450

**British Library Cataloguing in Publication Data**

A catalogue record for this book is available from the British Library


Printed in the United States on acid-free paper.

ISBN: 978-1-84545-665-8 Hardback

# ❧ CONTENTS ❧

# ⚡ FIGURES ⚡

# ❧ PREFACE AND ACKNOWLEDGEMENTS ❧

This book is a result of activities within a four-year research project based at Humboldt University Berlin funded by the German Research Foundation, DFG. Under the title 'Urban culture and ethnic representation: Berlin and Moscow as emerging world cities' my colleague Alexa Färber and I endeavoured to research various aspects of urban culture in two capitals during a process of transformation since the fall of the Berlin Wall and the collapse of the Soviet Union respectively. Both can be regarded, and in fact present themselves, as world cities but this status has different connotations in each city with respect to the weighting of the role of culture and cultural production vis-à-vis the economy and politics. We examined different facets of urban culture in connection with ethnic representation in the metropolis of late modernity. In particular we looked at how cultural production and ethnic representation are being instrumentalised in discursive strategies on the level of urban policy and city marketing, how cultural production plays an increasing role within the economy in forming niches for small and micro businesses especially for cultural groups outside the social urban mainstream, and how cultural production opens up spaces of participation in and identification with the city.

The project included several workshops and cooperation with other researchers, as well as with practitioners and artists from different countries. One of these workshops, *Public/private spaces – an urban culture of diversity?*, which we organised in Moscow at the Russian State University for the Humanities (RGGU), served as starting point for this volume. A number of ethnographic case studies of cultural practices from Moscow and Berlin were presented, some of which appear here. As the book took shape over the following years, more contributors joined us at a later stage.

The research project and, by extension, this book project has greatly benefited from the cooperation in particular with the RGGU as our Moscow base, with the researchers at REGION Research Centre in Ulyanovsk and with the researchers at the Centre for Independent Social Research in St. Petersburg. Organising workshops is one thing, but putting together an edited book quite another. I am indebted to Anika Keinz for her great editorial assistance and her encouragement to see this book project through to the end. Working together with the authors has been a valuable experience and I am thankful that they contributed their interesting case studies. I am also grateful to Graham Stack for his translation work and to the copy editors at Berghahn Books for polishing the manuscript. And, last but not least, I would like to thank Alexa Färber for her inspiring collegiality over the course of the project and since, as well as Wolfgang Kaschuba as project leader for his support.

# ⚜ 1 ⚜

# Cultural Diversity between Staging and the Everyday

*Experiences from Moscow, St. Petersburg
and Other Russian Cities.
An Introduction*

## CORDULA GDANIEC

A poster depicting flowers – but, interestingly, not people – and bearing the caption 'the city consists of different people (*gorod – edinstvo nepokhozhikh*)' can be seen in every Moscow metro station. The original Aristotle quote continues 'similar people cannot form a city'. This implies that urban culture is necessarily diverse, multi-faceted, often contradictory, even conflicting. Cities are built on and develop through cultural diversity. More specifically, this poster indicates a unique situation in Moscow where, as the mayor quotes on the website of the House of Nationalities, 'diversity is our wealth and beauty, and not a problem'[1], but where immigrants, or so-called *priezzhie* (newcomers, people who have moved to Moscow), are increasingly made to feel that they are only visitors or passers-by, who will not be given rights of the city or made to feel at home. These two quotes and the way they are presented are indicative of how cultural diversity is *managed* in Moscow, and in Russia more generally, on a discursive, official level that largely bypasses the realities of the multicultural everyday[2] in Russian cities and that also constitutes a global form of cosmopolitanism (Evans/Foord 2006). At many intersections of the urban landscape with its temporal axes these three levels, of course, merge or overlap, and cultural diversity is socially produced, implicitly, or even as part of the city's image strategy, by actors from the various groups of interest. Still, in every city there remains a discrepancy between an official rhetoric embracing on the one hand cultural diversity as cultural capital for the city and social capital for its inhabitants, and on the other hand the everyday experience of exclusion and racism or homophobia by the people embodying diversity. In Russian cities today this discrepancy appears to be greater compared to Soviet times and different in its causes and manifestations in comparison with cities in western Europe. However, many trends are rooted in current global flows and transformations, highlighting emerging similarities.

## Diversity as Cultural Capital

Every city manages its intrinsic ethnic and cultural mix in a different way. While all cities are spatial and cultural manifestations of their multicultural society, representing a heterogeneous urban landscape as well as multiculturalism or cultural-diversity politics, some actively foster this cultural capital on several levels. With respect to the policy terms (and tools) 'diversity management' and 'diversity mainstreaming' (Fager 2006; Jung 2003), managing cultural diversity, in the context of this introduction, plays out on three levels: 1) that of city government and policy as well as public discourse facilitated by economic agents, state-run or private media; 2) that of organisations representing, or claiming to do so, ethnic or cultural minority groups; and 3) that of everyday social, economic or cultural practices. In Berlin, for instance, cultural diversity plays a central role in city marketing, in urban policy and in people's choice to either move to or visit Berlin (Färber 2005). The city authority's self-representation as an attractive business location and tourist spot, or the events listings (see *Zitty* and *tip* magazines), are testament to this cultivation of diversity as a positive and profitable aspect of Berlin culture (Knecht and Soysal 2005; Lanz 2007; Berlin Partner). Other cities promote their multicultural aspects only on an official and discursive level, and the existing multitude of different lifestyles and groups is tolerated rather than seen to actively constitute cultural capital. Moscow, for example, belongs to this latter group. In an age of cultural and economic globalisation and increasing transnationalism of people's lives, cultural diversity in the city is becoming an ever more important topic within certain branches of the economy, in politics, and, not least, in the everyday lives of the city's inhabitants (Hannerz 1993, 2000; McDowell 1999). It is also an increasingly urgent item on policy agendas as social and economic problems are becoming more and more racialised.

Beneath the official and public discourse of multiculturalism and tolerance in cities there lies, of course, an everyday where these discourses are taken as given and 'function' without any problem but are also experienced as intolerance and racism. Certain groups that do not form part of mainstream local or national culture (e.g., beggars, labour migrants, gays, subcultural youth) are forced to, or choose to, carve out their own, separate spaces within the city, construct urban niches for themselves, and negotiate visibility or rights within physical or media space. There is always a public sphere in which problems of intolerance and exclusion *can* be discussed and criticised, when they are addressed at all. By public sphere I mean the media, including the Internet and meeting places, such as cafés, NGOs (non-governmental organisations), events or demonstrations.[3] This leads to two important questions for researchers: first, how do city governments and public discourses deal with this increasing multiplicity of urban culture, especially where it results in greater fragmentation of the urban landscape? and, second, how are the different cultures inscribed into the urban landscape? When and where are they present in public space? Where and how do they (have to) carve out their private spaces? The interaction between city governments and 'cultural groups' and the interaction between the appropriation of public space and of private spaces, which involves negotiations about contested spaces and cultures, is a crucial element of urban culture and the development of the social, economic and spatial fabric of the city. These are the questions that the authors in this volume are exploring in their respective case studies.

The authors in this collection present case studies of qualitative ethnographic research in a number of Russian cities on the theme of cultural practices and their spatial manifestation in the city, which I define in this context as urban culture (cf. Hannerz 1993; Zukin 1995). They examine four different perspectives of cultural practices within the urban context: ethnicity, lifestyle/subculture, gender and economic practices. The contributions explore the chances and limitations of various groups in Russian cities, as well as the official discourse on cultural diversity or cultural identity. Through this, they help to imagine how 'open' or 'closed' the respective city might be for diverse groups. A comparison with Western notions of the multicultural city, which was subject of the workshops in Moscow which this collection is based on, highlights the problematics as well as different approaches that can be found among Russian and Western researchers (cf. Malakhov 2007). More precisely, these essays give some insight into the spatial practices of groups of people beyond the Russian cultural mainstream – where and how they become visible (e.g., youth subcultures as explained by Irina Kosterina and Ulia Andreeva), if they choose to be visible at all (which is not necessarily desired, as in the case of lesbians and gays, explored by Katja Sarajeva), where they enter contested spaces (e.g., the spaces of street-level economy in Maria Scattone's contribution) and where they are (or want to be) part of a Russian social space (e.g., African volunteers in social projects as described by Svetlana Boltovskaya or labour migrants in the city as in the chapters by Olga Brednikova, Olga Tkach and Larisa Kosygina).

Because cities foster the development of culturally diverse environments, providing spatial and social niches for diverse cultural groups, the urban context is central to this book, and the various case studies seem to illustrate the concept of the city as assemblage (Venn 2006). Different temporalities and spatialities exist in cities side by side, which means urban niches for some and problems for others. In terms of governance this means management – in other words, control – of those elements of urban culture that fall outside the accepted, official (or mainstream) idea of the city. Those city dwellers *in* the perceived other spatialities or temporalities form part of the city, representing a normalcy of urban culture through their own everyday experience but also sometimes being aware of their anathema standing vis-à-vis the hegemonic structure. These Others, sometimes self-identified marginals, are not only migrants – i.e., representatives of the globalised or transnational urban population who are most visible – but also, and not to be neglected, other cultural minorities such as lesbians and gays, youth in subcultures, members of alternative cultures, members of minority religions, the disabled or representatives of low socio-economic status which together make up the social fabric of the large city. When looking at these populations and their positioning within the social space of the city one automatically also addresses policy issues and issues of power structures. With the city in a constant state of transformation, and not only in post-Soviet transformation, it is difficult to answer questions; or rather, the researcher keeps on discovering new important questions.

## Managing Cultural Diversity in Moscow – Official Discourse, Public Rhetoric and Everyday Practices

'There is this nationality: gastarbaiter' ran the headline of an article in *Komsomolskaya Pravda* discussing the newly published novel, entitled with the Russian term for labour migrants leaned from the German word *Gastarbeiter* ('guest worker', Steshin 2007). The autobiographical novel by Eduard Bagirov appeared at a time when the issue of labour migrants and social problems associated with their increasing presence in Russian cities had reached a peak in the Russian and foreign media. The year 2006 was marked by a number of incidents involving migrants and people perceived as such, including numerous attacks and even murders based on racist motives (see Boltovskaya in this volume and Gdaniec 2008). Furthermore, the *Rodina* (Homeland) party created negative headlines during the Duma election campaign in autumn 2005 with a video that expressed the allegedly grow-

**Fig. 1.1:** 'The city is made up of different people', Moscow. Photograph by the author, 2006.

ing public sentiment that 'Russia belongs to Russians' (Siegl 2005; WCIOM Sep. 2006). Bagirov's story of arriving in Moscow from Turkmenistan and finding first work through small ads in the papers in the semi-legal world of dubious retail firms in the mid-1990s is interesting not only for its insider description of this part of the post-Soviet retail and service economy but also for its frank account of the personal experience of everyday racism (see, e.g., 105f, 125ff). Thus, at a time of a steep increase in violent incidents, real and reported, there has also come a heightened awareness of xenophobia in Russian cities, especially St. Petersburg and Moscow. The novel's publication was accompanied by a large-scale media and advertising campaign, prompting critical discussions of the subject in the media, the quality of which was new in the otherwise conservative Russian media not renowned for their awareness of this subject. Indeed, the media have been proven to play an important role in reproducing stereotyping and prejudices through their use of language and slant in reporting (based on discourse analysis of Moscow media within the Berlin-Moscow research project; see also Karpenko 2002; Malkova 2005). The book title alone is a confrontation of this subject in the 'megapolis' Moscow that has an estimated 12 million inhabitants, an increasing proportion of whom have moved there, but where native residents (*korennye Moskvichi*) still maintain a certain snobbism (Bagirov 2007: 84; see also Gdaniec and Ovchinnikova 2006) that places 'Others' firmly in a separate category.[4] In popular discourse they are not even considered residents of the city, a fact that was sorely brought to attention through comments by Moscow mayor Yuri Luzhkov in response to the accident at Baumansky Market in February 2006. The roof of the market building collapsed under a heavy load of snow in the very early hours, which meant that those who were buried under the rubble had slept at their work place. There were many casualties, injured and several dead, and the mayor very quickly announced that 'only a few Muscovites had suffered' (various press, e.g., Tichomirowa 2006). While it emerged in subsequent media coverage that the deceased were originally from Azerbaijan it is also clear to those who know how Russian markets are run that these transnational migrants have a base in Moscow, that they may well consider Moscow their home and that they are spending or have already spent a considerable amount of time, part of their life in Moscow (cf. Brednikova and Tkach in this volume; see Gessen 2006). It is an unwieldy bureaucracy and popular discourse that prevent migrants from acquiring citizens' rights or even legal status as resident. Even when they have the necessary documents they are still discursively constructed as outsiders, as marginals, as the term 'gastarbaiter' indicates.[5] This trend to exclude migrants from city spaces culminated in a law preventing people not holding a Russian passport from working in markets. It came into effect in April 2007, with the immediate result of some markets closing altogether and the others being left half empty (see Brednikova and Tkach in this volume).

It is within this setting that we need to consider the current official staging of the multicultural city. The most prominent space on the official multicultural scene is the Moscow House of Nationalities (*Moskovskii Dom Natsional'nostei*, or MDN), which opened after long and heated discussions in October 2003 (Khabenskaya and Filippov 2007). This House is a representational object of Moscow city government for its multicultural commitment and a physical space for associations of ethnic communities. However, it provides room only for associations that claim to represent the interests of their respective diaspora by trying to preserve the traditional ethnic culture, and many are shaped by the personal interests of their chairmen (Khabenskaya and Filippov 2007: 3). When visiting the MDN I found it difficult to access and was provided little information. On entering the restored nineteenth-century *usadba,* or manor house, you are greeted by two security guards who will permit your entry only if you have an appointment or are on the list of invited guests for an event, and only after they have checked your passport. I had an appointment with one of the higher-ranking civil servants there to find out about their programme, their aims. After a near interrogation about the Berlin House of World Cultures (HKW), which the civil servant regarded as a model for the MDN and sought to establish contact with, I was offered a little book about the history of the building and an issue of the city government bulletin which included information about the administration of the MDN. I also got a tour of the building with its conference hall, offices and the corridors which would host exhibitions by artists representing various ethnic cultures. What I did not receive was a programme or mission statement, and subsequent research revealed that there is none. The events taking place at the MDN are not open to the *general* public, as they are not generally advertised and they lack a common theme. Like the atmosphere in the House, they exude a Soviet-style, hierarchical and ideological quality. Events included a seminar series 'Inter-ethnic consent and safety in society', a round table on 'Spiritual and material culture of the Buryats', a concert to celebrate the Day of the Defender of the Fatherland and a meeting of the group organising the 'Days of Slavic Writing and Culture in Moscow' (Khabenskaya and Filippov 2007: 7). Interviews with members of various ethnic minorities in Moscow indicated that this sort of paternalistic representation of ethnic communities was not desired by many representatives and that they clearly did not (want to) belong to a community, or that one cannot speak of 'the Armenian community', etc. Except in virtual space, that is, on the Internet, the House of Nationalities is largely invisible in Moscow as it does not figure on the cultural landscape, neither in the *What's On* magazines nor on posters.

Once a year the official multiethnicity of the city does enter a visible central stage, though: The official celebrations of City Day (*Den' Goroda*) take place on Tverskaya, Moscow's main street, in front of the mayoralty. Only invited guests are allowed on the tribune and the entire section of Tverskaya is closed off for half the day, heavily guarded by police and OMON.[6] Those who are interested can watch the show on *TV Tsentr,* City Hall's television station. In this highly staged event the mayor presents himself not just

alongside other Moscow political figures but also next to the Patriarch of
the Russian Orthodox Church. On the stage, below the statue of Yuri Dol-
goruky, the city's founding father, dance ensembles and bands perform traditional folkloristic pieces. Apart from traditional Russian costumes, music
and dance there are some performances of Other ethnic folklore, which
amounts to an official demonstration of the multiethnicity that is the city's
'wealth' (see above). Another item on the programme is the annual award
ceremony for 'the best in their professions', in which a number of citizens
are rewarded for outstanding professional achievements. The pictures thus
produced form part of the city's imaginary that is still deeply rooted in
Soviet iconography and policy: Moscow as the centre of the multinational
Soviet Union and the communist world, with connotations of the capital
of an empire, which it clearly was before the Russian Revolution. Whether
this stage is in actual fact more visible than the MDN is debatable. The programme of all the festivities includes many stages throughout the central
city and at least one in each administrative district with different musical
and other shows which are not explicitly dedicated to the multicultural city.
Most central streets are closed to traffic for the day, which renders the city
almost eerily quiet for usually it is teeming with traffic. People walk along
them selling small Russian and Moscow flags. Many families with children
and groups of youth enjoy a day out. At the same time as people are stroll-

Fig. 1.2: One of the many posters advertising City Day, Moscow. Photograph
by the author, 2005.

ing around, workers of the municipal services are already out there sweeping the streets, collecting the litter. They are conspicuous not only because of their bright orange vests but also because they all appear to be migrant workers from Central Asia. This is one indication that the 'real' – i.e., lived – multiethnic city is to be found in a different space, at a different level from that constructed on the city government stages. Still, the festivities of City Day do constitute a platform, albeit temporally and spatially restricted, on which certain meaning is inscribed in the city constituting a cultural practice that I call urban ritual.[7]

An interesting comparison to these annual festivities is the 1000th anniversary celebrations of Kazan, the capital of Tatarstan in August 2005. As the largest of the republics in the Russian Federation, and with Tatars representing the largest non-Russian ethnic group in Moscow and other cities and regions, Tatarstan and its capital have been imbued with symbolism to represent the multicultural nature of Russia. In her analysis of the Kazan millennium, Kate Graney demonstrates how this date was used as a stage for cementing Tatarstan's political status in the Federation in a show for Moscow's benefit and also for a local public. Within this staging from above, the multiethnic composition of Kazan played a key role. In the run-up to the anniversary many historic buildings were restored and new buildings were constructed in order to revive historic meaning – Kazan as the 'ancient Tatar metropole' – and simultaneously to align the city in a global network of modern cities. Central to this was the restoration of the Kazan Kremlin, symbolising the multicultural nature of the city in which Tatar and Russian, Muslim and Orthodox, Eastern and Western and/or Asian and European cultures have existed side by side for centuries (Graney 2007). This image is especially significant in view of the fact that Tatars form a minority in Russian cities, that there *they* present the Eastern 'Other', albeit the largest and arguably most assimilated group, with the most visible and historically rooted cultural landmarks in Moscow's cityscape – historic mosques and the historic Tatar district in the city centre.

The way in which multiculturalism is staged in Moscow on the official level seems to reflect a post-modern type of urban 'imagineering' (Kaschuba 2005; Färber 2008) that is found in most large cities that today need to draw on their cultural capital to be successful in political and economic terms. Moscow differs, however, in terms of a world or global city with the Western notion of producing an image of a positive urban multiculturalism and cultural creativity in order to generate economic clout. This type of city marketing (the example of Berlin as mentioned above) seems to be unnecessary in Moscow at this stage (Medetsky/Mereu 2006, Leonov et al 2006). Researching Moscow as a world city in the cultural sense (Hannerz 1993) and looking through the Berlin perspective has revealed the limitations of this concept and the fact that it is a very Western concept. The positioning of Moscow not on the periphery of the Western cities network but at the centre of the post-Soviet space (including countries in Africa, Asia and Latin America) and on the periphery of a burgeoning Asian urban and economic sphere invites considering a different analytical lens: Moscow could be regarded as a postimperial city (King 2006). Russian cities seem to evade the euro-centric dichotomy of Western / non-Western, European / colonial. Rather, they can be constructed as forming part of their own system of central / peripheral, Russian / non-Russian within the post-Soviet space. The phenomenon of increasing labour migration of people from the former Soviet Union to Russian cities, in particular the two capitals, Moscow and St. Petersburg, supports this perspective. Continuing migration of people from the global south – for higher education, business and a minority as refugees – together with an increased wealth generation in and migration of labour migrants from the Western world (who are not called such but 'expats') to the two capitals is, in the particular form it takes, another indicator of a post-colonial city. Furthermore, there are increasing numbers of Russian 'expats' abroad, often based on settlements dating back to Soviet times, such as 'Petit Moscou' in Conakry, the capital of Guinea, for instance. This analytical perspective requires further exploration, but not within this book.

As mentioned above, the setting in which the articles in this volume need to be read is one of prejudice and intolerance on a generalised level in Russia. It might be that the number of incidents of racial or other harassment have not actually increased but that reporting and discussion of this topic have. While the novel *Gastarbaiter* was a well advertised piece of literature critically dealing with this topic, the subject matter has also found its way into Russian films recently. Here it is shown only in certain scenes rather than as theme of the whole film. In '*Mne ne bolno*' (It doesn't hurt, Alexei Balabanov 2006), for instance, there is a scene of everyday life, almost in the background which makes it all the more striking: In a fast food pavilion, one of the better kiosks, not quite shops or restaurants, by a metro station in central St. Petersburg on Navy Day (*Den' voenno-morskogo flota*) the main protagonist of the film witnesses a couple of sailors racially abusing the Uzbek-looking woman serving them. In a bold statement by the filmmakers, the protagonist is appalled and decides to teach one of the sailors a lesson, picking up his food and tipping it out into his lap.

It is in these mundane places of the city where cultural diversity is managed without any statement, without any programme of multiculturalism, where it is 'lived' – on the metro, around kiosks, in art galleries, in restaurants, at university, at home and on markets. In my research I have chosen markets and shopping malls as places within the urban structure in which one can observe everyday practices of consumption and leisure, official representation strategies as well as manifestations of the post-Soviet migration phenomenon. Moscow's food markets – the former Kolkhoz markets – have become symbols of the city's multiethnic composition and of post-Soviet migration processes. The markets, together with their managers and traders, evoke strong 'ethnic' connotations in the minds of many (Russian) Muscovites, and are often associated with the 'migration problem' (Vendina 1999; Malkova 2001). It is particularly since the first bombs were detonated in Moscow in 1996, the start of a series of terrorist attacks in the city, that the markets have been negatively associated with 'Caucasians' (not to be confused with the English term for whites) in popular discourse, and thus with crime and terrorism. The markets represent everyday life and routine shopping practices. Although the food and atmosphere contain ethnic, even exotic references through the produce on sale and the form of display, they do not seem to add any symbolic value to the actual goods or practices, as is the case with less everyday goods sold in restaurants, cafés or specialist shops: meals, shishas, accessories. Inside the produce markets I noticed a feeling of normality rather than marginality, reminiscent of the Soviet situation when people from the Caucasus and Central Asia were, just like Russians, Soviet citizens. They still represented the 'Other' and the East but, as they were not foreign citizens and movement within the Union was state-controlled, they were framed differently. Since the break-up of the USSR citizens of the other republics have become de facto foreigners in Russia, even if they feel completely at home there, and are framed as migrants, thus becoming marginals not only discursively. Outside this setting of the market, the space of everyday consumption, however, people from the Caucasus or Central Asia become part of a mass of people who many Russians find, if not threatening, at least suspicious. The markets, paradoxically, represent two types of space in Moscow today: one in which migrants are accepted, within the defined social space of trading, which is in contrast to the city space at large; and another that represents a non-place (Marc Augé 1994) which many Muscovites try to avoid because they associate it with crime and fear or, if they have to go there, pass through it with the least possible contact.[8]

In the perception of African students I interviewed at the Peoples' Friendship University (RUDN), the city of Moscow as a whole appears as a non-place. Marc Augé describes places of transit and transport, as well as places of consumption, as non-places to contrast them with anthropological places which are marked by identity, relations and history (Augé 1994: 92), inscribed with meaning and produced socially. Two important features of a non-place are control at the point of entry and exit of such a place and the loss of individuality and relation (Augé 1994: 120f). These characteristics apply also in the case of the African students in Moscow. For African students, Moscow is a stepping stone in their biography. They intend to move through the city on their way from Africa to the West where they expect to find better career prospects than in Africa or Russia. They need to legitimise themselves not only on entering and leaving the city and/or the country, involving a lot of bureaucracy with obtaining entry as well as exit visas, grants, registration, but are subject to random document checks by the Moscow police and easy targets for bribe extortion because of their distinct Otherness and unfavourable socio-economic situation (Amnesty International 2003).

For fear of racist attacks, of which every interviewee could tell a tale, the students had constructed their own Moscow world, on campus and within a transnational social network heavily dependent on the Internet. The RUDN campus has evolved into a microcosm city within the city which the interviewees do not often leave (Gdaniec 2008). Nevertheless, African students do not represent themselves within a discourse of victimisation. Their 'village' (*studenchesky gorodok*) possesses all important amenities, even specialist shops (e.g., 'Indian Spices') and a rich cultural life attracting an audience from outside its boundaries. For example, on May Day every year the students organise a big international festival, where there are regular sports competitions and numerous groups organise cultural events on campus or tour the country. On the one hand this represents normalcy of life in a city of Moscow's scale, on the other the pictures thus produced can be used to reinforce the marginalisation of RUDN students. The May Day festival, for instance, is described as turning the campus into the 'model of an ideal world' (Mozhaev 2005) which is at once reminiscent of the socialist International and an example of post-Soviet cosmopolitanism. Although this is Moscow, it is 'already not Moscow', representing a completely different form of urban culture, of cosmopolitanism than what can be witnessed in the city as a whole (Mozhaev 2005). Thus, cultural diversity in Moscow is produced and managed continually by a whole range of actors – actors on the official level, in the media and research institutions – as well as on the level of everyday practices.

## Post-Soviet and Global Trends: Cultural Diversity in Russian Cities

The development of policies concerning cultural diversity and of urban cultural practices themselves is clearly shaped by global cultural flows (Hannerz 1993), but also by what I describe as post-Soviet practices, as indicated in the examples above. This intertwining of post-Soviet and global developments is also clearly visible in retail patterns and consumption culture more generally, including café and restaurant scenes, as well as in the music, youth and subcultural scenes and can be found not only in Moscow and St. Petersburg but also in other Russian cities. The articles in this collection each describe and analyse certain perspectives on the current state of cultural practices in urban space. Each delivers one case study on a group, a phenomenon or a space that is a constituent part of cultural diversity and that can be described as diverse in itself. This is framed within a wider discussion of (urban) policy and theoretical concepts, tracing the ways in which public spaces are used and private spaces are constituted. As the articles demonstrate, analyses of cultural diversity – i.e., of policy as well as social, economic and cultural practices which all produce diversity – have to pay careful attention to representation and image(s).

The authors presented in this collection come from different disciplinary backgrounds – geography, sociology and anthropology – and from different cultural backgrounds – Russia, western Europe and the USA. This reflects cultural diversity on another level – in the composition of the articles and in the different approaches to the research subjects and to writing about the findings. The ways in which issues of ethnic and cultural groups, migrants and implicit marginality are framed differ in each chapter, thus inviting the reader to reflect on discursive production or deconstruction of marginals rather than offering a set opinion (cf. note 5).

All case studies refer to the three levels of analysis introduced above – policy and public discourse; organisations and lobbies; everyday practices, albeit with different emphasis. A subject on which all three levels of analysis meet is urban development projects which involve city government, planning commissions, large businesses, investors and medium-size enterprises and, at the other end, the consumers. Developments for the rapidly growing retail, service and finance economies are the most conspicuous in Russian cities today. While the building boom, which continues unabated, encompasses an enormous volume of housing construction, it is the (semi-) public buildings that have a bigger impact on the city's image, representation and the divisions of urban space, affecting people's everyday practices directly. The topic of urban planning thus forms a background to all articles to a certain extent, and one article deals with this topic in more detail. Megan Dixon's discussion of 'Chinese' spaces in St. Petersburg goes beyond the level of state involvement and large-scale business, focusing on Chinese restaurants in the central city landscape and on everyday practices of Chinese businessmen and students in relation to their uses of urban space. Her empirical data and analysis show clearly how complex the situation is concerning Chinese migrants. On the one hand they are representatives of an economically successful country and themselves have a high social status (middle class, successful business owners, university students) associated with Western lifestyle, but on the other hand they represent the Eastern Other and become subject to discrimination. 'Chinese' spaces in central St. Petersburg are simultaneously perceived as exotic and as threatening to Russians. Restaurants reproduce the commodification of ethnic and hybrid culture and are thus a component part of the contemporary urban fabric accessible to everybody. This perception, however, can shift very quickly, and the spaces labelled 'Chinese' by Russians can as easily be read as exclusive and inaccessible to Russians. This chapter also highlights another interesting issue – the position of Russia vis-à-vis (western) Europe and Asia. While Russia is western Europe's 'East', it constitutes the 'West' in some of the Russians' narratives presented here, thus legitimising a cultural, moral and racial differentiation of Chinese. This shows again that the East is not a geographical but a cultural concept.

In her chapter on racialisation of migrants from former Soviet republics Larisa Kosygina picks up the concept of an imagined East from a different angle. She describes how some of her informants use the racial stereotyping they are confronted with in Russia to their own advantage. This occurs within the setting of commodification of ethnically marked symbolic capital – that is, in restaurants serving Central Asian or Caucasian cuisine or as performers of Oriental art. While the interviewees in Moscow and Novosibirsk all report experiencing everyday racism, they still prefer to stay as foreigners in Russia because of a more favourable economic and social situation (for women, importantly, a more liberal gender order). It can be argued, therefore, that by appropriating the label Eastern/Oriental (*vostochnyi*) for themselves these migrants also contribute to the reproduction of the stereotyping and that this act is not just about empowerment.

Another chapter describes the experiences of labour migrants from the former Soviet Union, in particular, women working on markets in St. Petersburg: Olga Brednikova and Olga Tkach explore the concept of home as produced by these transnational migrants. These women consider themselves as migrants even if they have been living in St. Petersburg or Russia for a number of years because they are not making it their permanent home, instead moving between their place of origin – usually the place where their family lives – and their place of work on a regular basis. The city space for them does not play an important role as their movement through the city is restricted by very long working hours and limited financial means. However, the small social spaces they create within the city at their places of work and residence are all the more important. And yet these too lose significance when put in the context of the women's postmodern nomadic lifestyles.

Another group of people moving in transnational spaces are Africans studying or working in Moscow and St. Petersburg. Svetlana Boltovskaya describes two social spaces within which Africans are trying to make the respective city their, albeit temporary, home. While access to city space for them is characterised by difficulties, the NGO African Unity in St. Petersburg and the Protestant Chaplaincy in Moscow constitute important 'third places' for the Africans active in these organisations. Here they are not only accepted but also needed. For their efforts, they earn not only respect but also material subsistence (e.g., meals in the Soup Kitchen). Furthermore, these niches allow them firstly to mingle with Russians and with other Africans, thus breaking out of their marginalisation as Africans as opposed to city residents; and secondly, to get out of a compartmentalisation of their country of origin and into a wider community of pan-African solidarity, which strengthens their position in Russian society.

As mentioned earlier, cultural diversity in cities is produced not only through ethnic references but through other cultural practices that diverge from a publicly accepted norm or mainstream. The most obvious examples for this category of urban culture are probably youth scenes and alternative subcultures which can be found in public spaces at certain times but which also leave (subtle) visual traces around the streets and buildings, such as grafitti.[9] Irina Kosterina and Ulia Andreeva describe such a place in their chapter – the Fun Box in the centre of Sochi. As a social space this is where identities of different youth scenes are played out and where being a *marginal* provides positive cultural capital. The city of Sochi is of great interest itself because of its geographical location on Russia's border in the Caucasus and its resulting highly charged ethnic mix. Whether this multicultural asset, which is regularly used by (Western) cities in international competitions to host events, has played a part in Sochi's successful bid to stage the 2014 Winter Olympics, is, however, not clear.

One other aspect of cultural diversity that city governments like to use to their advantage in the competition for events and resources is sexual orientation. Tolerance towards lesbians and gays, especially in the visible and marketable form of a gay village or gay pride events are considered cultural capital by many Western city authorities. For instance, the annual gay pride parade in Berlin, Christopher Street Day, was postponed in 2006 in order not to clash with the Football World Cup so that no visitors (i.e., revenue) would be lost. In the same year, gay activists tried to stage the first Russian gay pride event in Moscow which did not even get permission by the city government. In contrast to Berlin, here sexual orientation does not form part of the accepted or visible range of cultural diversity or urban culture nor does it play a positive role in the representations of the city. This (non-)event has, however, sparked a heated debate among gay activists in Russia as to whether this type of outing, perceived as clearly representing Western values and lifestyles, is at all necessary in Russia. This is particularly interesting to researchers because it questions the normative views of tolerance, civil society and democracy as reproduced in EU regulations and public discourse.[10] Katja Sarajeva analyses the geographies of lesbian spaces in Moscow which are produced both in public and in private spaces but which remain largely invisible in the city's landscape, thus producing new aspects of privacy and public-ness. Sarajeva includes a first-hand account of the failed parade and analyses this particular form of representation and use of public and media space by the opposing agencies and national and international media.

Visibility of cultural practices and of individuals representing the Other varies considerably, not only in urban space but also across social tiers. Within the higher social status groups, differentiation on the basis of ethnicity or migrancy is often less explicit or does not have such a negative impact as in the case of lower status groups. Another group constituting urban cultural diversity seems to fall between all these categories. Beggars, or actors within the street-level economy, as Maria Scattone terms them, are visible yet invisible right in the city centre and they exist only in one, the lowest, social tier, constituting a social Other without any ethnic connotations. In her description of two places in central St. Petersburg, an underpass on Nevsky Prospekt and the steps of Kazan Cathedral, Scattone analyses the ways in which beggars appropriate these public spaces and pinpoints different types of social spaces thus produced. This is set against the backdrop of the dramatic developments in St. Petersburg's historic centre regarding retail, service economy, housing and conservation, which is described from different angles in the chapter by Megan Dixon.

Much has been written about multicultural society, and increasingly critically so (see Parekh 2000). This book does not aim to add to this body of literature. Rather, it aims to offer an ethnographic perspective on cultural diversity in Russian cities, which is much more than a diversity of ethnic cultures, by focusing on spatial manifestations of cultural representation and cultural practices. Furthermore, through arranging these particular articles this volume is intended to give food for thought, to strengthen a research perspective that combines Western and Russian points of view. Research on Russian and East European cities often stresses post-socialist aspects as manifested in the vanishing or dismantling of Soviet-era practices and structures, a 'catching-up' with the West or in the re-coding or obliteration of socialist urban landscapes, thereby emphasising their important differences to Western cities. Sometimes, these are stressed at the expense of the growing similarities caused by economic globalisation and global structural changes that affect East and West equally. By focusing on qualitative research, examining cultural, social or economic practices as well as discourses and patterns of representation rather than on the post-Soviet theme, this volume aims to bring post-Soviet and, by implication, East European cities into the wider scholarly arena of urban research. The theme of the book is the interplay of different levels of managing cultural diversity: public and official discourse, staging of cultural diversity and everyday practices which all make up the more or less visible manifestations of cultural diversity in the city. The practices and representations on all three levels are played out in public and private spaces in the city and the points at which they meet – spatially and temporally limited, yet overlapping and blurring boundaries become public spaces of either accord or conflict, as the case may be. The ensuing friction as well as fruitful cooperation occurs, naturally, in every city – East, West or South – but, as with other global phenomena, these processes also have their distinct local flavour.

## NOTES

1. 'Mnogonatsional'nost – eto nashe bogatstvo i krasota, a ne problema', Yu. M. Luzhkov, http://www.mdn.ru/, last accessed 27.01.2008
2. I am using the term 'multicultural' here not in its policy sense (as in 'multiculturalist') but in its de facto meaning of a culturally diverse population. A discussion of this term and its applications is not the subject of this book (see the vast literature on this subject – e.g., David Bennett (ed), *Multicultural States. Rethinking Difference and Identity*, London, 1998).
3. Comparing the various practices of urban culture and ethnic representation in Moscow and Berlin on three levels has shown that the manifestations of cultural diversity and its reverse side, intolerance and exclusion, are largely the same in both cities, currently shaped by the same global processes but that the origins of both and the handling of diversity policies and regulations of intolerance differ, a fact that can be attributed to the different political systems (cf. Kaschuba 2001; Niedermüller 1999; see also final report of the research project or http://www.euroethno.hu-berlin.de/forschung/projeckte/abgeschlossene/berlinmoskan/text).
4. On the book cover Bagirov is called 'best counter-cultural author of the year'; see www.gastabaiter.ru for interviews with the author and newspaper articles, last accessed 07.02.2008.
5. The term 'gastarbaiter' is not necessarily employed in a pejorative way by the speaker. It is routinely used by Russian academics in discussions and in print. The choice of language, however, as well as a certain approach to researching ethnic minorities and diversity issues which reinforces Othering have sparked intense discussions at our workshops. The approach of using politically correct and non-racist language as well as actor-centred research emerged as a west European concept that was clearly at odds with the approach of many

Russian researchers that I spoke with or whose work I read. This topic is by no means exhausted and is reflected in the differing positions of the authors in this collection. (See also V. Voronkov, O. Karpenko, A. Osipov (eds), 'Rasizm v yazyke sotsialnykh nauk' (Racism in the language of the Social Sciences), St. Petersburg, 2002).

6. OMON (acronym for *Otryad Militsii Osobogo Naznacheniya*) is a special force of the *Militsiya* or police, mostly in action as riot squad.

7. City Day brings the contrast between official rhetoric and everyday experiences to the fore but it also allows meeting with otherwise barely visible subcultures, in this case members of the Hip Hop scene, in Russia even marginal among the subculture. To them, it offers the unusual opportunity of celebrating right in the city centre. Both sides are differently inscribed in the city, and inscribed by it.

8. Based on data gained through a survey conducted at *Okhotny Ryad* shopping mall in central Moscow, September 2003, and interviews.

9. For a description of the local manifestations of global alternative cultures and protest movements (DIY cultures) in Moscow and other Russian cities, see the work of Olga Aksyutina, e.g., 'Yesli vy khotite izmenit' gorod – vam nuzhno kontrolirovat' ulitsy'. Prostranstva protesta i udovol'stviya v Moskve' ('If you want to change the city you need to be in charge of the streets'. Spaces of protest and pleasure in Moscow), in Etnicheskie protsessy v stolichnom megapolise, ed V. R. Filippov, Moscow, 2007, 225–24.

10. For more on this discussion see, for instance, Anika Keinz, 2008, Polens 'Andere'. Neu-Verhandlungen von Geschlecht und Sexualität im post-sozialistischen Polen, Bielefeld.

## References

Amnesty International, '*Dokumenty!' Discrimination on grounds of race in the Russian Federation,* London, 2003. (Also: http://www.amnesty.org/russia)

Augé, Marc. *Orte und Nicht-Orte,* Frankfurt a.M. 1994.

Bagirov, Eduard. *Gastarbaiter,* Moscow, 2007.

Berlin Partner GmbH, http://www.berlin-partner.de/index.php?id=642&L=0, accessed 14.05.2008.

Evans, Graeme and J. Foord. 'Rich Mix Cities. From Multicultural Experience to Cosmopolitan Engagement', in *Multicultures and Cities,* eds G. Arvastson and T. Butler, Copenhagen, 2006, 71–84.

Färber, Alexa. 'Vom Kommen, Bleiben und Gehen: Anforderungen und Möglichkeiten im Unternehmen Stadt. Eine Einleitung', in *Hotel Berlin. Formen urbaner Mobilität und Verortung, Berliner Blätter* 37 (2005): 7–21.

Färber, Alexa. 'Urbanes Imagineering in der postindustriellen Stadt: Zur Plausibilität Berlins als Ost-West-Drehscheibe', in *Selling Berlin. Imagebildung und Stadtmarketing von der preußischen Residenz bis zur Bundeshauptstadt,* eds T. Biskup and M. Schalenberg, Stuttgart, 2008, 279–96.

Fager, Sangeeta. 'Diversity Management. Ein Überblick über Definitionen und Umsetzungsbeispiele', Heinrich-Böll-Stiftung, http://www.migration-boell.de/web/diversity/48_462.asp (2006) (last accessed 26.02.2008)

Gdaniec, Cordula and Julia Ovchinnikova. 'Megapolis Moskau. Die russische Hauptstadt zwischen Multikultur und Russifizierung. Künstlerische Annäherungen', documentary film, Moscow, 2006.

Gdaniec, Cordula. '"Ordinary Young Hooligans" or Moscow Geographies of Fear: Spatial Practices in and around the Peoples' Friendship University of Russia', in *Hierarchy and Power in the History of Civilizations. Cultural Dimensions*, eds. L. Griffin and A. Korotayer, Moscow, 2008, 3–15.

Gessen, Masha. 'Roof Collapse Exposes All That is Rotten', *The Moscow Times*, 02.03.2006, 8.

Graney, Kate. 'Making Russia Multicultural: Kazan at Its Millennium and Beyond', *Problems of Post-Communism* 54, no. 6 (November–December 2007): 17–27.

Hannerz, Ulf. 'Thinking about culture in cities', in *Understanding Amsterdam. Essays on economic vitality, city life and urban form*, eds Leon Deben et al. Amsterdam, 2000, 161–78.

Hannerz, Ulf. 'The Cultural Role of World Cities', in *Humanising the City? Social Contexts of Urban Life at the Turn of the Millennium*, eds A. Cohen and F. Katsuyoshi, Edinburgh, 1993, 67–84.

Jung, Rüdiger. 'Diversity Management – Der Umgang mit Vielfalt als Managementaufgabe', in *Vielfalt gestalten – Managing Diversity*, eds R. Jung and H. Schäfer, Frankfurt /Main, 2003, 89–110.

Kaschuba, Wolfgang. 'Geschichtspolitik und Identitätspolitik. Nationale und ethnische Diskurse im Kulturvergleich', in *Inszenierung des Nationalen. Geschichte, Kultur und die Politik der Identitäten*, eds Beate Binder et al, Köln, 2001, 19–42.

Kaschuba, Wolfgang. 'Urbane Identität: Einheit der Widersprüche?', in *Urbanität und Identität zeitgenössischer europäischer Städte* (Dokumentation der Fachtagung vom 11.11.2003 an der ETH Zürich), ed K. Hasenpflug, Ludwigsburg, 2005, 8–28.

Karpenko, Oksana. 'Yazykovye igry s 'gostyami s yuga': 'Kavkaztsy' v rossiiskoi demokraticheskoi presse 1997–1999 gg.' (Language games with the 'Guests from the South': 'Caucasians' in the Russian democratic press), in *Multikulturalizm i transformatsiya postsovetskikh obshchestv* (Multiculturalism and transformation of post-Soviet societies), eds V. Malakhov and V. Tishkov, Moscow, 2002, 162–92.

Khabenskaya, Elena and Vassily Filippov. 'Strategies of Ethnic Representation: The Moscow House of Nationalities as Socio-Cultural (Non-)Space', unpublished manuscript, 2007.

Knecht, Michi and Levent Soysal (eds). *Plausible Vielfalt. Wie der Karneval der Kulturen denkt, lernt und Kultur schafft*, Berlin 2005.

Lanz, Stephan. *Berlin aufgemischt. Abendländisch, multikulturell, kosmopolitisch? Die politische Konstruktion einer Einwanderungsstadt*, Bielefeld, 2007.

Leonov, Aleksandr, et al. 'Gorod – antigeroi. U Moskvy uzhe yest imidzh 'vesyologo goroda'. No stolichnye vlasti khotyat ee sasushit' (City – Antihero. Moscow already has the image of a 'party city'. But the city authorities are trying to 'dry it out'), in *Russkii Newsweek* 33 (2006): 12–17.

Malakhov, Vladimir. 'Etnizatsiya fenomena migratsii v publichnom diskurse i institutakh: sluchai Rossii i Germanii' (Ethnitisation of migration in public discourse and institutions: The case of Russia and Germany), in *Ponaekhali tut ... ocherki o natsionalizme, rasizme i kulturnom plyuralizme* (They're coming over here ... Essays on nationalism, racism and cultural pluralism), V. Malakhov, Moscow, 2007, 104–24.

Malkova, Vera. *"Ne dopuskaetsa razzhiganie mezhnatsionalnoi rozni...' Kniga ob etnicheskoi zhurnalistike'* ('We will not allow kindling of interethnic hatred...' A book on ethnic journalism), Moscow, 2005.

Malkova, Vera. *'Moskva mnogonatsional'naya: konflikt ili soglasie? II. Russkie moskvichi i inoetnichnye migranty: vzglyad drug na druga'* (Multiethnic Moscow – conflict or consent? II. Russian Muscovites and non-Russian migrants: Mutual look at each other), Moscow, 2001.

McDowell, Linda. 'City life and difference: negotiating diversity', in *Unsettling Cities,* eds J. Allen, D. Massey, M. Pryke, London, 1999, 95–135.

Medetsky, Anatoly and F. Mereu. 'Luzhkov Tackles City's PR Problem', in *The Moscow Times,* 19.07.2006, 1.

Mozhaev, Aleksandr. 'Internatsional', *Bolshoi Gorod,* 11 May 2005, 28–29.

Niedermüller, Peter. 'Visualisierung, Ästhetisierung, Ritualisierung. Die Politik der kulturellen Repräsentation im Postsozialismus', in *Ethnische Symbole und ästhetische Praxis in Europa,* eds R. Johler et al, Vienna, 1999, 97–107.

Parekh, Bhikhu. *Rethinking Multiculturalism. Cultural Diversity and Political Theory,* Basingstoke, 2000.

Siegl, Elfie. 'Fremdenfeindlichkeit und Rassenhass in Russland', *Russlandanalysen* Nr. 75 (07.10.2005), www.laender-analysen.de/russland/

Steshin, Dmitry. 'Portret yavleniya: Migranty. Yest' takaya natsional'nost – gastarbaitery' (Portrait of the phenomenon Migrants. There is such an ethnicity – Gastarbaiter), *Komsomolskaya Pravda,* 17 July 2007, http://kp.ru/daily/23935/70166/ accessed 08.02.2008.

Tichomirowa, Katja. 'Schreie aus dem Trümmerberg', *Berliner Zeitung* 24.02.2006, 8.

Venn, Couze. 'The City as Assemblage. Diasporic Cultures, Postmodern Spaces, and Biopolitics', in *Negotiating Urban Conflicts. Interaction, Space and Control,* eds H. Berking et al, Bielefeld, 2006, 41–52.

WCIOM, press release No. 533 (15.09.2006) Itogi Kondopogi: Rossiyane o mezhnatsionalhykh otnosheniyakh (Results of Kondopoga: Russians on interethnic relations), www.wciom.ru/?pt=47&article=3189 accessed 08.02.2008.

Zukin, Sharon. *The Cultures of Cities,* Cambridge, MA, 1995.

# ⚜ 2 ⚜

# Is Chinese Space 'Chinese'?

## *New Migrants in St. Petersburg*

### MEGAN L. DIXON

## Introduction

I met Mei when I had lunch in a small Chinese restaurant on Gorokhovaya Street in St. Petersburg. It turned out that we both lived nearby, and it was a short walk for us both to reach Nevsky Prospekt, the downtown's main street. At one of our later meetings, we ordered lunch at a mid-priced self-serve cafeteria at the corner of Nevsky and Griboedov Canal. I was impressed by her fearless interaction with the girl at the cash register: at a similar stage of learning Russian, I spoke timidly and barely at all unless I was certain that I was saying something with complete grammatical correctness. Mei showed no timidity; she was clearly used to making her way around. Yet when I proposed a walk to the Mikhailovsky Garden, my favourite park two blocks away, she said she had never been there. She certainly had never been to Marsovoe Polye (Mars Field), a park two blocks further; neither place was on her daily trajectory or fell into spaces that made her comfortable.

When I told this story to Russian friends, no one was surprised. This could happen with anyone, they said; there are Russian residents of Petersburg who still haven't been to Mars Field! To me, though, it was a hint of the complexity of my young interviewee's location in St. Petersburg Russian society, and an indication that the position of Chinese in the city is not as simple as marginalisation or confident integration. Certainly, no one was barring Mei from walking in Mikhailovsky Garden or Mars Field. Other friends of hers seemed to range more widely, and probably had been to those places. Mei herself, although she lived downtown when I met her, had once lived north of the Neva River in a more distant district that required her to travel to her classes on the subway. Mei felt fully confident and at home in the cafés near the main avenue, but hadn't learned about the culturally significant sites (good for walking, too) that lay within five blocks of her dormitory. She and other Chinese students with whom I later spoke mentioned Pushkin and Pavlovsk as favourite sites – yet these famous parks are located outside the city, requiring a bus or train ride. How could she be so unfamiliar with the green spaces right around her residence, if she liked parks so much?

My research provided only a preliminary answer to this question, but observing Mei's reactions to these spaces made me more alert when I was conducting formal interviews. I did discover that my Chinese research subjects in St. Petersburg occupy a kind of liminal space between confidence and constraint, and that their experience has a lot to say about Russia's response to multicultural phenomena.[1] Like other work in this collection, this chapter examines the negotiation of one 'cultural group' with local spaces and practices in a Russian city – in this case a growing population of Chinese. This chapter seeks to examine the experience of new Chinese residents of St. Petersburg and tell a part of their story. It also seeks to refute a common Russian expectation that arriving Chinese will concentrate themselves into 'Chinese' spaces, often anticipated as densely-inhabited 'Chinatowns', where Chinese residences and services concentrate. (This phenomenon/stereotype stems from a range of factors operating in cities where Chinese migration has concentrated in Western cities during recent centuries; see, e.g., Anderson 1991 on Vancouver, Canada. Other famous examples in the USA are New York and San Francisco.) This expectation mistakenly views new Chinese immigrants as socially and economically identical to their historical predecessors, and also ignores local conditions that affect the options open to migrants. The chapter proposes that new Chinese migration to Russian cities (among others) should actually be seen as a feature of new economic globalisation, and thus that the social and economic identity of new Chinese migrants will differ significantly – and thus that the way they inhabit Russian space cannot be anticipated based on historical stereotypes. However, I still want to recognise the persistence of these stereotypes as a factor in Russia's globalising process. St. Petersburg currently seeks to become a 'global' space, but in studying this process we must acknowledge the uneven texture of local receptivity to globalisation as both an economic and cultural phenomenon, since this will affect how all city residents will negotiate and inhabit urban space.

At a time when many studies of Russian cities measure them against models of economic success, it is helpful to use the additional criteria offered by Ulf Hannerz to gauge their cultural adaptation to globalisation. Hannerz writes,

> some [cities nowadays] appear to be prominently engaged in transforma-
> tions and recombinations of meanings and meaningful forms which are
> changing the cultural map of the earth, and perhaps the way we think
> about the relationship between culture and territory (1993: 67–68).

According to this approach, we should pose the question: is a given city able to transform and recombine cultural meanings? Hannerz reconsiders the terms 'orthogenetic' and 'heterogenetic' suggested by Redfield and Singer and notes that the idea of a heterogenetic global city in today's world would be a place 'to which people in different parts of the world look ... as fairly durable sources of new culture' (1993: 68). Since my topic here is the arrival and integration of Chinese migrants into St. Petersburg, I will consider whether the experience of Chinese interviewees in Russian space suggests that St. Petersburg operates more along heterogenetic lines, allowing the integration of Others, or whether Chinese tend to see Petersburg as an orthogenetic space where local cultural patterns are rigidly maintained and closed to outsiders. Put another way, this approach allows us to consider to what extent Petersburg functions as an urban node of anonymous culture, wealth and opportunity, and to what extent it resists this identity and pushes to remain 'provincial' and closed.

In fall 2006 and March 2007, I conducted research on urban change in St. Petersburg. My data on Chinese migration to that city include semi-structured interviews with ten Chinese subjects, interviews on a focused topic with two Chinese employees of the Baltic Pearl development firm and fifty-two written responses in four different focus groups with Chinese students at an institute south of the city centre. (These proved useful for establishing possible parameters for sending locations in China and for general impressions of St. Petersburg among the Chinese.) This article is based on this qualitative data; I also include relevant comments from Russian interviewees.

Of the ten Chinese residents with whom I conducted extended semi-structured interviews, three were locally established businessmen (two own restaurants); one was a local professor; and six were students, two of whom had at least part-time work in the city, one in a local Chinese restaurant and one as a tour guide. As is clear from this list, all of my interview subjects were in the country legally and were engaged in white-collar or educational pursuits. While there are rumours of large numbers of Chinese in the countryside, on construction sites and in markets, I was not able to research this.

My interview subjects cannot be considered part of the 'great mass' either of Chinese or Russians. Most were well educated or in the process of seeking more education, and many were representatives of that part of any population that is curious and willing to learn about other cultures. Under these circumstances, the results of my interview research showing potential friction in Russian-Chinese interaction are all the more significant, since in many cases my interviewees were people who are doing their best to facilitate interaction between the two groups.[2]

My methodology, as a foreign visitor to Russia myself, was to consult my Chinese interviewees as expert outsiders, treating them above all as urban dwellers, as powerful subjects with the ability to evaluate Russian society and St. Petersburg's services and infrastructure. This approach perhaps minimised what the subjects might have said about harassment in public areas, and magnified their agency. However, the criticisms (as well as praise) of Russia offered by my subjects thus seemed to me to be freely offered.[3]

As a geographer, my interest lies in the effect of local administrative policies and resident attitudes on the spatial distribution and behaviours of Chinese city residents. While migrants of any group have agency, their choices depend on the range of possibilities offered to them by local economic conditions (e.g., available space for rent/purchase, rent costs) and their perception of safety based on host resident attitudes. Kay Anderson makes an important point in her work on Chinese migration to Vancouver during the twentieth century. She maintains that local prejudice and rulings on land use did as much to form a 'Chinatown' as did the supposed Chinese desire to live together. While she concedes that economic benefit might have made this clustering advantageous, she adds that 'there is little doubt that the force with which the racial category was being wielded … convinced many Chinese of the wisdom of locating together' (1991: 69); she reinforces this assertion by quoting a report commissioned in 1901: 'the Chinese live in aggregation, but this is more a matter of necessity than choice' (69). In the Russian cities of Moscow and St. Petersburg, Chinese residents there are not clustered into a 'Chinatown' – at least not yet. Vilia Gelbras, an expert on Chinese migration to Russia (see 2001, 2004), noted that his extensive surveys of Moscow populations did not attempt to learn about residential location since 'there is no pattern…. they don't settle together' (interview March 2007). Chinese restaurants in Moscow also seem to be scattered in the city with no particular pattern.[4] While some generalities can be made about the distribution of Chinese restaurants in St. Petersburg (the subject of this chapter), this most probably depends on cost factors; distribution of residence does not seem to correlate. As a professor of Chinese language and culture at St. Petersburg State University told me, 'in Petersburg you couldn't say, the Chinese are *there*' – that is, it is not possible to point to one district or set of city blocks as 'Chinese' space or the centre of Chinese residence; there is no 'Chinatown' (Starozhuk, interview March 2007).

Thus, the Russian assumption that Chinese will automatically cluster into one space does not match the evidence uncovered in my research. The question is, then: how and where *do* Chinese migrants access and use space in St. Petersburg?

## Chinese Migration to Russia

According to various estimates from several interviewees, the number of Chinese currently residing in St. Petersburg is 7,000–8,000. A large proportion of this number is made up of students, although some of these students reportedly work in addition to (or instead of) studying. The official census records somewhere from 900–1000 registered Chinese residents (depending on which table is consulted).[5] A Chinese businessman, asked about whether this number could grow in the future, said it was likely that quotas would be instituted long before the number of Chinese in Petersburg got close to the reported number in Moscow – 30–40,000 by some expert estimates or 70–80,000 according to rumour or records of work visas issued. Numbers of Chinese immigrants and students in Russia have been on the rise continually since the late 1980s when China and Russia were both moving towards more openness internationally.

The issue of Chinese migration to Russia has drawn increasing attention among Russian scholars.[6] In order to increase the interpretive potential of my own findings, I consider here some major features of Chinese-Russian interaction as described by a Russian scholar. In this first section I draw on an interview conducted with Vilia Gelbras in March 2007, combined with information provided in his 2001 study compiled from extensive surveys of Chinese resident in Russian cities. Although Gelbras's comments are controversial, conveying views that often seem oversimplified, his studies represent some of the most active Russian-initiated analysis of and interaction with the Russian Chinese community. My interview findings partly reinforce these stated features, but, as discussed further below, suggest interpretations that hint at persisting cultural practices on both sides which reinforce separate – rather than integrated – spaces.

Gelbras made a series of related points about the effect of scale on Russian-Chinese relations in urban space. The first point that drew my attention related to the scale of individual interactions and small groups; this was Gelbras's comment that there are increasing issues with the isolation of Chinese students in Russian university dormitories. The quantity of Chinese students has recently increased in Russian cities due to the relative cheapness and low competitiveness for Chinese youth of the education here compared to North America and Europe, and university administrations, eager for the income, have accepted this trend (a Russian interviewee made this point, and it was confirmed by my survey data). However, the latest wave of students often seems interested in entrepreneurship outside the classroom (a situation mentioned by interview subjects in St. Petersburg), and not in a deep study of Russian language and culture. Unlike Chinese students who arrived in Russia with the first government exchange programmes which were renewed in the 1980s (two of my interview subjects had participated) and, critically, unlike North American and European students who often seek active contact with Russian peers, many of the current students speak Russian poorly and do not make quick progress in their fluency. This leads, Gelbras asserted, to the students clumping together and not mingling with their Russian counterparts. (This sort of comment emerged in numerous interviews with both Russian and Chinese students as well as professors throughout my research, not just in conversation with Gelbras.)

As a second related point, Gelbras asserted that the lack of student-student contact during the educational process makes integration into the Russian workforce difficult. Chinese educated in Russia often do not want to return to China, where unemployment in their socioeconomic rung is high, but they also have trouble keeping jobs in Russia: their lack of contact with Russian peers means that they have low fluency in Russian customs and habits of interaction.

A third point growing out of the first two is a related difficulty for Chinese who remain in Russia after their education. The importance of interpersonal relations in Russian life and business means that any individual without a reliable network of acquaintances and business contacts has a hard time making progress in Russian society. As Gelbras put it, 'if you don't have a network of unofficial contacts which protect you, you're done for' (see also Gelbras 2001: 64).[7] That is, this network of contacts is part of what allows a Chinese migrant to occupy Russian space successfully; access to space may depend on adherence to these local cultural norms.

Intriguingly, scholars have noted that Chinese society and business practices also rely heavily on personalised business networks, or *guanxi* (roughly, 'connections') (Olds and Yeung 2000: 14–15). A successfully integrated Chinese businessman with whom I spoke mentioned the efforts he made to keep contact with all of his Russian network (and how much he had to drink as a result); during our interview, the local chief of the fire station was holding a birthday party for his 21-year-old daughter in a nearby private dining room, and made repeated cell phone appeals to the businessman to join the party for champagne. This businessman had extended experience living in a mostly-Russian dorm in the mid-1990s; he called the Russian people 'fun-loving' (*veselye*) and praised their ability to celebrate life in the midst of hardship. I would hypothesize that this man's participation in the Russian dorm allowed him to transfer his interpersonal skills into his business practices in 'Russian' space. This suggests an 'orthogenetic' character to St. Petersburg's local culture, requiring significant preparation and familiarity before the newcomer is entitled to create new spaces. The Chinese then might be expected to form their own, more exclusive spaces as a way of establishing a base from which to 'recombine' elements of local culture.

A fourth point raised in the conversation suggests that such an option for the Chinese might not be welcome among local people. Questioned about a plan for a combined high-rise centre for Chinese business and residences in Moscow (Huamin Park), Gelbras worried that this was a poor strategy for the Moscow Chinese. This kind of project, he said, 'will not make sense' to locals (*ne budet vosprinimat'sia*). He noted that it is a natural tendency of people to settle around institutions that are significant to them (such as a church), but that 'this group would do better not to concentrate themselves' (*etoi publike vygodnee ne kontsentrirovat'sia*, interview March 2007). In his 2001 study he observes that the Chinese 'inevitably strive to settle compactly' (2001: 46) and that this can be a successful economic and social strategy for entering Russia (such as Chinese businesses in the Russian Far East[8]); yet in regards to the example of Huamin Park, he suggests that Chinese should not draw attention to themselves by clustering together in prominent locations. Gelbras's first several points recognise the complexities of building trust in local spaces, but this final comment implicitly acknowledges the xenophobia in contemporary Russian society. In order to be among the creators of new meaning that Hannerz indicates as a feature of world cities, individuals and groups must have a place to be. How, in light of these obstacles to their access, do Chinese migrants appropriate and occupy space in Russian cities?

The Chinese currently in Russia present an interesting population for an ethnographic researcher. While they are regarded as outsiders, the recent prosperity in China has reversed the former 'elder brother' relationship that Russia (as the USSR) had to China. (At the beginning of Mao Zedong's rule, Russian and other Soviet specialists went to China to aid the new Chinese communist government in rebuilding its war-torn economy and in training specialists for new industries.) Now, many Chinese realise that they have assumed the position of 'elder brother' to the less successful Russian attempts at post-communist reform. Today, in spite of Russia's oil wealth, China as a whole is the more successful economy, and individual Chinese are very much aware of this. They have an economic power and a familiarity with globalised spaces that many Russians do not.

Their overall access to space, though, is affected by a contradiction at the central governmental level: support of large-scale international cooperative economic projects on one hand, and on the other inaccurate information about Chinese migration and negative depictions of the effect that migrants in general have on Russians and their society. On the one hand, the central government favours the establishment of concentrations of Chinese capital – but does not make efforts to remove stereotypes about what 'concentrations of Chinese people' would mean at the local level.

In the rest of this chapter, I consider some modes of accessing and using space in St. Petersburg by Chinese migrants, both discursive and practical. I then draw on qualitative interview data to produce a picture of Chinese experience at a finer scale. During my research, I perceived certain Russian expectations for the effects of Chinese presence on the local landscape – i.e., an appearance marked by traditional 'Chinese' signs such as red lanterns or traditional architecture. A major point is that Chinese appropriations of space are frequently *not* marked by these stereotypical signs. In fact, my research shows that Chinese people tried to treat Petersburg space as heterogenetic – open and ready for anonymous appropriation – while the perception of them often seemed based on a more closed orthogenetic cultural system.

## Chinese Places in Russian Space

In surveying the ways that Chinese city residents accessed and used space based on my observations during fieldwork, I have two types of questions. First, is there a regularity in where they locate themselves? Is their location imposed on them by local policy? Second, are these modes of accessing space discernibly 'Chinese'? Examining these questions for restaurants and for residences will help to answer whether St. Petersburg maintains rigid orthogenetic norms or offers a way for Chinese people to create spaces with new meanings in the urban landscape.

### Restaurants as Chinese space

First, I will consider the distribution of Chinese restaurants in the city. According to an expert Russian interview subject, the first Chinese restaurant opened in St. Petersburg early in the post-Soviet period, in 1991. It was initiated through joint cooperation between the Shanghai and St. Petersburg city administrations, and was staffed equally by Russians and Chinese; however, a diffuse, inefficient management style prompted the restaurant to close after six months. The next restaurant was opened by one of my interviewees in about 1994, just west of the city centre. Another Chinese interviewee told me that there were 'capricious' obstacles such as demands to provide Russian food in addition to the Chinese menu. In spite of resistance from the city committee which approved the plan, the restaurant did open and became successful; it is now the anchor establishment for several restaurants owned by this interviewee. Chinese restaurants suffered along with other small businesses in the 1998 economic default, but many survived and new ones continually opened.

The number of restaurants has grown since that time, today counting as many as 150–200 throughout St. Petersburg. The online yellow pages list ninety restaurants; many of them are mapped in figure 2.1.[9] While the restaurants are spread fairly evenly throughout the city space, the highest number per district occur in Admiralteisky, particularly concentrated around the area of Sennaya Square (see figure 2.2). Svetlana, a Russian interviewee who formerly worked in elite real estate, commented that this was 'the centre, but not the expensive centre' (interview, March 2007); the area lies about thirty minutes' walk from the true downtown. Svetlana said that she and her husband once walked from their apartment near the Fontanka River to St. Isaac's Square and counted over a dozen Chinese restau-

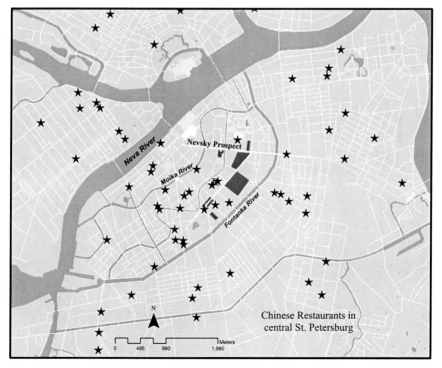

**Fig. 2.1:** Chinese restaurants in central St. Petersburg. Cartography by M. L. Dixon, 2008.

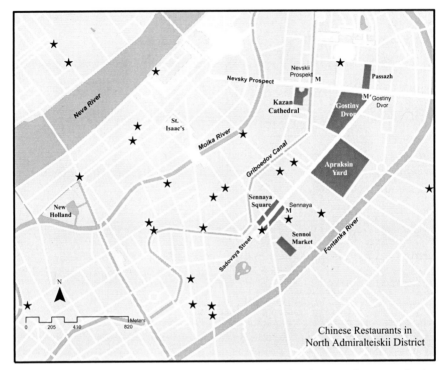

**Fig. 2.2:** Chinese restaurants in north Admiralteisky district. Cartography by M. L. Dixon, 2008.

rants. This information might make it seem as though the Sennaya area is a potential 'Chinatown'.

There are factors here, however, which indicate that the choice of Chinese restaurants to locate here in larger numbers does not result specifically from the desire to cluster as Chinese per se. In contrast to Nevsky Avenue where many of the shops and restaurants are highly priced, the Sennaya area offers two modern-style indoor malls as well as numerous small shops; unlike the Nevsky area, the area has many inexpensive small grocery markets and small cafés along the side streets. Thus, one hypothesis that can be offered fairly quickly is that this area favours the location of Chinese restaurants just as it favours the location of other small businesses that benefit from high traffic and less pressure on rent rates. Yet ongoing evidence indicates that the city administration would like to see this area gentrify – i.e., acquire a population of larger, high-priced businesses and residences controlled by more elite residents of the city. As this process continues, all sorts of small businesses in the district may close, including

Chinese restaurants. Indeed, the restaurant where I first met Mei was planning to close and relocate when I last visited in March 2007. [10]

Second, it is useful to consider to what extent Chinese restaurants constitute an expected kind of 'Chinese' space, i.e., to what extent restaurants are populated and used by Chinese. A certain non-Chineseness of these spaces is suggested by a challenge I ran into early in my fieldwork: my plan had been to frequent several Chinese restaurants in order to become familiar to owners and waitstaff, and then to attempt contact for interviews. While I was lucky in my very first visit to a tiny two-room restaurant, meeting Mei, I soon found that this was an exception. Almost every other of the ten restaurants that I surveyed had young Russian women as waitresses. Only one of these young women seemed at all familiar with Chinese language; she (and one other hostess) did express fierce loyalty to the owners, and reprimanded me for seeming to copy down the menu. But on the whole, the atmosphere that I found inside the restaurants reminded me of Mudu's (2007) description of interiors of Chinese restaurants in Rome, complete with standard silk dresses for the Russian waitresses. Most had the same red lanterns outside (see figure 2.3), and had some kind of Chinese décor inside. In fact, the medium-level Chinese restaurant had multiple halls containing several tables, with Chinese furniture, carved wood panelling and a fairly standard menu (this usually had lemon chicken, sweet and sour dishes, noodles, soup and often a special wok dish

**Fig. 2.3:** A Chinese restaurant near Moskovsky Prospekt. Photograph by the author, 2005.

called 'teban'). Some variety came in tiny establishments such as the one where Mei worked – these had minimal authentic décor – or at the high end, where the Chinese décor was deliberately pronounced.

I decided later that a truly comprehensive survey of the 'Chineseness' of Chinese restaurants would have to include multiple visits at differing times of day, in order to test usage of the spaces by Chinese residents. In almost all cases, the other patrons of the restaurants that I surveyed, usually somewhere between 2:00 PM and 6:00 PM, were Russians. During one visit to a restaurant near the Mariinsky Theatre, a group of Chinese tourists came in; the larger part of the group went into a private dining hall while the leaders sat together at a small table in the main room. In this restaurant, also, when I came in a television set had been tuned to a Chinese-language channel with what appeared to be Chinese news. A woman who appeared to be the owner's wife left and returned with a small girl, their daughter, coming from school. This restaurant seemed to have a degree of authenticity and intimacy that other restaurants did not seem to have (especially those which I discovered were part of a chain). This observation suggested to me that some less standardised restaurants do function as cultural space for local Chinese. I never saw a karaoke evening, although I gathered that they occur, since the Chinese association holds a yearly competition for finalists in a citywide contest (according to interviewee Li). In more standardised restaurants, the Chinese are in the kitchen as chefs, cooks, and preparatory staff, while the dining areas become more 'Russian' space.

An intriguing aspect of Chinese restaurants in St. Petersburg is the number of chains that exist; these are not concentrated in one area, but, as any good entrepreneur chooses, they are spread out in different profitable locations in the city. One chain, Harbin, has as many as fifteen restaurants; another, Tan Zhen, also has numerous restaurants that stretch from the Sennaya area to Vasilievsky Island to the Five Corners area south of Moscow Station. While 'Chinese' restaurants, such as the chain of tea stores named Sea of Tea, may in many cases be owned by Russians, at least two of these chains are owned by Chinese; I could gauge this from interviews with their owners. The strategy of one interviewee, an early restaurateur in the city, has been to create a chain of 'fast-food' Chinese cafés along the model of other popular Russian-style restaurants: while one is located in the Sennaya area – in the mall – the others are located at the city's peripheries, also in new malls. This behaviour contradicts the idea that Chinese businesses will mostly try to take advantage of an exclusively Chinese audience in seeking clientele, and also the idea that they feel the need to cluster in order to prosper. Restaurants are certainly a different sort of business than other services that have often made up the 'Chinatown' profile (food shops, tailors, laundries), but the point is still an important one: rather than

Fig. 2.4: An ad for the souvenir store Feng Shui near the restaurant. Photograph by the author, 2005.

necessarily behaving according to some 'ethnic' imperative, Chinese entrepreneurs seem to be following the market.

In fact, while Chinese restaurants probably do provide some measure of comfortable space to Chinese residents, they also function within the local urban economy as a new kind of space for everyone. Interviewee Li had almost fifteen years' experience in St. Petersburg, and remembered the immediate post-Soviet period. As he said, 'As far as going to restaurants, people didn't use to do it. Now people go often. It's developing very fast in Piter. In 1993, in 1990, there weren't very many. In the Soviet time you had to pay a bribe to go.' His comments indicate that he sees himself as providing a new, market-type opportunity for all city residents (cf. discussion in Färber and Gdaniec 2004); he is participating in the general resurgence of restaurant life in Petersburg, and not in a perceived 'ethnic economy'. His vision, however, is hampered by the perception of his restaurants as 'Chinese' space. Svetlana, a thirty-eight year old lucratively employed in a foreign-based service company, seemed to express distaste when she mentioned that the previous summer she had come across a group of Chinese tourists in what turned out to be Li's flagship restaurant. Svetlana – who has the new Russian habit of going out to eat frequently – used to like that restaurant, she said, but the 'large group' of tourists made her think that it was part of a 'closed economic space' that the Chinese had created. She perceives an ethnic quality in something businesspeople with a migrant background assert is generic good business; the choices she makes based on this assumption are not only part of discriminating practices or discourse but also effectively prevent such spaces from inscribing themselves into the urban landscape, to contribute new meaning to St. Petersburg.

## Residential Chinese Space

In considering residential space, I start again with the broader question of whether there is any discernible regularity to where Chinese live in St. Petersburg. As mentioned above, a Russian expert interviewee asserted 'in St. Petersburg, you can't say that the Chinese are *there*' (Starozhuk, interview March 2007), that is, in any one particular spot. My own research confirmed this. The residential locations of the six students whom I interviewed were mostly constrained by the location of dormitories. The responses of the fifty-two students surveyed also confirmed that most lived in dormitories either southwest of the center, along Marshal Zhukov Avenue, or northeast of the centre, near Ladozhsky Train Station. Two of the businessmen and the professor, those with greater economic means, lived near the centre but not in the most expensive area, in a kind of triangle from Vasilievsky Island to Peter and Paul Fortress to the Sennaya area. The other businessman preferred his location in the Moskovsky District because of the greenery, cleaner air and gentler demeanor of the population. None of those interviewed mentioned any specific desire to live near other Chinese, although they often mentioned sharing food and spending time (especially with fellow students).

Are residential interiors 'Chinese' in any noticeable way? Given the modernisation trends in China, I already knew that living structures there had become more and more Western. I had the opportunity to see a residential interior of just one Chinese person – a successful businessman. This apartment was larger than those of even my most successful Russian friends, with a spacious great room and kitchen. The interior décor was not noticeably 'Chinese'; while the businessman obviously obtained food items from China on a regular basis (such as a rare green tea, which he served to me), the furniture and layout resembled other Russian apartments I had seen.

While the apartment almost certainly functioned as a safe familial space, the businessman did not appear to need particular 'Chineseness' when he was in it. Indeed, he frequently expressed his enjoyment of Russian culture and markedly 'Russian' spaces; he liked to tell the story of his daughter's demand to have Russian fast food at least once a week (often from 'Chainaya lozhka', a popular chain that serves Russian-style vegetable salads and stuffed pancakes).

More important points about Chinese residences seem to be that, while they are dispersed throughout the city and may not be especially 'Chinese' inside, the relationship between local conditions and the tendency of Chinese to choose residences according to standard criteria (per my interviewees: cleaner air, accessibility of transport and architectural appearance) may be distorted in the long term by the behaviour of Russian neighbours (just as Anderson suggested about early settlements in Vancouver).

One example of such behaviour emerged in an extended interview with Mei and her friend Jun, who unlike other students I interviewed had also rented rooms at various times and in various locations in the city. Students tended to share rooms in order to save money; they also tended to cook for themselves at their residences, both in order to save money and because they found restaurant food (both Russian and Chinese) unappealing. Mei mentioned several instances of Chinese students being evicted suddenly by their Russian landlords, without a clear economic reason. Evidently, the desire for rent income does not always overcome what is probably a prejudice against what is seen as 'foreign' behaviour.

This example is confirmed and extended by the comments of a Russian interviewee, a woman employed along with her husband in a Western-connected financial firm; the couple has often rented their apartment in a historical building in order to earn money during the summer or while they travel. Svetlana described a time when she was screening applicants to rent the apartment; a Chinese family came with a Russian real estate agent and stood in the courtyard below while the agent negotiated. They offered double the requested rent. Other agents, Svetlana said, called her and said: 'Surely you aren't going to rent to Chinese?' She decided in the end to let the apartment to an Icelandic couple. 'After all, it's the European mindset, you know what to expect', Svetlana explained. This second example makes especially clear an issue that even educated, professional and successful Chinese might continue to face in Russian cities: they are regarded as 'Oriental' (*vostochnyi*), in spite of the economic might of China – in spite of the fact that the latest architecture is being built in China – in spite of the fact that they are often well travelled, wealthy and have expensive Western-style tastes. Members of the Russian elite often associate themselves with Europe as the model civilisation. Svetlana was clearly anxious that she would destabilise this association, which also reinforces her higher status vis-à-vis other Russians. This local dynamic may act as did the attitudes of city fathers in nineteenth-century Vancouver to limit their possibilities for spatial dispersion, making Chinese clustering a material option/constraint even though it was not an original choice. (For other ways of exercising identity as '*vostochnyi*', see Kosygina, this volume.)

In my fieldwork I saw hints of some types of intentional clustering. While interviewing a businessman, I discovered that a Chinese specialist in massage offered his services in an unmarked apartment in the same block where the businessman lived. This apartment was in an older section of the building, with high ceilings and small rooms. One room had been designated as the waiting room, while another was furnished with a massage table and large posters of the human body with labels in Chinese, and an additional surtitle in English stating that the posters came from a Shanghai medical institute. The masseur did not speak Russian; a Chinese woman asked questions in Russian about sore areas, and conveyed this information to the masseur. This apartment hints at a web of 'Chinese' spaces hidden from street view, where the Russian language becomes less necessary and Chinese residents get Chinese-style services from each other. A more open attitude from Russians would support the businessman's creation of a Chinese medical centre, where such services could be available to all city residents (this is one of his plans); anxiety about the appearance of Chinese might only increase these less visible spaces.

## The Baltic Pearl as Chinese in National and Local Space

St. Petersburg has another excellent example of the contradiction between the national and local levels in confronting Chinese migration. In 2004, the administrations of St. Petersburg and Shanghai signed an agreement about the transfer of a large parcel of land at the city's southwest to a consortium of investment firms from Shanghai and Hong Kong. The consortium, which formed an investment company called 'Baltic Pearl', planned a multi-use district with housing, retail and business space, hotels, and recreational attractions. Evidence from presentation materials prepared for investors suggests that the Chinese firms saw this project as an investment venture, and also as an important service to the city of St. Petersburg, providing a model of modern European-style construction and linking the city centre by water with Peterhof Palace. Concept drawings for the earliest design books show Western-style promenades along water features, pedestrian zones and even photos from selected European cities (London, Amsterdam, Paris, Berlin).

Protest over this plan arose immediately, since many Russian residents of the city saw this investment project as a covert project for mass Chinese migration to St. Petersburg. Early media coverage of the development project suggested that it would become a 'Chinese space' in a physical sense, including 'a branch of the Peking opera' and a 'Buddhist temple'.[12] Such features do not appear in an August 2004 design book prepared in Shanghai. No religious spaces at all appear in the lists of planned services; and while the materials do mention a theatre, the text makes it clear that the kind of theatre envisioned is on a 'Scandinavian' model. The first designers of the quarter researched the city thoroughly, and presented all elements as modelled on local and northern European norms, showing that in this sense at least the 'Chinese' vision of St. Petersburg was as European space.[12]

A chat room provided by the online newspaper *Nevastroyka* has over one thousand comments archived from the very first responses registered after the public announcement of the project. Fearful readers stereotyped Chinese migrants as living packed in together (a far cry from the spacious quarters of the businessman I interviewed, and closer to the often forced conditions in 'Chinatowns' outside China). They envisioned a dark, forbidding space off limits to Russians – again, a far cry from the spacious Swedish-looking concept drawings for the Baltic Pearl.

Will the Baltic Pearl, when built, turn into a 'Chinese space' in any meaningful sense? In fact, there is no reason why it should become the kind of stereotyped 'Chinatown' that many Russians describe and fear. Members of the Baltic Pearl consortium have produced some of the most contemporary housing projects in China, with international standards of architecture and services; thus, as an investment project, the 'Baltic Pearl' development in St. Petersburg will have no particular 'Chinese' signature. The company claims that housing in the quarter will be available to any prospective buyer, and repeat that they intend the housing supply to alleviate the shortage in St. Petersburg. Contrary to the fearful expectations stated on the newspaper chat room mentioned above, it is unclear that Chinese buyers would be at all interested to acquire real estate in St. Petersburg, since the kinds of conditions drawing Hong Kong Chinese buyers to developments in Vancouver as studied by Olds (2001) do not apply here; there is no logical reason for PRC Chinese to migrate to Petersburg. There does seem to be a hope among the Baltic Pearl officials that they will succeed in gathering a community of Chinese businessmen to the Baltic Pearl business centre, which was completed in June 2007.

However, when I asked my three Chinese business interviewees about any intention to relocate to the Baltic Pearl, two said no. Only one, the entrepreneur with the highest diversity of business ventures, and possibly the most financially successful, indicated that he would keep a small office open in the new location in order to keep an ear to the ground; this seemed as much a savvy business decision as a desire to be near other Chinese. The two smaller-scale businesspeople whom I interviewed both said that the location was too far from the centre of the city, and that it would be too inconvenient for them to travel there. Neither wanted to live in the new quarter. The interviewee who lives south of the centre expressed fondness for his neighbourhood and its accessibility to the centre; the other said that the Baltic Pearl would be too far away to accommodate the social life of her daughter, who is fluent in Russian and whose daily activities are closely articulated with the neighbourhood of St. Petersburg State University (on Vasilievsky Island, right near the city centre). The evidence of these opinions to me indicates that these individual Chinese interviewees were thinking of their location and activity in a kind of 'market' way, prizing convenience and business success over location near a conglomeration of other Chinese. They persisted in regarding Petersburg as heterogenetic urban space, open to new meanings and to their desires.

## Response to Russian Space –
## Categories Derived from Interviews

Given these general remarks, I would like to go more deeply into the interviews I completed with Chinese city residents in order to probe the questions of whether they perceived St. Petersburg to be accepting or resisting them.

The interview structure that I used with Chinese subjects was similar to that used with Russian subjects during my research project. The goal was to discover which parts of the city prompted interest or loyalty among the interviewees, and also to elicit critiques of the city infrastructure. With Chinese subjects, I also invited them to compare St. Petersburg to their native cities in China.

### Spaces of affinity

A question that I posed to Russian and Chinese interviewees alike asked them to name favorite places in St. Petersburg. In the case of Chinese subjects, I hypothesized that this question would allow me to evaluate their familiarity with the city and also the kind of affinity they would feel. In the context of this chapter, the comments quoted below reveal how the Chinese interviewees accessed space discursively – that is, claimed locations in St. Petersburg as familiar and attractive to them without regard to the attitudes of Russians about whether that space is actually open to them.

Zhang, 25 years old, is an artist whose choice of St. Petersburg was inspired by studies in China of European art. He attends classes and works as a tour guide. Asked about what he liked in St. Petersburg, he answered:

> Here I was happy right away. I love it! It was my dream inside. Because I wanted to go to Europe – to Florence, to Italy. There it's a good city of course, but small. Not like Piter, so much of everything! A big city, going on and on and on!

Particular places that he liked to visit were St. Isaac's Square, between the cathedral and the city legislature building, and the Griboedov Canal:

> There's lots of interesting history there. Inside [the cathedral], it's really interesting. And the widest bridge [in the city] is there. On the right it's red, on the left it's green. The bridge is called Blue Bridge. Therefore, there are a lot of feelings here.... I also love to walk along Griboedov. There are small buildings there, like in Venice. First left, and then right. I don't like walking straight – I like it when it bends.

Interviewee Jihan, forty-five years old and a businesswoman, told me that she likes the cemetery at the Aleksandr Nevsky Monastery.

> Besides museums, I like most of all to see the monument at the Aleksandr Monastery. To see who is there. Not just musicians, but also Dostoevsky. I read a book at home in Chinese, and then looked at all the monuments. I stood and thought for a long time.

In these comments it is striking that the Chinese mention the way that they feel intimate emotions in St. Petersburg through connection with particular places. Interviewee Yifang, a 19-year-old student, also noted that there were places in St. Petersburg that could even comfort her, such as the catwalk under the cupola of St. Isaac's Cathedral and the Hermitage museum.

> I like to go to Isakii, the tallest of all, to see the whole city. And I like to go to the Hermitage. If I know that I don't have a very good mood on some day...
>
> *What do you do?*
>
> I need to walk through the Hermitage, to look at the paintings.

It is clear from these comments that at least some Chinese residing in St. Petersburg – particularly those, of course, who have the opportunity to study and who have the discretionary time to spend in appreciating cultural spaces – find places that create a sense of emotional attachment for them.

## Support for preservation

Another aspect of Chinese residents' affinity for the city of St. Petersburg came in their comments about the good state of preservation of the historical center, and the comments of a few interviewees about the modern style of the proposed Gazprom Corporation headquarters, Okhta Centre, which was being widely covered in the press at the time of my interviews. Such comments point to the interviewees' appropriation of a local discourse of pride and historical preservation. Li, a businessman who had lived in the city for many years, expressed the general sense of Chinese reactions to St. Petersburg:

> I like the whole city! It's a good city. Of course mostly the old district, the central district. Typical European architecture is good, especially for us, easterners (*vostochnye*), this is very interesting.

An employee of the Baltic Pearl firm mentioned that he appreciated that St. Petersburg was 'a very whole historical city', with little change in its centre. In Beijing, he said, 'a lot of things were changed, old areas destroyed'. Although many people wanted to build the newer modern buildings further from the old centre, 'finally they were defeated. A lot of districts were destroyed. It is very regrettable'. Of St. Petersburg he added, 'you cannot build another one in the world'.

Although this employee's words might be put down to the need for good public relations with city residents, he was not the only Chinese person I talked with who expressed exactly the same opinion. Interviewees who addressed this topic all made comparisons with the loss of historical districts in Chinese cities. Asked about the Gazprom skyscraper, Jihan said,

> I don't know whether it's bad or good. If it's for the economy, that's good, but it doesn't match Piter at all.... This isn't New York. I know they already did this in Shanghai. There was an old city, and they built over everything. ... Here it's very good, the parts that are historic – they did the repair well, it's beautiful, they didn't destroy it. It's too bad in Beijing, they've already destroyed a lot of historical buildings. It's too bad.

As she expresses, the Chinese people with whom I spoke hoped that the aggressive building practices from their native country would not affect St. Petersburg in the same way as it already had Chinese cities. Asked what he thought Chinese people might like to change in St. Petersburg, Zhang made an intriguing comment:

> If a lot of Chinese come here, maybe for ten years it will be fine, it will still be beautiful. But if more, maybe fifteen years, they will want to change things. It's bad, I don't know how to explain it. In Chinese it's called *lan fei*. It means, 'While I have it, I don't want it.'[13]

Thus, many of my Chinese subjects had lived in the city long enough to know certain of its historical places and to appreciate its historical character, and had become confident critics of a possible tendency in the city administration to follow the Chinese model of reconstructing historical sections of cities. They had a sophisticated approach to dispersing newer buildings away from the centre, as another interviewee put it: '[The officials] need to put new sorts of districts further from the centre, around the edges, and in the city, especially in the centre, they should preserve these [historical] styles.' They could perceive a local tendency to preserve the architectural aspect of the culture and align themselves with this local attitude.

These three types of comments indicate the potential of St. Petersburg to be an anonymous urban space that can generate attachment among people who come to the city. In that way, it seems to be a city with heterogenetic potential, allowing newcomers to identify with its local culture and to appreciate its physical features. However, most of my Chinese interviewees expressed reservations about Russian people in general and about particular experiences in public space.

## Street anxiety

Many of the interviewees with whom I spoke raised the issue of feeling anxiety on the street owing to a rise in Russian xenophobia; this prevented them from accessing or using many spaces in a way that they otherwise would. Of the fifty-two students in focus groups, almost half mentioned 'bad people', 'skinheads', or 'hooligans' as a problem. Interviewee Wei, who had lived in Russia since 1986, mentioned that she had been used to walk frequently around the city, but that now she did it only in the evenings in the summer, when there were fewer people. She also commented that she lived within walking distance of her workplace, but preferred to drive so as to avoid contact with Russians on the street.

Jihan developed this theme:

> When you're home you feel safer. Especially now. Before, I didn't feel this. But now there are attacks all the time. I'm nervous all the time. I'm always

worried, what time is it. [I tell my daughter], don't go anywhere, go to the dorm or come home. So I never feel calm.

Jun noted that he preferred summer because he felt more vulnerable during the dark winter; the early evenings changed how public space felt to him. Both Jun and interviewee Yifang said that Chinese students avoided staying out after dark due to frequent attacks on foreign students. While the students interviewed generally expressed appreciation for St. Petersburg's parks and main streets, they pointed out the way that anti-foreigner aggression constrains their ability to be there.

This aggression may be more common in congested commercial areas at St. Petersburg's centre and in certain outlying districts, where xenophobic Russians tend to congregate. At least, interviewee Chaolin noted that he felt safer in the Moskovsky district where he lived, at mid-distance from downtown. He brought up the attitude of Russian residents after describing the physical characteristics that he liked about that district:

> The buildings are Stalinist there, they're better built, and the population there is more ... mostly old Petersburgers live there, there aren't many migrants. It's a more expensive district. The real estate. The people there are local, native (*mestnye, korennye*). Migrants can't afford apartments there.[14]

This sort of comment, of course, does not mean that a large number of Chinese could congregate in the Moskovsky district without drawing any negative attention. And while Chaolin seemed to have adapted to Russian street etiquette and travelled each morning by metro, he did mention travelling home each evening in a car with a hired driver, thus avoiding street contact in the evening. Clearly, the possibilities for Chinese to occupy public space are drastically reduced by their fear and by the incidents that take place. And even at the level of ordinary interactions, other anecdotes related by interviewees indicated that minor incidents in daily spatial etiquette could produce friction between Russians and Chinese.

## Specific incidents

Yifang was the most open and simultaneously thoughtful with me in relating her experience of the city. In recounting to me her daily route from her dorm to classes, she described a situation that I recognised as standard etiquette on public transportation – but in her retelling, it surfaced as a moment of cultural misunderstanding even as it reflects a basically shared tenet in both cultures.

Yifang described what happened in busses when an elderly person entered the bus. In Russian cities, younger people are supposed to give up their seats to these senior citizens, and often do; the older people often also have the additional moral authority of having been veterans or survivors of the siege. In Chinese culture, respect for elders is a strong principle in intergenerational relations: two interviewees actually mentioned this idea to me as something distinctly, and unpleasantly, lacking in Russian culture. Therefore, Yifang might have been expected to respond to this element of Russian transportation etiquette with alacrity.

> For example, a grandmother [says], I want to sit in this seat! Because they're old. You have to change with me! So I stand. Usually they kindly say thank you, but if it's a bad grandmother, we changed, they just think, they don't have to say thank you, you have to stand. I don't like them, I don't know, they are old, I have to change places ... but if I don't want to, if I also want to sit ... I think you should say thank you!

Yifang saw her access to the seat on the bus as interrupted by this kind of street rudeness which, while it may also be a result of poverty and the decline of public etiquette since the turmoil of the 1990s, she perceived as characteristic Russian behaviour. Even though it may not be specific anti-Chinese feeling, it would not matter to her as a visitor with only brief opportunities to absorb Russian cultural practices.

In the focus groups, some of the specific comments that fell under the question 'What do you not like about Russia?' were as follows: 'Some young generation are rude and their manners are bad'; 'the way people treat each other', 'Russians aren't polite'. These comments could be imagined as quotations from the older generation of native Petersburgers about the younger generation; in fact, I heard comments about young people's rudeness from my older Russian friends in casual conversation. Clearly, though, this general perception among a small group of Chinese students indicates a difficulty that faces the local authorities as they seek to increase the city's readiness for increasing numbers of migrants.

Gelbras noted in March 2007 that Chinese students tended not to mingle with Russian students, and that this would likely create problems for them if they tried to stay in Russia for work. Both Chinese and Russian students themselves seem to sense this problem – without, however, knowing how to solve it. Russian students in a small focus group gave an example of how their efforts to include Chinese students in their social activities failed.

> Usually the doors in our dorms are open. The floors where the Chinese students live are called 'Chinatowns' because their doors are always locked.

They look out and won't open if it's not 'one of ours.' They're so reserved that it's not just a problem to learn about their culture, it's just impossible to start a conversation. There was one Chinese guy in our dorm, the only one, we invited everyone but they all refused except for him. He said, 'Oh, I love Russians! Just to socialise, Russians are so open, they're always smiling...' But then he never came back.

From the other 'side', Yifang noted to me that she wanted to learn Russian better and to overcome the separation, but didn't seem to know how.

We are foreigners, so we live together all Chinese. We speak Chinese. This isn't very good. In classes, too, you saw us, there are just two foreigners [non-Chinese], we talk Chinese there too. This isn't good. I want to speak Russian.

Further questioning revealed more about why Yifang couldn't quite overcome the divide. In his 2001 study, Gelbras asked all survey respondents whether they would marry a Russian or whether they would approve of a Chinese friend marrying a Russian. Since the overwhelming response was negative for all locations surveyed, Gelbras concluded that Chinese were unwilling to embrace Russians and their culture. However, it is not quite so simple. When I asked Yifang why she found it difficult to get into more situations where she would have to speak Russian, she mentioned different attitudes to social behaviour that held her back.

I'm a girl, but here girls are different. They drink, they smoke. In China ... In my family, my mother said that I shouldn't drink beer. I shouldn't smoke. I shouldn't sleep with men. But here the girls are different. They drink beer, vodka, they smoke ... they do a lot of things. But I don't want [to be] with that kind of girl. I don't know whether she's good or not. If she's good, we can be friends. But if not, then what later? ... I don't want a Russian man. They just want sex.

The characteristics that Yifang describes here could hardly be ascribed generally to Russian and Chinese women; there are young Russian girls who would share her behavioural preferences. Her experience, however, does point to the fine scale at which cultural differences must be confronted if Russians want to ease the transition of migrants into their society. Combined, the inertia of shared language and habits and the fear of criminality tends to circumscribe Chinese presence and acts to limit them to their dorm rooms, apartments, and certain restaurants. Creating more spaces where both groups feel safe and in which individuals can make contact with each other would seem to be two goals that tolerance advocates might pursue.

## Conclusions

Chinese who migrate to Russia do not form a monolithic group, just as Russians do not all hold the same opinions about their arrival. There are surely intentions for Chinese investment in Russia that come from the state level which would try to create clusters of Chinese people in order to maximise business cooperation and sustain cultural practices. However, the evidence from individual interviewees – except in one case, located quite distant from the vector of Chinese government intentions – suggests that young Chinese come to Russia, as to other places, hoping to better their lives educationally and economically. Yet here is where individual people are caught between scales: there is an economic contradiction between the governments' intentions to share projects and investments, and the Russian government's failure to improve conditions for life at the microscale (Gelbras 2001: 110). This means that individual Chinese, operating under the broad understanding that the Russian government welcomes their presence as an extension of the state-to-state cooperation, may find their hopes for successful interaction with individual Russians and local Russian conditions to be disappointed. Additionally, the very characteristic of the governments that causes this situation (neglect of the individual, overriding concern with large investments and big spaces) means that it is unlikely that successful efforts will be made to remove the inaccurate portrayal of individual Chinese at the microlevel – to uncover the reality that Chinese want apartments in the same way that Russians do, that they also travel to Europe as tourists, that they also want to shop, and in general enjoy urban space.

More research could be done to explore the types of spaces that Russians want, expect, and use in their daily urban lives in order to compare these desires, expectations, and uses with those of Chinese migrants. The fear of closed Chinese spaces coincides in present-day Russia (certainly in St. Petersburg) with a closing-off of previously 'public' spaces for semi-private use, especially courtyards. While some see this as a negative trend in a city that knowledgeable residents could formerly navigate without ever using main streets, it is also a reaction against petty criminal activity and neglect that has little to do with loss of public space as political freedom.

In fact, the larger context of this research suggests that resentment against Chinese is partly a function of the poverty that is still persistent in St. Petersburg (and other Russian cities). While wealthy Russians who have no Chinese friends express a decided prejudice against them (as did Svetlana), they also express a great deal of prejudice against the Russian poor; it is also common for successful Russians to want to exile the poor to the periphery of the city and to remove them from the centre, which has gone from being a deliberately constructed space of idealised Soviet populism to a recreated symbol of urban wealth and prestige.

Certainly, there are elements in Russian policy towards all migrants that also affect Chinese and that make them feel unwanted. A few Chinese students in focus groups mentioned harassment by police. Jihan said, 'we here, as foreigners, there are always problems. First this and then that. We don't understand'. But she noted that this was a function of general policy, and it could be partly avoided by careful attention to detail: '[Unlike] other Chinese, I notice, I have fewer problems. We do everything according to the law. If we need to do something, we know, we read'. As Chaolin put it, bureaucracy is a general brake on economic development in Russia, since it takes up so much time and money to do things legally. A transparent, simplified set of regulations would thus seem to facilitate easier integration of migrants.

Many St. Petersburg residents fear increased immigration. Many also worry about the influence of modern architecture and investment as threats to the familiar landscape and the existing balance of economic power. Yet, as described above, students surveyed about the city and all my interviewees expressed admiration for local architecture and culture. This indicates that many Chinese might be open to adopting the culture of preservation (which is tied with the local tradition of civil society) that allowed the buildings to stay. Recognizing this common opinion might help support the city's heterogenetic identity as an urban node of anonymous culture, wealth, and opportunity without losing the local tradition that residents prize. By contrast, many of the Chinese students noted that they loved Russian culture but didn't like the people (on the streets). The confrontation between the Russian projection of their stereotypes onto Chinese does not meet the desire of Chinese (students and businessmen, at least) to admire the achievements of Russian culture.

Urban loyalty was once one of many that individuals could feel without excluding entirely other scales of loyalty (Holston 1999). The contradiction between engendered national loyalty to Russia (which still militates against the idea of Chinese entering Russian space) and the fluidity of urban loyalty (which was turned into orthogenetic rigidity by deliberate neglect and political as well as military besiegement) creates problems, but could also point to solutions: since the national level promotes cooperation with China as an economic opportunity for Russia, the local history of multiculturalism at the city scale might enter to enable better understanding of what in-migration really means, and also suggest solutions for spatial conflicts. At least, the 'normal', market and location-based reasoning of individual Chinese could be recognised so that Petersburg does not end up forcing a kind of clustering on its Chinese migrants that many do not even want themselves.

## NOTES

This material is based upon work supported in part by the U.S. National Science Foundation under Grant No. 0623599. Any opinions, findings and conclusions or recommendations expressed in this material are those of the author and do not necessarily reflect the views of the U.S. National Science Foundation.

1. Throughout this article I use first-name pseudonyms for non-expert interviewees, both Chinese and Russian.
2. In this article I discuss at length the work of V. G. Gelbras, the most prominent scholar of Chinese migration to Russia. In both of his books, Gelbras attempts to interpret the attitudes and status of the 'great mass' of Chinese entering Russia; his survey subjects include low-skilled workers as well as highly educated managers and entrepreneurs. In his 2004 book, Gelbras sees the 'great mass' of potential migration as more threatening to Russia in connection with the formation of *zemliachestva*, or Chinese ethnic business organisations. This more negative view contrasts with the tone of the 2001 work. I still see my interview subjects as important informants for the development of the Chinese experience in Russia, especially in order not to lose sight of the desires of individuals that help to shape the larger phenomenon; see Appadurai 1996.
3. Another example of such fieldwork in St. Petersburg is Patchenkov (2004), who points out that if the researcher 'reminds informants that they are ethnic persons' she can 'collect data about ethnicity but lose information about the real life of migrants' (2004: 72). I hoped that my framing of interviewees as urban residents helped to minimise this potential fallacy.
4. Another scholar, consulted briefly by phone, mentioned that there was one road in Moscow with a high number of Chinese restaurants but could give no more detailed description of Chinese clustering.
5. To obtain this data I used the Rosstat website (http://www.perepis2002.ru/) and accessed documents on 9 October 2007. See for example 'natsionalnyi sostav', TOM_04_03, which notes 1064 registered Chinese residents of St. Petersburg.
6. In addition to Gelbras, see for example Larin 2003, Galenovich 2003, Zaionchkovskaya 2005, Vitkovskaya and Zaionchkovskaya 2005.
7. This idea refers not necessarily to corruption as monitored by international agencies such as transparency.org, but even more importantly to the way that opportunities in the Russian economy are still shaped by personal relationships and affiliations, such as family ties and educational profiles (see Ries 1999, 2002). This factor emerged during the research in interviews with Russians as well as with Chinese subjects.
8. Gelbras notes in his study of Chinese migration to the Russian Far East that a successful strategy for settlement in the cities he studied have been mini-

fiefdoms run by Chinese businessmen, where the entrepreneurs maintain closed compounds for workers and their small manufacturing facilities. Gelbras suggests that these compact self-governed units – at once a protection from anti-Chinese feeling and a way of avoiding inefficient Russian work practices – may be a 'new form for mastering the Russian expanses' (*novaya forma osvoeniya russkikh prostorov*, 2001: 54). That is, he suggests that these separate spaces are a way of achieving economic success and negotiating the potential resistance of Russians to Chinese presence.

9. I drew the list of Chinese restaurants used here from *www.yell.ru* on 4 October 2007.

10. The policy of the city administration is to 'clean up' the historical centre to make it more profitable and attractive to tourists. Among other policies, the city administration has introduced new regulations that make it harder for small groceries and kiosks to exist, and have closed for 'reconstruction' Apraksin Yard in the Sennaya area – a cheap, centrally-located goods market in the city – partly because it is seen as a haven for illegal migrants. In late December 2007, the commission to redesign Apraksin Yard was granted to international architectural superstar Sir Norman Foster.

11. The temple and Peking Opera were mentioned in a description of the project on the Nevastroyka web-newspaper site as early as 18 November 2004 (accessed 7 January 2005). They are *not* mentioned in a document – archived on the same site – that was presented to the city's legislative assembly by the Committee on Investments and Strategic Projects on 23 March 2005; however, the temple and Chinese theatre remain in the description to this day (February 2008). (*www.nevastroyka.ru*)

12. Given Shanghai's attempts to become a 'world city' in financial terms (see Gu and Tang 2002), St. Petersburg's cooperation with the Shanghai city administration for this project suggests adoption of some Chinese financial models to accomplish this, even as the nominal architectural model is Europe.

13. The accepted translation into English for *lan fei* is 'waste'.

14. In addition to non-Russian migrants to Petersburg, Chaolin may be referring to disgruntled Russian migrants who come from the economically impoverished Russian north or from former Soviet republics where there was ethnic conflict between Russian settlers and local people during the breakup of the Soviet Union. These segments of the population were mentioned to me in an interview as the source of much of the current aggressive xenophobia in Petersburg.

## LITERATURE

Anderson, K. *Vancouver's Chinatown: Racial discourse in Canada, 1875–1980*, Buffalo, NY, 1991.
Appadurai, A. *Modernity at Large: Cultural Dimensions of Globalization*, Minneapolis; London, 1996.

Färber, A. and C. Gdaniec, 'Shopping Malls and Shishas: Urban Space and Material Culture as Approaches to Transformation in Berlin and Moscow', *Ethnologia Europaea* 34, no. 2 (2004): 113–28.

Galenovich, Iu. M. *Rossiya-Kitai: shest' dogovorov* (Russia-China: six treaties), Moscow, 2003.

Gelbras, V. G. *Kitaiskaya realnost' Rossii* (Russia's Chinese reality), Moscow, 2001.

Gelbras, V. G. *Rossiya v usloviyakh global'noi kitaiskoi migratsii* (Russia and global Chinese migration), Moscow, 2004.

Gu, F. R. and Z. Tang, 'Shanghai: reconnecting to the global economy', in *Global Networks, Linked Cities*, ed. S. Sassen, New York; London, 2002, 273–307.

Hannerz, U. 'The cultural role of world cities', in *Humanising the City? Social Contexts of Urban Life at the Turn of the Millennium*, ed. A. P. Cohen and K. Fukui, Edinburgh, 1993, 67–84.

Holston, J. 'Spaces of insurgent citizenship', in *Cities and Citizenship*, ed. J. Holston, Durham, NC, 1999, 155–73.

Larin, A. G. *Kitaitsy v Rossii, vchera i segodnya: Istorichesky ocherk* (The Chinese in Russia, yesterday and today: A historical study), Moscow, 2003.

Mudu, P. 'The people's food: the ingredients of 'ethnic' hierarchies and the development of Chinese restaurants in Rome', *GeoJournal* 68 (2007): 195–210.

Nevastroyka. (www.nevastroyka.ru) Online newspaper. Articles, November 2004–January 2008.

Olds, K. *Globalization and Urban Change: Capital, Culture and Pacific Rim Mega-Projects*, New York, 2001.

Olds, K. and H. W. Yeung, 'Globalizing Chinese business firms: where are they coming from, where are they heading?' in *Globalization of Chinese Business Firms*, ed. K. Olds and H. W. Yeung, 2000, 1–30.

Patchenkov, O. 'The life of ethnic migrants: primary groups vs. imagined communities (based on case-study research of Caucasian migrants in St. Petersburg, Russia)', in *Times, Places, Passages: Ethnological Approaches in the New Millennium*, ed. A. Paladi-Kovacs, 2004, 65–74.

Ries, N. "Honest Bandits' and 'Warped People': Russian Narratives about Money, Corruption, and Moral Decay', in *Ethnography in Unstable Places. Everyday Lives in Contexts of Dramatic Political Change*, eds. Carol J. Greenhouse et al., Durham/London, 2002, 276–315.

Ries, N. 'Business, Taxes and Corruption in Russia', *Anthropology of East Europe Review* 17, no. 1 (1999): http://condor.depaul.edu/~rrotenbe/aeer/issues.html.

Vitkovskaya, G. and Z. Zaionchkovskaya, "Kitaiskoe vtorzhenie' v Sibir i na Dalnyi Vostok: mif o zheltoi ugroze i realnost', in *Rossiia i ee regiony v XX veke. Territoriya – rasselenie – migratsii*, Moscow, 2005.

Zaionchkovskaya, Z. 'Pered litsom immigratsii. Sosedstvo Kitaia pomozhet reshit obshcherossiiskuyu problemu ostrogo defitsita rabochei sily', *Pro et contra* (2005): 72–87.

## ❖ 3 ❖

# Constructions of the 'Other'

### Racialisation of Migrants
### in Moscow and Novosibirsk

#### LARISA KOSYGINA

### Introduction

This chapter presents some results of my research on the Russian migration regime and migrants' experiences.[1] In this project I investigate how the
migration regime – legislation, institutions and discourses – constructed
in Russia in response to immigration from other Newly Independent States
(NIS), impacts on the experience and identities of migrants from this
region.

In spring and summer of 2004, I conducted thirty-nine in-depth interviews with migrants, who had settled in Moscow, and in Novosibirsk, a
large city in Western Siberia with approximately one and half million inhabitants. I approached respondents through my friends, acquaintances
and relatives as well as thorough NGOs working for migrants' rights.[2] I
chose to approach people in this way to be able to gain their trust, which
was very important considering that many of them were so-called 'illegal
migrants' and therefore in danger of deportation if exposed to the authorities.[3] Among my respondents were people who had migrated to Russia for
various reasons: some of them had come to work and planned to return
home as soon as they had earned enough money; some came to study; some
were people forced to change their place of residence due to threats to their
life and livelihood and/or the lives and livelihood of their relatives; some
could be defined as repatriates; and some had migrated to live together
with their families (their spouses, children, parents) etc.[4] They differed in
age, gender and ethnicity. They also differed in terms of their legal status
on the territory of the Russian Federation. There were two factors, though,

which they all shared: they were former Soviet citizens and at the time of interview they had been living in Russia for more than one year. My interviews started with the open question 'Please tell me the story of your life in Russia', which aimed to prompt respondents to produce a narrative about their life in Russia. After a migrant told me his/her story, I asked questions to develop topics mentioned in that particular interview as well as in previous interviews. In this chapter, I examine two topics that came up in my conversations with migrants. The first one is racialisation, or, in other words, the differentiation of people based on their phenotypic features. I investigate how this differentiation is reflected in the experiences of my respondents in Russia. Another theme I will address in this chapter is the emancipation experienced by women who migrate to Russia from societies with a different gender order.[5] Drawing on the example of two young women who migrated from former Soviet republics in Central Asia, I investigate the themes of racialisation and emancipation to show the complexity of migrants' experiences, where they encounter both exclusion and inclusion.

## Racialisation of Migrants in Russia

At the beginning of the twentieth century the term 'racialisation' denoted the process of 'race building' based on so-called 'race-feeling' – the putative mysterious ability of people to feel other people who belong to 'their kind' – which was considered to be implanted into mankind by Nature (Barot and Bird 2001: 602–6). After being out of use for some time, the term 'racialisation' was rethought and reintroduced into academic discourse by social scientists who questioned the appropriateness of such categories as 'race' and 'race relations' (Banton 1977; Fanon 1968). Although the new interpretation of 'racialisation' also refers to 'the process by which groups of persons come to be classified as races' (Cornell and Hartmann 1998: 33), nowadays 'racialisation' is conceptualised as a representational process of constructing the 'Other' by ascribing meaning to real and imagined biological characteristics of people. This new concept of racialisation is accepted both by those who completely reject the category of 'race' as useless and moreover harmful, and by those who still employ the notion of 'race', but emphasise that 'races' are socially constructed groups of people, with borders that change through time (Barot and Bird 2001: 608–9).

Racialisation is a dialectical process. 'Ascribing a real or alleged biological characteristic with meaning to define the 'Other' necessarily entails defining the Self by the same criterion' (Miles and Brown 2003: 101). Hence, racialisation means not only excluding people by defining them as different 'Others' from 'us', but also defining people as 'Ours'. Those people who are defined as 'Others' are not passive recipients of external categorisation. They can resist it through denial, negotiation and transformation of meanings (Cornell and Hartmann 1998: 113–21). Racialisation as a concept is employed in theorizing about racism. Robert Miles defines racism as a mode of racialisation 'that represents the world's population as divided biologically, and negative evaluations are made about some groups constructed by this division' (Miles and Brown 2003: 65). Thus, racism as a representational phenomenon is analytically distinguished from practices of exclusion. In other words, for Miles racism is not an act of exclusion; rather, it is an ideology of exclusion (Miles and Brown 2003: 104). That analytical distinction, however, does not deny that exclusionary practices can go hand in hand with an ideology of exclusion (Miles and Brown: 109). As illustrated in the literature, the differentiation of people according to their phenotype made on the level of representation can result in their social exclusion – in other words, in deprivation of rights and resources allocated in the society where they live and/or operate (Solomos 2001).

Analysing my interviews allows me to argue that my respondents experience racialisation in Russia. Migrants in their stories reveal that in the receiving society they encounter differentiation based on their appearance. 'Russian'-looking people are assigned to one group, while people who have features (colour of skin, form of nose or eyes, etc.) which are defined as 'non-Russian' find themselves ascribed to another group.[6] As became apparent through analysis of the interviews, 'non-Russian' looking migrants experience negative appraisals, while 'Russian'-looking migrants are perceived more or less positively. My respondents report that locals do not distinguish them according to their ethnicities. Instead they call them pejoratively 'non-Russians' (*ne-russkiye*), 'blacks' (*chernye*), 'persons of Caucasian nationality' (*litsa kavkazkoi nationalnosti*), or worse. The majority of these names have strong negative connotations. Migrants talking about the experience of being perceived as 'non-Russians' recall the negative stereotypes encountered in Russia. Among these stereotypes are those which represent 'non-Russians' as a threat to the security of Russian society. Leyla, a 23-year-old woman living in Novosibirsk, but originally from Uzbekistan, told me about the suspicions she encountered in Russian shops where she would be watched as if she were a thief.[7] My respondents in Moscow pointed out that every terrorist act caused intensified police checks of 'non-Russian' looking people. Migrants from Tajikistan in their interviews frequently mentioned that they were associated with drug trafficking.

Negative stereotyping of 'non-Russians' is reproduced by the Russian mass media. According to the results of a research project 'Hate Speech in Russian Mass Media', launched in 2001 by the Informational Analytical Centre 'Sova' and involving analysis of national and regional newspapers as well as national TV programmes, 'non-Russians', 'Caucasians' and 'Asians' are among the most popular targets for 'hate speech' supported by the Russian mass media. Researchers note that, while such extreme elements of 'hate speech' as calls for violence and discrimination are usually condemned by journalists in their presentations, other elements of 'hate speech' such as creation of negative images, statements about inferiority, criminality and lack of morality are taken for granted by presenters (Verkhovsky 2007). The reproduction of negative stereotypes linking 'non-Russian' looking people with criminality, drug trafficking, epidemics, competition on the labour market and so on is indicated by those researchers, who have studied representations of migrants in Russian newspapers (Titov 2004; Mkrchyan 2003; Kosygina 2007).

The differentiated attitude towards 'Russian'-looking people and 'non-Russian' looking people revealed in my interviews is also reflected in the results of studies of public opinion. They show that the Russian population expresses a higher level of aggression and suspicion towards 'non-Russian' looking migrants than towards 'Russian'-looking migrants. A survey conducted by the Levada Centre in 2002 revealed that 73 per cent of the local population had negative feelings towards migrants from the Caucasus and 63 per cent of the locals expressed unfavourable sentiments towards migrants from Central Asia. At the same time, only 17 per cent reported a negative attitude towards migrants from Belarus, Ukraine and Moldova (Leonova 2005). These results are supported by the research carried out by the International Organization of Migration in a range of Russian regions. It was revealed that while so-called 'Slavs' are welcomed by 40 per cent of the local population, ethnic groups united in the survey by the name of 'Caucasians' are welcomed only by 9 per cent of the locals. According to this survey 39 per cent and 19 per cent of the respondents express negative feelings towards 'Caucasians' and 'Asians from NIS countries' respectively, while negative feelings towards 'Slavs' are not mentioned at all (IOM 2005). Nationwide surveys conducted annually by the Levada Centre show that the above-mentioned differentiation in the attitudes of the Russian population towards migrants has been steady over the past few years (Levada Centre 2006).

The stories migrants from former Soviet republics told me revealed that the racialisation experienced by foreign citizens in Russia is intertwined with their social exclusion, or, in other words, with their deprivation of rights and resources allocated in the society where they live and operate[8]. The next part of the chapter is focused on this issue.

## Social Exclusion of Migrants in Russia

Analysis of interviews with my respondents suggests that migrants' access to resources and rights in the receiving society occurs simultaneously at three interconnected levels – the level of state, the level of the economy, and the level of social networks. Being excluded at one level, people can still find opportunities to be included at other levels. These findings are in line with other literature which points out that the process of social exclusion is a multi-layered process (Saraceno 2001; Burchart, Le Grand, Piachaud 2002).

The exclusion of migrants at the level of the state occurs through legal regulations imposed on them by the receiving society. Access of citizens from former Soviet republics to rights and resources, as well as their participation in the economy of the Russian Federation are regulated by international law, bilateral agreements between Russia and other Newly Independent States (NIS), and Russian national legislation.[9] In Russia, my respondents, being non-Russian citizens, were limited not only in their political rights, but also in social rights that mediate access to such social goods as health care provision, education, pensions, social benefits, etc. Imposed regulations not only indicate which rights and resources can be or cannot be accessed by any given category of migrants, but also prescribe certain ways of obtaining access to these rights and resources (where to apply, what documents to submit, and to which organisation, how much to pay, how long to expect a decision, how to appeal, etc.) These regulations constitute formal channels of 'getting things done'. The majority of my respondents as 'illegal' migrants were excluded from these channels.

Exclusion of migrants at the economic level means deprivation of opportunities to earn money and to spend it on goods and services. Using the criterion of the presence or absence of legal regulation, researchers subdivide the economy into the formal and informal sectors (Tickamyer and Bohon 2000: 1338f). The migration regulation in place in Russia today limits the participation of non-Russian citizens in the formal economy of the Russian Federation. In order to be officially employed in Russia, those who do not hold permanent resident status have to obtain a work permit. They are restricted in their choice of jobs (there is a list of jobs which foreign citizens may not undertake) and opportunities to change workplaces. Those migrants, who for some reason cannot meet the requirements prescribed by law, are pushed into the informal economy, where their working conditions are not protected by contracts or state regulations. It was the case that the majority of migrants interviewed in the framework of this research worked informally.

The exclusion of migrants at the level of social networks refers to disruption of their informal connections with other people, which can handicap

СРОЧНО СНИМУ КОМНАТУ В ЭТОМ РАЙОНЕ

ДЕВУШКА, РУССКАЯ.ОБРАЩАТСЯ В МАГАЗИН

"КАЗКА" В ОТДЕЛ -РЕМОНТ ОБУВИ ИЛИ

ТЕЛ.     3-491-80-28 *(без посредников)*

**Fig. 3.1:** Stating one's Russianness is important in small ads looking for or offering accommodations. Photograph C. Gdaniec, Moscow 2005.

their participation in the receiving society. A social network consists of ties constructed and reproduced among social actors and operates according to unwritten rules. These ties and rules constitute informal channels of 'getting things done'. Numerous studies of Russian society outline the importance of social networks for access to resources allocated in it (see, for example, Clarke 2002; Rose 1999). In the following paragraphs, I explore how racialisation experienced by my respondents intertwines with their exclusion at each of above-mentioned levels – the level of state, economy and social networks.

## *Racialisation and social exclusion at the level of the state*

Russian legislation does not differentiate migrants according to their physical appearance, but its implementation is racialised. This racialisation stems from the fact that meanings constructed and reproduced in Russian society in respect to real and imagined biological features of people can be shared by officials responsible for the implementation of legislation (Roman 2002; Amnesty International 2003). Interviews with migrants show that the whole system created in Russia to regulate migration makes it difficult for migrants to secure their legal status in Russia. 'Transformation' of 'legal' migrants into 'illegal' ones often occurred due to the inability of migrants to meet the requirements prescribed by legislation, regulating the process of their registration on the territory of the Russian Federation.[10] Additional difficulties were caused by the 'creativity' of officials, whose interpretations of the national legislation can prevent migrants from obtaining registration on the territory of the Russian Federation. Among respondents pushed into realms of 'illegality' were both 'Russian'-looking migrants and 'non-Russian' looking migrants. However, the literature describes cases when 'non-Russian' looking migrants were not able to secure their legal status in Russia because of direct discrimination by officials (Roman 2002).

Migrants who have not managed to secure their legal status in Russia and who decided to stay on 'illegally' find themselves in a very vulnerable position. They are excluded from formal channels of 'getting things done'. Their rights are not protected by Russian legislation. In fact, they can be persecuted as lawbreakers. Both 'non-Russian' looking people and 'Russian'-looking people without proper documents will face trouble if the authorities find them. However, my research shows that 'non-Russian' looking 'illegal' migrants are more vulnerable than 'Russian'-looking migrants in the same situation.

Russian legislation allows the *militsiya* (police) to stop people on the streets in order to check their documents – passports and registration.[11] These routine checks help police find those in violation of the migration regulations. These people are fined or taken to the station for further questioning, perhaps extortion and possibly subsequent deportation. From my observations, it seems that the police tend to approach 'non-Russian' looking people more often than 'Russian'-looking people. This selectiveness of police officers is also noticed by other researchers (Caldwell 2003). My respondents noticed it, too. In their interviews they outline the importance of appearance. For example, a 25-year-old woman from Belarus who defines herself as a Russian Jew does not experience document checks and puts this down to her 'Slavic' appearance. At the same time, a young woman arrived from Central Asia revealed to me how she is adjusting her appearance to merge with 'Russian'-looking people

It is often argued that a 'non-Russian' appearance makes migrants more visible in Russia, so they can be easily detected as a migrant, while Russian-looking migrants can successfully hide themselves among Russian citizens because of their similar appearance. However, there are a lot of 'non-Russian' looking citizens of the Russian Federation (for example Bashkirs, Buryats, peoples of the North Caucasus, etc). Taking this into consideration, 'non-Russian' looking migrants are not more visibly foreign than 'Russian'-looking migrants. What makes them more vulnerable for document checks by the *militsiya* is a negative attitude towards 'non-Russians' which is widespread in Russia. 'Non-Russian' looking citizens of the Russian Federation are also often stopped and checked by the police in Russia (Gdaniec and Ovchinnikova 2006). 'Non-Russianness' is a marker of the 'Other'. The greater the degree of 'Otherness' attached to a person, the more trouble for the society is expected from him/her.

The fact that 'non-Russian' looking people are stopped more often by police than 'Russian' looking people means that they come into contact with the police more often and are thus more likely to have bad experiences with them. Migrants often remark on the rudeness of police officers. They also express fear that police officers could turn violent towards them. Such fear is well founded. The reports of international and national NGOs detail facts of abuse undertaken by Russian police.[12] The situation is worsened by the fact that migrants do not have mechanisms to protect themselves against this violence, because they can complain about the police only to the police. The young woman from Uzbekistan cited above expressed the vulnerability of migrants, especially 'non-Russian' looking 'illegal' migrants, vis-a-vis the Russian police. She perceives Russian policemen as a threat, not only because they can catch her as an 'illegal' migrant and deport her from the country, but also because she expects violence from them.

> For example, they [police] will say let's go to the police station ... I am afraid because they can take you anywhere ... People say, and newspapers write that ... they [policemen] beat and rape ...
> *(Leyla)*

Unprotected by Russian law, abused and persecuted by law-enforcement agencies, 'illegal' migrants are vulnerable to unlawful behaviour on the part of the local people. As far as Russian society is infected by xenophobia, those of 'non-Russian' appearance are even more vulnerable. Some migrants interviewed during this research revealed that they experienced acts of violence undertaken by locals only because they were defined as 'non-Russians'. Other 'non-Russian' respondents expressed fear of possible violence towards them.

### Racialisation and social exclusion at the level of economy

It is often argued that the post-Soviet Russian economy is characterised by the emergence of 'ethnic' niches – in other words, economic activities operated by entrepreneurs of the same ethnicity and their co-ethnic workers (Snisarenko 1999; Tyuryukanova 2006: 52–53). This phenomenon is presented as a side-effect of migration from abroad, especially from former Soviet republics. Data collected during my research, however, support those researchers, who argue that there are no 'ethnic' niches in Russia (Brednikova and Pachenkov 2000; Voronkov 2000). All my respondents work in multiethnic environments, and in their search for jobs they do not rely solely on social networks based on shared ethnicity. At the same time, some 'non-Russian' looking migrants provide information that allows me to say that their experience in the labour market is racialised. Apparently, in Russia 'non-Russian' appearance can help in finding a job in certain circumstances. Such was the case of a young woman from Tajikistan who started her new carrier as belly dancer soon after her arrival in Novosibirsk. In Russia, where belly dancing is associated with the Orient (*vostok*) and is called 'oriental dance', to look 'oriental' (*vostochnyi*) is an advantage for its performer. Nona, a 23-year-old woman from Tajikistan, who started her career as a belly dancer in Russia without any previous experience, reported that she did not need any certificate, diploma or videotapes with records of her performance to get her first place as a dancer in an oriental restaurant. According to her story, she got this work simply because she looked 'oriental'.

Otherness of the 'non-Russian' looking people has become an object of consumption for the locals. The demand for the 'oriental look' which exists in the Russian entertainment and catering industries is reflected in interviews with other respondents. Both 29-year-old Arif and 39-year-old Abron, migrants from Tajikistan with whom I spoke in Moscow, told me that they were employed as 'oriental men' to make *Shaurma* (the Russian version of *Döner Kebab*). Not all places that sell the 'Orient' have 'oriental'-looking staff. However, competition in this market prompts entrepreneurs to start paying attention to this aspect. According to Leyla, she was approached many times by the owners of such places who promised to hire her without proper papers and even suggested their help in the process of legalisation. In her interview, Leyla expresses understanding of this situation:

> It is profitable for them [owners of 'oriental' places]. The restaurant is 'oriental' and waitresses there also 'oriental'. Imagine, you enter a [restaurant] and [find] the 'Orient' in Siberia...
> *(Leyla)*

Although migrants defined as 'non-Russian' can be included in the economy through involvement in production of goods and services, they also face barriers as consumers, especially when it comes to housing. My respondents report that a 'non-Russian' appearance significantly complicates the search for accommodation. Many landlords express their unwillingness to have 'non-Russians' from former Soviet republics as tenants. In both Moscow and Novosibirsk, it is usual to see advertisements about rental accommodations which clearly state that only Slavs are wanted. Each of my 'non-Russian' looking respondents had a story to tell of a potential landlord rejecting him or her as tenant merely on the basis of their 'Otherness',

**Fig. 3.2:** The Uzbek restaurant Chaikhona No.1 Lounge in central Moscow. Photograph C. Gdaniec 2005.

their name or (perceived) origin. The evidence provided by my respondents is supported by findings of other researchers about the experience of migrants in Russia (Pain 2003; Vendina 2005; Mukomel' 2005, 234–43).

### Racialisation and social networks

My research revealed the importance of migrants being included in social networks. Although, among my respondents, there are people excluded from the receiving society at the level of the state and/or the economy, there is nobody who did not use social networks. Moreover, according to interviews with migrants, inclusion at other levels seems to be impossible without inclusion at this level. They use their social networks to meet requirements imposed on them by Russian legislation on migration and naturalisation, to find jobs, accommodation, and gain access to other resources. Besides, social networks not only secure their material well-being but also provide the psychological comfort of not being alone.

The data I collected does not suggest that social networking among my respondents is racialised. The results of the interviews suggest, rather, that in Russia construction of difference among people through ascribing meaning to their real and imagined phenotypic features, does not result in the exclusion of 'non-Russian' looking people from the social networks of 'Russian' looking people, and vice versa. Although my respondents recognise that stereotypes and prejudices existing in the receiving society about 'non-Russians' can complicate initial contacts with some locals, they also indicate that personal communication and getting to know each other better make people change their attitudes towards 'Others' and can result in very close relationships (see also Caldwell 2003).

Analysis of interviews with migrants suggests that factors facilitating creation of new connections include shared space[13] and shared interest. The latter could be understood as an initially shared interest in something (for example, in the process of legalisation) or as a negotiated interest (for example, interest between employer and employee; landlord and tenant). Belief in shared ethnicity also played a significant role in the development of social networks for some of my respondents. However, it is worth noting that their social connections stretch far beyond the borders constructed through ethnicisation.[14] Migrants have friends and acquaintances among people assigned to different so-called ethnic groups. Moreover, my research reveals cases when people preferred to avoid inclusion in social networking based on shared ethnicity. Two such cases are presented by the stories of the young women discussed below.

## 'Oriental Women' in Russia

While conducting my fieldwork in 2004, I met two 23-year-old women who had been living in Novosibirsk for several years. Both women were born and spent all their lives in urban areas. Leyla hailed from Uzbekistan and identified herself during the interviews as Uzbek. Nona was originally from the Pamir region of Tajikistan but she did not talk about herself as Tajik, instead she used the category 'oriental woman'. Neither of the women had Russian citizenship. Moreover, they were 'illegal' immigrants, as they did not manage to obtain the official registration in Russia. Neither of them had proper documents allowing them to work in Russia, so they were working in the informal economy. In as much as their employers hired them unofficially without any contract, Leyla and Nona as employees were not protected from possible mistreatment. Leyla had finished medical college in Uzbekistan, but in Russia she could not find a job befitting her qualification. She was working as a waitress in a café serving fast food. There was nothing oriental at this workplace. Nona, who had completed only ten years of school, was working as a dance tutor in numerous fitness centres as well as a dance performer in restaurants and at different kinds of events such as weddings and birthday parties.

Leyla came to Russia with her husband, who had studied for a medical degree in Novosibirsk before they married. She got to know him in Uzbekistan, when he came for a short time to work at a hospital where she was employed as a nurse. They met in a dramatic period of her life. Her parents had arranged a marriage for her. Leyla told me that she was very doubtful about getting married to a person whom she had never seen before. So she was happy to avoid this by marrying a person whom she at least knew. After the wedding, the couple left Uzbekistan because Leyla's husband had to continue his studies in Russia. At the moment of the interview with Leyla, her husband was taking an internship as a newly qualified doctor in one of the Novosibirsk hospitals. Because of her husband's social embeddedness and legal status in Novosibirsk, Leyla 'arrived' in a social network that provided a basis for her new life in Russia. This initial network was not based on ethnicity. It consisted of the colleagues of her husband.

Nona, on the other hand, came to Russia alone. She did not tell me why she left her hometown at the age of seventeen and came to a place where she did not know anybody. She never visited or contacted her family after she came to Russia. I could only make assumptions from her references about the society she had left behind, that the reasons had been serious. Nona's story about her life in Russia showed the importance of social networks for survival. She had some very hard times in Novosibirsk because she knew nobody when she arrived. However, despite her difficulties, she never approached other Tajiks who lived in Novosibirsk to get help. Contact with compatriots was not something that she or Leyla were looking for in their new life in Russia. Leyla and Nona experienced significant constraints as 'illegal' migrants and as people classified as 'non-Russians'. In their narratives, they pointed to the prejudices of the local population against 'non-Russian' looking people. They also told me about the discrimination, which they experienced in Russia because of their 'non-Russian' appearance. Both Leyla and Nona had unpleasant encounters with Russian police. Both of them expressed fear of violence and vulnerability. Nevertheless, they stated that they liked being in Russia because of the freedom that they experienced there as compared to life in their countries of origin. That feeling of freedom resulted largely from the differences between the gender orders in their countries of origin and the gender order in Russian society. According to Leyla and Nona, gender order, as it exists in Uzbekistan and Tajikistan, is restrictive towards women, especially towards young women in marriage.

If Nona in her interview depicted a patriarchal family model in which women are oppressed by men, what Leyla told about young married women in Uzbekistan revealed a much more complicated picture of hierarchy within the family. In this pyramid of power, the daughter-in-law who has to live with her husband's parents is at the bottom, and the parents of the husband are at the top. A woman must obey her husband, and both of them have to obey his parents. She has to ask permission for everything, and the decision of her husband to grant permission has to be approved by his parents. According to Leyla, a husband cannot even give a present to his wife without asking permission from his mother. The figure of the husband's mother is powerful. She rules the household, her children and the wives of her sons. This rule of the older woman appears to be restrictive towards the younger women in the household. As Leyla put it in her interview:

> To get married means to send yourself to prison.... It is a cage, it can be a gold cage but it is still a cage.... You cannot even visit the neighbours without permission.... I cannot explain it; to understand me you need to experience this atmosphere where all are waiting for the word of mother-in-law...
> *(Leyla)*

Both Leyla and Nona outlined how parents tended to give their daughters to marriage when the girls were very young. According to Leyla and Nona, family life does not allow young women to invest time and effort in further education. Young women may also be prohibited from employment. Their prime responsibilities are giving birth to children and working as housewives.

> If I had married there, I would have had to sit at home and give birth. That is all, my tasks would be to give birth and look after the house ... no studies, no employment
> *(Leyla)*

The gender order in Russian society has its own regulations producing unequal treatment of persons of different gender (Ashwin 2000; Kay 2000). Researchers who study gender relations in Russia describe, for example, gender inequality in both the economic (Jyrkinen-Pakkasvirta 1996; Kozina and Zhidkova 2006) and the political spheres (Temkina 1996). However, Russian gender order seems to be much more liberal than the gender orders that Leyla and Nona left behind. Taking into consideration their accounts about regulations imposed on women in the societies of their previous residence, it was no surprise that they perceived Russia as a country where women had freedom.

> I feel freedom here ... I like being here ... Someone who has lived in the atmosphere where I lived before will understand me ... Nobody tells me

what to do, who to speak with ... I am learning by my own mistakes. I like that I am independent now. I like to be independent ...
*(Leyla)*

Leyla and Nona expected that other Uzbeks and Tajiks (women and men) who migrated to Russia would carry in their minds and in their social practices the traditional norms and regulations of gender order, which they had left behind and were afraid could be re-imposed on them. As a result, these two young women tried to avoid other compatriots and did not seek out an Uzbek or Tajik 'community'. When compatriots approached them, Leyla and Nona tried to conceal their origin by pretending that they did not know the language. While Leyla expressed that she could not explain to herself why she did this, Nona was quite sure about what could happen as a result of communication with people from her ethnic 'community'

I do not communicate with my diaspora, because there will be questions, why you are here alone, why you [are] without husband, I could get real problems ...
*(Nona)*

Instead of networks based on ethnicity, Leyla and Nona constructed connections with people whom they did not identify as belonging to their 'ethnic groups'. At the time of the interview, both of them had extensive social networks of friends and acquaintances that helped them to organise their life in Russia and feel at home. Later, people from new networks promoted further liberation of these women from the gender orders they left behind. Sometimes migrants, being socialised in a society with a particular gender order, could not see opportunities open to their gender in the society with a different gender order. Constructing relations with people who were socialised in Russia, they could start to see these initially 'hidden' opportunities and try to use them. For example, in the case of Nona it was her new Russian friends who showed her opportunities for constructing a career for herself as a dance performer and tutor.

Liberation from internalised gender regulations, inherent to the society of departure, was no one-day process. For example, in her interview, Leyla expressed her happiness at having the freedom to make her own decisions and to communicate with people without first seeking permission; but as she noted, it took some time to get used to this freedom and stop asking her husband if she could do this or that particular thing. It was her husband who encouraged her to express more independence. According to Leyla, he told her that people would laugh at him if she continued to seek his permission for everything. The support of close people was apparently very important for both women to be able to rethink internalised regulations of their gender orders. Nona said she was afraid at the beginning of her teaching career. It was so unusual for her to tell other people what to do and how to do it. She said that she was even afraid to look in the eyes of her students or to correct them. However, with time she became more relaxed and confident in class. She was encouraged by her own progress and that of her students and also by their respect towards her. Some of them became her friends and supported her in the development of her career. Through her teaching and communication with students, she began to feel that her skills and knowledge were important for others, and that made her '*feel fulfilled in all senses*', in her own words.

Despite the racism and the bureaucratic problems they experience in Russian cities, women from societies with more restrictive gender orders than Russia's prefer to live in Russia than in their country of origin. Experiencing liberation from regulations imposed on them in the former society, these women link their future to Russia. They expect that the gender order of Russian society will provide them with the necessary opportunities to realise their dreams of personal development and achievements.

> There is hope that some day I will study and will have a career ... that I will be able to achieve something, to do something for myself, not for somebody else or by somebody's order ...
> *(Leyla)*

# Conclusion

In Russia, migrants from former Soviet republics encounter racialisation, or, in other words, differentiation of people through ascribing meanings to their phenotypic features. The main division line runs between so-called 'non-Russian' looking people and 'Russian'-looking people. In Robert Miles' terms, this could be defined as racism because not only are people in Russia assigned to different groups in accordance with their real or imagined biological differences, but also 'non-Russian' looking people are subject to negative stereotyping (Miles and Brown 2003).

Racialisation experienced by migrants in Russia intertwines with their social exclusion and inclusion, which occurs at three interconnected levels: the level of the state, the level of the economy and the level of social networks. People defined through racialisation as 'non-Russian' looking experience exclusion at the level of the state through discriminatory practices by officials implementing legislation. At the same time, racialisation has both positive and negative impacts on the participation of my respondents in the economy of the receiving society. On the one hand, representation of the 'Other' as different and 'exotic' creates additional opportunity for those 'non-Russian' looking people whose appearance is defined as 'oriental' to participate in the economy through selling their 'Otherness' to the local population. On the other hand, negative meanings ascribed to 'Otherness' result in barriers for consumption for people defined as 'non-Russian' looking. Interviews with my respondents do not provide evidence that racialisation influences the construction of their social networks. Taking into consideration the importance of social networking for access to resources and participation in Russian society, this fact might alleviate the consequences of social exclusion at the level of the state and at the level of the economy as experienced by 'non-Russian' looking foreigners in Russia.

My research reveals that, although social networking based on ethnicity is practiced by migrants to overcome constraints imposed by the receiving society, young women arriving from societies where the gender orders are more restrictive than in Russia, still prefer to avoid inclusion in these networks. They expect that such inclusion will impose on them the gender order that they wish to leave behind. Instead, they construct social networks with people they consider not to be from their 'ethnic group'. In the case of young women from Central Asia I interviewed, interaction with people socialised within a different gender order leads to revision of their gender beliefs and transformation of their social practices in the public and private spheres. Although the life of these women is complicated by the fact that they do not have legal status on the territory of the Russian Federation, and by the racism which exists in Russian society, they report that as women, they feel much more freedom in Russia than in their home countries. They link with Russia their hopes to realise their dreams about personal development and achievements in the future.

## NOTES

1. This research was supported by the Ford Foundation International Fellowships Program (IFP).
2. I approached my respondents through the following NGOs located in Moscow: Forum of Migrants' Associations (http://www.migrant.ru/), The Civil Assistance Committee (http://www.refugee.ru/), Fond Tajikistana (no web site).
3. The glossary on migration issued by the International Organization for Migration contains several terms to indicate migrants 'who, owing to illegal entry or the expiry of his/her visa, lack legal status in a transit or host country ... who infringe a country's admission rules and ... not authorized to remain in the host country'. They are called 'clandestine / illegal/ undocumented/ irregular' migrants or 'migrants in an irregular situation' (Perruchoud 2004: 34). This variety stems from discussion of ethical issues around migration and attempts

to grasp the variety of reasons leading migrants to the so-called 'irregular situation' (Koser 2005: 5; Parker 2005: 8–9). In Russia, the term used by officials, academics, journalists and other social actors to define the above-mentioned category of migrants is 'illegal migrants'.

4.  In the Russian Federation, after the break-up of the USSR, there was no unified position regarding how to define people whose ethnicity was defined as Russian, migrating from former Soviet republics to Russia for permanent residency. Some commentators tended to see them as 'forced migrants', or, in other words, as people who had to move to Russia because they and their relatives experienced threats to their lives, health and livelihood on the ground of their ethnicity in the countries of departure. Others perceived them as people who voluntarily returned to the country of their birth and/or origin and so called them repatriates. An analysis of this debate can be found in Flynn (2004: 38–53) and Pilkington (1998: 23–34).

5.  The gender order is described by Connell as 'an historically constructed pattern of power relations between men and women and definitions of femininity and masculinity' (Connell 1987: 99).

6.  Division into 'Russian'-looking people and 'non-Russian' looking people indicated by my respondents points out that 'colour of skin' is not the only marker involved in racialisation, although the literature discussing racialisation in post-Soviet Russian society tends to speak only about this marker (see, for example, Roman 2002).

7.  Names of respondents have been changed.

8.  For a discussion on the definition of 'social exclusion' see Saraceno 2001.

9.  Current legislation which regulates issues linked with migration can be seen at http://www.consultant.ru

10. Before 2002, migrants from former Soviet republics had to obtain a registration, the so-called 'propiska' (temporary or permanent) in order to obtain rights and get access to resources in Russia. Nowadays to secure legal status in Russia they have to obtain a different kind of registration in the migration card. This registration expires within ninety days. Problems arise owing to rejection by the *militsiya* of application to extend this registration for another ninety-day period.

11. In Russia, the police force is called *militsiya*.

12. See publications at the web site of Informational-Analytical Centre SOVA (http://xeno.sova-center.ru/4CBA78E/4CBA7FD/500A658 , http://xeno.sova-center.ru/45A29F2/8B967ED, http://xeno.sova-center.ru/45A29F2/76FECEA, accessed 08.12.2007)

13. For example, migrants and their new friends and acquaintances work in one firm, study in one educational institution, live in one area (flat, house), visit one church, etc.

14. 'Ethnicisation is the making of an ethnic group. It is the process by which a group of persons comes to see itself as a distinct group linked by bonds of kinship or their equivalents, by a shared history, and by cultural symbols' (Cornell and Hartmann 1998: 33–34)

## REFERENCES

Amnesty International report *'Dokumenty!' Discrimination on Grounds of Race in the Russian Federation*, London, 2003.

Ashwin, S. 'Introduction: Gender, State and Society in Soviet and post-Soviet Russia', in *Gender, State and Society in Soviet and post-Soviet Russia*, ed. S. Ashwin, London and New York, 2000, 1–29.

Banton, M. *The Idea of Race*, London, 1977.

Barot, R. and J. Bird. 'Racialization: the Genealogy and Critique of a Concept', *Ethnic and Racial Studies* 24, no. 4, 2001: 601–18.

Burchart, T., J. Le Grand, and D. Piachaud. 'Introduction', in *Understanding Social Exclusion*, ed J. Hills, J. Le Grand, D. Piachaud, Oxford, 2002, 1–12.

Brednikova, O. and O. Pachenkov. 'Etnichnost' 'Etnicheskoy Eknomiki' i Sotsial'nye Seti Migrantov', in *Etnichnost' i Ekonomika*, eds O. Brednikova, V. Voronkov, E. Chikadze, St. Petersburg, 2000, 47–54.

Caldwell, M. L. 'Race and Social Relations: Crossing Borders in Moscow Food Aid Program', in *Social Networks in Movement: Time, Interaction and Interethnic Spaces in Central Eastern Europe*, eds D. Torsello, M. Pappová, Šamorín, 2003, 255–73, (www.vmek.oszk.hu/01800/01847/01847.pdf, accessed 31.01.2008)

Clarke, S. *Making Ends Meet in Contemporary Russia: Secondary Employment, Subsidiary Agriculture and Social Networks*, Cheltenham, 2002.

Connell, R. *Gender and Power: Society, the Person and Sexual Politics*, Cambridge and Oxford, 1987.

Cornell, S. and D. Hartmann. *Ethnicity and Race: Making Identities in a Changing World*, London, 1998.

Fanon, F. *The Wretched of the Earth*, New York, 1968.

Flynn, M. *Migrant Resettlement in the Russian Federation: Reconstructing Homes and Homelands*, London, 2004.

Gdaniec, C. and J. Ovchinnikova. *Megapolis Moskau. Die russische Hauptstadt zwischen Multikultur und Russifizierung*, documentary film, Moscow 2006.

Human Rights Watch. *Moscow: Open Season, Closed City, 1997* (http://www.hrw.org/reports/1997/russia/ accessed 08.12.2007)

International Organization of Migration (IOM). 'Iz Vsekh Rossiyskikh Phobiy Sil'neyshchaya – Kavkazskaya', *Demoskope Weekly*, no. 203–4, 2005 (http://demoscope.ru/weekly/2005/0203/analit03.php, accessed 14.07.2007).

Jyrkinen-Pakkasvirta, T. 'Women's Work and Threat of Unemployment in St. Petersburg', in *Women's Voices in Russia Today*, eds A. Rotkirch and E. Haavio-Mannila, Brookfield and Aldershot, 1996, 3–32.

Kay, R. *Russian Women and their Organizations: Gender, Discrimination and Grassroots Women's Organizations, 1991–96*, London, 2000.

Koser, K. *Irregular Migration, State Security and Human Security*, London, 2005 (http://www.gcim.org/attachements/TP5.pdf accessed 13.06.07)

Kosygina, L. 'Rossiyskie gazety o migrantakh iz byvshih sovetskikh respublik SSSR: analyz reprezentatsiy', *Vestnik Novosibirskogo Gosudarstvennogo Universiteta: Filosofiya* 5, no.1, 2007: 81–83.

Kozina, I. and E. Zhidkova. 'Sex Segregation and Discrimination in the New Russian Labour Market', in *Adapting to Russia's New Labour Market: Gender and Employment Behaviour*, ed S. Ashwin, London and New York, 2006, 57–86.

Leonova, A. 'Migrantophobia: Srez obshchestvennykh nastroenii: 'Rossiya dlya Russkikh' – Strakh ili stremlenie k izolyatsionizmu?', *Demoskope Weekly*, no. 203–4, 2005 (http://demoscope.ru/weekly/2005/0203/tema03.php accessed 14.07.2007).

Levada Centre, 'Rossiya dlya russkikh?' in Informational bulletin 25. 08.2006 (http://www.levada.ru/press/2006082500.html accessed 14.07.2007)

Miles, R. and M. Brown. *Russism*, London, 2003.

Mkrtchyan, N. 'Migratsiya i sredstva massovoi informatsii: real'nye i mnimye ugrozy', *Kosmopolis* 3, no. 5 (2003): 108–115 (http://demoscope.ru/weekly/2004/0179/analit05.php accessed 14.07.2007)

Mukomel', V. *Migratsionnaya Politika Rossii: Postsovetskie konteksty*, Moscow, 2005.

Pain, E. *Modernistskii Proekt i ego traditsionalistskaya al'ternativa v natsional'noy politike Rossii*, Moscow, 2003.

Parker, J. International Migration Data Collection, 2005. (http://www.gcim.org/attachements/TP11.pdf, accessed 13.06.07)

Perruchoud, R. *International Migration Law: Glossary on Migration*, Geneva, 2004.

Pilkington, H. *Migration, Displacement and Identity in post-Soviet Russia*, London, 1998.

Roman, M. L. 'Making Caucasians Black: Moscow Since the Fall of Communism and the Racialization of Non-Russians', *Journal of Communist Studies and Transition Politics*, 18, no.2, 2002: 1–27.

Rose, R. 'Modern, Pre-Modern and Anti-Modern Social Capital in Russia', *Studies in Public Policy*, no. 324, 1999: 1–36.

Saraceno, C. 'Social Exclusion, Cultural Roots and Diversities of a Popular Concept' in *Conference on Social Exclusion and Children*. Columbia University: 2001. (http://www.childpolicyintl.org/publications/Saraceno.pdf, accessed 8.12.2007)

Snisarenko, A. 'Etnicheskoe predprinimatelstvo v bolshom gorode sovremennoi Rossii (na primere issledovaniya azerbaijanskoi obshchiny v Peterburge)', in *Neformalnaya ekonomika. Rossiya i Mir*, ed T. Shanin, Moscow, 1999, 138–155.

Solomos, J. 'Race, Multi-Culturalism and Difference', in *Culture and Citizenship*, ed N. Stevenson, Thousand Oaks, CA and New Delhi, 2001, 198–211.

Temkina, A. 'Entering Politics: Women's Ways, Gender Ideas and Contradictions of Reality', in *Women's Voices in Russia Today*, eds E. Haavio-Mannila and A. Rotkirch, Brookfield and Aldershot, 1996, 206–234.

Tickamyer, A. and S. Bohon, 'The Informal Economy', in *Encyclopedia of Sociology*, eds E. F. Borgatta and R. Montgomery, New York, 2000, 1337–44.

Titov, V. 'O Formirovanii obraza etnicheskogo immigranta (analiz publikatsii pressy)', *Demoskope Weekly*, no. 179–180, 2004.(http://www.demoscope.ru/weekly/2004/0179/analit03.php, accessed 14.07.2007)

Tyuryukanova, E. *Forced Labour in the Russian Federation Today: Irregular Migration and Trafficking in Human Beings*, Geneva, 2005.(http://www.ilo.org/

wcmsp5/groups/public/---ed_norm/---declaration/documents/publication/
wcms_081997.pdf, accessed 14.07.2007)

Vendina, O. *Migrants in Moscow: Is Moscow Heading towards Ethnic Segregation?*,
    Moscow, 2005.

Verkhovsky, A. ed Yazyk vrazhdy protiv obshchestva, Moscow, 2007.

Voronkov, V. 'Sushchestvuet li etnicheskaya ekonomika?', in *Etnichnost' i Ekonomika*,
    eds O. Brednikova, V. Voronkov, E. Chikadze, St. Petersburg, 2000, 42–47.

# ❧ 4 ❧

# Reshaping Living Space

## Concepts of Home Represented by Women Migrants Working in St. Petersburg

### OLGA BREDNIKOVA and OLGA TKACH

## Introduction

The subject of this article was prompted by 'misunderstandings' occurring during conversations with our informants. While studying labour migrants in St. Petersburg who sell goods on the markets and shop pavilions, we often had to stand for hours on end beside the stalls where our informants worked. During interludes when there were no customers we talked to the migrants, and our topics of conversation ranged from their customers' characters to their own housing problems, from the vagaries of weather to how it is to be a woman migrant. As is usual in conversation, our partners referred to their own experience, using phrases such as, 'But where I'm from ...' or 'Where we're from ...', etc. It quickly transpired that the meaning of these apparently simple phrases was not always clear. They often required additional qualification – *here, there, earlier, in my previous apartment, before moving to Petersburg*, etc. A particular source of confusion were phrases such as 'back home', since the context did not always make it clear what was meant: Where do you mean by 'home'? This question regularly cropped up in conversation and finally became the starting point of this study: Where is a migrant's home, and what indeed constitutes home for a woman labour migrant?

When they change location, migrants do not just move from one place to another. They reshape their living space and significantly broaden the horizons of their own life. Contemporary migrants are now already defined as transmigrants, because they develop and support numerous family, economic, social, organisational, religious and political ties across borders (Glick Schiller, Bash, and Blanc-Szanton 1992: ix)[1]. They inhabit a number of places simultaneously and belong to more than one society or community. Migrants' social networks create special delocalised and diffuse social spaces. In these spaces, ideas of what home is change greatly: 'home' does not simply relocate with the migrant, or 'multiply', but changes its meanings.

Contemporary research on the phenomenon of 'home' comprises three basic directions or dimensions: 1) specific studies of physical space (housing, interior, material environment, etc.); 2) studies of people's experience, the routine daily practices that define their being in a certain location as 'being at home'; 3) reconstruction of different meanings attributed to 'home'. Prior to the current age of global migration, researchers took 'home' to be synonymous with the house inhabited: a physically defined, restricted place. From the mid-1980s onwards, research on 'home' has focused mostly on conceptions about home and on social practices connecting identity with home. As Berger describes, for a world of travellers, of labour migrants, exiles and commuters, 'home' comes to be found in a routine set of practices, a repetition of habitual interactions, in styles of dress and address, in memories and myths, in stories carried around in one's head. People are more at home nowadays, in short, in 'words, jokes, opinions, gestures, actions, even the way one wears a hat' (Berger 1984: 64 cited in Rapport and Dawson 1998: 7).

The existing literature on 'home' reveals an ongoing tension between definitions pertaining to physical places and those referring to symbolic spaces. 'Home' includes not only territorial attachment, but also adherence to transportable cultural ideas and values. It is not only national, cultural and social belongings, but also a sense of self, of one's 'identity', which corresponds to various conceptualisations of home. Sometimes 'home' can be recognised in an abstract ideal, a longing for a nostalgic past or a utopian future (Al-Ali and Koser 2002: 7).

This study will follow our informants in understanding 'home' as a life space, or rather a localised, but nevertheless very mobile space of practices. This space is assigned the special symbolic status of being 'one's own' – appropriated and privatised, comprehensible and safe, etc. Female migrants' accounts distinguish between three overlapping levels or concepts of home:

1. Home as housing
2. Home as place of residence, in this case the city
3. Home as a place of origin, or 'homeland'

There is also the fourth, rather significant dimension of 'home', which combines and connects all three previous levels – 4. *Home as a space of social ties.*

## Social Context of Labour Migration in Russia

This study focuses on female labour migrants from the countries of the former Soviet Union in St. Petersburg. Labour migration to Russia is now a widespread phenomenon. Its main sources are Ukraine, Belarus, Moldova, Azerbaijan, Tajikistan and Uzbekistan. Labour migration on the territory of the former Soviet Union is caused by a combination of economic contrasts between former Soviet republics and the relative openness of borders between the new nation states. In addition, as our previous studies have shown, migrants often still perceive the territory of the former Soviet Union as 'their own' space, and interpret the conditions and rules of life across the territory as more or less uniform, thus predictable and understandable (Brednikova and Pachenkov 2002: 43–89).

Saint Petersburg is a Russian metropolis with a large need for migrant labour. However, official institutionalised channels of entering the labour market are still only poorly developed, and are subject to constant change. This legal uncertainty affecting labour migrants pushes them onto the informal labour market, with its restricted range of opportunities, low-paid and low-status work, usually not requiring professional skills and capacities. As numerous studies of migrant or ethnic economies show (e.g., Waldinger 1995), diverse forms of small-scale entrepreneurialism constitute the traditional economic niche for migrants. In Petersburg, and many other Russian cities, labour migrants' basic sphere of activities is on construction sites and in petty retail.[1]

Labour migration to Russia is mostly individual male migration. This gender slant is connected mainly to traditional roles. The man is 'responsible' for his family, and thus compelled to take risks and take active steps to improve their economic situation. This makes migration an option. Sometimes an entire family emigrates, but usually women and children only move to a new location after the man has done so and found work there. According to the newspaper *Inostranets* ('Foreigner', 3.10.2004) in the first half of 2004, nine times more men than women arrived in Russia as migrant labourers. However, this statistic is not very reliable owing to the methodology employed, and it is certainly true that the number of female migrant workers employed in retail in St. Petersburg is considerable. They simply remain invisible to the authorities because they are not regarded as a threat to the security and stability of the host society. When checking registration documents, for instance, the police stop men far more often than women. With a few exceptions, female migrants also remain unnoticed by researchers, and most Russian publications on migration are gender-blind and implicitly focus exclusively on male migration.[2]

It is, however, precisely female labour migration that interests us. For women from the post-Soviet space, migration constitutes a radical experience of independence, in a certain sense even a spontaneous feminist project. Their biographical narratives and discourse on migration often contain motifs of liberation and gaining independence – freedom from tyranny in the family, financial freedom, or the freedom to take decisions for oneself (cf. Kosygina in this volume). Studies of how female migrants navigate and appropriate new places, of how they restructure the space of their life, and create a 'new home' and 'new location' are particularly interesting, since it is precisely women to whom traditionally an attachment to home is attributed. This attachment becomes problematic in the situation of migration.

## Conceptualising the Migrant Home

Our study followed the qualitative sociological approach of participant observation and included a series of in-depth interview-conversations.[3] Our main informants were five women who had moved to Petersburg from post-Soviet republics as migrant workers. They were women between thirty and fifty-five years old, employed in the retail sector as vendors by so-called 'owners' of the stands on the markets and retail centres. They had all been working here for at least five years (see Appendix for details).

As a rule, we looked for informants on the food markets and shop pavilions located near metro stations.[4] The market atmosphere and spatial structure (constant flow of shoppers, high counters, closed kiosks) unfortunately made it difficult to form close acquaintanceships with vendors and to conduct lengthy conversations. It became much easier to form acquaintanceships when we assumed the role of regular customers, to whom vendors grew used and whom they came to trust. This enabled us to gradually form friendly and frank relationships with them. However, the basic problem was that in the course of a 10–14 hour working day, our informants had almost no time to meet us outside the market. These factors determined the form of the investigation – frequent informal meetings and chats with female migrants at their workplace, subsequently recorded in field diaries. Conversation usually occurred in interludes when vendors were not occupied with customers.

Besides conversation, we also gathered information through observation – for instance, of the market's spatial structure, the rules of interacting with the neighbouring stalls, with customers and with the owners of booths and our informants' employees. Whenever possible, we also visited our informants at home. Unfortunately there was little opportunity for this. Our

**Fig. 4.1:** Migrant woman selling greens at the market. Photograph by the authors, 2007.

informants' lengthy and uninterrupted working hours, with only a couple of days free each month on 'sanitary days' (*sanitarnye dni*)[5], meant that for a long time it was not possible to visit them at home. But the way such visits were postponed was informative. They led up to our visits by telling us about their home and about the places they frequented in the city. The way they justified not inviting us home revealed significant practices and motifs that contributed to the constitution of domestic private space (such as cleaning the rooms or due to the apartment's owner etc.).

### Housing and 'Home'

Two factors shape the idea of the migrant's home as housing: instability (frequent moves of apartment or rooms), and lengthy working hours meaning little time is spent at home. Prior to moving to Petersburg, our informants had their own accommodation – an apartment or village house. Past feelings of ownership ('there, everything was ours') and independence ('there were no bosses there and we lived as we wanted'), in conjunction with domesticity, form their conception of 'the ideal home' that they remember, talk about with enjoyment and in great detail, even mentioning such details as the colour of the wallpaper. When talking to us, informants' tales of their previous homes were often painted in nostalgic colours. However, that home was lost in the past, and in the new circumstances, the ideal was unattainable. The new life dictated new demands and new relations regarding private domestic space, and new practices of organisation of everyday life and arranging living space.

None of our informants, despite their lengthy period as migrants, having moved to Petersburg not less than five years previously, have sufficient means to buy housing. Women (whether alone or with families) rent rooms in hostels, in communal apartments or self-contained apartments, together with other newcomers. Almost all our informants had moved apartment multiple times during their years in Petersburg. Initially, rented accommodation serves only the purpose of a 'roof over one's head' and the only criterion is the lowest possible rent. Usually, these are rooms and apartments let only to immigrant workers. As a rule, the apartments' owners are 'marginal elements' who have no regard for basic comforts or hygiene. The women told us of atrocious living conditions where the plumbing did not work 'at home' and up to ten people might inhabit the same room, and every free square centimetre was filled with market goods such as vegetables, greens, etc. However, subsequent moves and relocations were only partly motivated by the desire to improve living conditions and/or gain some domestic space. Informants, rather, told us how they moved to be 'nearer to their place of work', and the problems of overcrowding or dirt were 'only secondary'. The search for acceptable housing was made more difficult by the lack of official registration and of economic and social capital. For instance, Veronika and her husband and two children live together in a twelve-square-metre room in an eleven-room apartment, where thirty people use one bathroom. This said, in their accounts of accommodation, we almost never heard complaints about their housing problems. They told us more about the positive aspects of their accommodation and of the means they employed to overcome difficulties, such as washing laundry in an apartment without bath etc.

Initially, they took little pain to make themselves at home in their living quarters: The only things they brought with them were clothes, and the only furniture was that provided by the owner. Women do not strive to make their accommodation homely, since they regard it more as simply 'a roof over their heads', a place to sleep, and gather strength for work. For example, one of them told us of her work schedule and consequent relationship to her home:

There's nothing at all in the apartment, not even furniture. There's some-where to sleep, and hot water – and that's enough. We get home at mid-night, take a bite to eat and then sleep. (Tamara)

Even where there is a degree of stability, such as staying at the same place for a sustained period of time, they basically take no measures to furnish or do up their accommodation. Migrants moving to a new location to earn money prefer to minimise expenditure on doing up their living quarters. For instance, furniture is usually provided for free by the owner of the room or apartment, of from neighbours in a communal flat, or employers. The women do not try to 'put down roots', to make themselves at home in yet another apartment. They leave themselves a space of mobility, and the op-tion of easily moving on, by 'living out of a suitcase', ready to move at any time. They avoid accumulating old and superfluous things, and also avoid buying bulky and expensive articles and domestic appliances (furniture or fridges, washing machines, etc). The only exception here is perhaps TV or audio equipment. Watching an evening TV series is the only form of rec-reation mentioned by our informants.

Any efforts to make their accommodation more homely are usually mo-tivated by the presence of children in the family. All long-term planning of everyday life is connected with them: redecoration of a rented apartment, purchase of furniture, cooking of food to last a number of days and even, when absolutely necessary, searching for more comfortable housing. When they do up their homes, it is to provide a bare minimum of comfort for their children – for play and for doing their homework. Rubina lives together with her husband and two school-age sons in a small room in a hostel. Dur-ing the seven years she has stayed in Petersburg, she purchased one single piece of furniture, to make things more comfortable for her children:

To start with, we slept on the floor a long time, then I bought a couch for the children that cost 11,000 roubles [approx. 300 Euros]. (...) Children need things to be as they should be, and I also bought them bed clothes. (Rubina)

The domestic space of the migrant's home does not constitute a 'mirror of identity'. In our informants' homes, everything has been acquired 'by chance'. They are purely functional, and not intended to match with any concept of an interior. Here there are virtually no superfluous objects or useless souvenirs that accumulate over the years and reveal something about the owners' personalities. About the only marker of identity in the homes of women migrant workers are the photographs that our informants were keen to show us. Revealingly, the story told by such photos is the 'story of a working woman'. Most of the photos are of the workplace and colleagues from the stalls, and not of any domestic interiors.

Domestic comfort and recreation rarely constitute a topic of discussion for the women themselves. Our informants aim to attain economic self-sufficiency and to have enough money for their children. As such, they are factually excluded from possessing private space as assiduous housewives. They do not create, they only use this space. It is only significant as a temporary space for briefly relaxing before the next working day begins.

> I get very tired, like a zombie, I can't see or hear anything any more. If I could be at home, I would go to bed. (Rubina)

In their efforts to avoid spending money, women seize every opportunity to work, neglecting domestic activities, relaxation and spending time with their children.[6] On public holidays – official time off for the rest of the city – their work is particularly long and arduous, since on these days selling food, flowers and cheap clothing is particularly profitable. Their rare days off on 'sanitary days' are also cleaning days at home, when the women do the washing, housework and cooking. A number of studies have shown that 'home' becomes synonymous with cuisine for migrants.[7] However, for these women migrants, cuisine is not very important. They initially retain a fondness for 'ethnic cooking'. For instance, the migrant from Moldova told us how in the beginning she and her husband went to the station to meet the trains from Moldova and buy Moldovan wine from the conductors. However, gradually, traditional dishes are reserved more and more for special occasions, and replaced by snacks and quickly cooked meals. National cuisine remains a cultural marker to impress the neighbours – a special 'exotic' resource used to build networks and make contracts:

> When we had just moved in to this apartment, I cooked *mamalyga*[8] from corn. All the neighbours came to taste it. (Veronika)

> Those people [from among the neighbours in a communal apartment] cook who have more time, and we eat together. We cook what we have. We fry the potatoes, and fry the meat, I don't have time any more for *satsivi*.[9] We eat what we have. At the start we cooked Georgian food, but now it depends. We cook Georgian food when we all gather together. (Tamara)

Our informants' lack of any spare time allows them to rewrite the traditional gender roles whereby the woman is responsible for domestic chores and raising the children. These tasks are shifted to the man, thus reversing the traditional gender order. A migrant from Azerbaijan told us that

My husband does not work, but stays at home. I have two sons – I think it's right that he takes care of them, there's all sorts of problems – drugs, etc. You can't let them go out alone before they're eighteen. My husband cooks. He's like a housewife. (Rubina)

Our informant in this case strategically planned the family structure most suitable for her: In taking on the 'male' role of provider, she still left it to her husband to teach her sons behaviour appropriate to 'a man'. Her economic self-sufficiency allowed her to question ethnic gender codes, and to revise the distribution of authority in the family.

A: Actually, where I'm from [in Azerbaijan], it's customary to fear your husband. My brother's wife fears him.

Q: And do you fear your husband?

A: That would be the day! Why should I be afraid of him, I'm the one earning money. If I wasn't earning money, I suppose I might pretend to fear him. (Rubina)

This study's result show that, even where the husband is responsible for domestic chores and raising the children, women migrants still have to exercise control and management over these spheres, and sometimes bear the double burden of providing materially for the family as well as housework and childcare. For instance, when we visited one of our informants, we witnessed her asking her husband to hang up the washing from the machine. But he could not carry out her request, since he did not know how to open the washing machine. As a result, our acquaintance had to hang up the washing herself.

One further feature of the migrant's home is, according to our observations, its relative openness. In homes we visited, we had the impression that the private sphere overflows from out of the room into its surroundings, as if it cannot be contained within the room's perimeters. Whenever the situation allows, the doors are thrown wide and stay open, washing is dried in the apartment's communal space or in the hostel's corridors, feast days are open 'to all comers' in the communal kitchen, and *shashliks* (lamb kabobs) are barbecued in the courtyard. Something like a privatisation and domestication of public space takes place. Here, 'home' is just as open and accessible – guests are invited in, the private sphere is permeable and 'transparent', and things that might be kept secret are revealed (for instance, neighbours learn not only about what the family eats and buys, but also the relationships among family members). Obviously, such a relationship between private and public is the result of a number of factors – a very real shortage of room; the habitus of villagers such as our informants, where such behaviour is perfectly normal; and the exigencies of communal living in terms of cooperation and thus openness. Doubtless the openness of 'home' is also connected with a feeling of security. The negative experience of encounters with authorities due to the lack of formalised status, or intolerance exhibited on the part of Petersburg inhabitants, results in the doors of the 'home' being closed. For instance, we attribute the consistent reluctance to invite us to their home in the room of a dormitory (Rubina) to an insurmountable distrust towards new acquaintances we could not overcome.

## The City as 'Home'

Generally, women migrant workers move to Petersburg from small settlements, and they learn about life in a large city here, in the already extreme situation of being an immigrant. The encounter with city life, orientation in and appropriation of the new space starts for almost all women migrant workers with their new place of work, the marketplace.

> My move to Petersburg was a gamble, I had no acquaintances here. I arrived, and immediately set off for Sennaya Ploshad [Haymarket], and that same day I found my first job, working for Tajiks. I started work. I lived in the railway station for the first week, and then managed to find an apartment. (Olya)

As described above, women migrant workers spend most of their time at work. This means that their workplace (stalls in markets, shop pavilions and booths) becomes their key point in space, their reference point in the space of the city, structuring and forming the remaining space and everyday life. This is where the city begins, and from where our informants start to familiarise themselves with and feel at home in the previously unknown territory. This said, usually only the space of the market and surrounding territory is particularly familiar to them. Our informants are largely uninterested in what lies beyond. In the mid 1990s, feminist geographers turned their attention to the fact that women usually look for work close to home, to facilitate their roles as carers for children and providers of domesticity (Hondagneu-Sotelo and Avila 1997: 548–71). In our study, we see the reverse logic – the women make their homes close to their place of work. Women migrants often try to move nearer to their work. This strategy is chosen with the aim of avoiding loss of time and money moving around town. Apart from that, minimisation of the home-work-home journey, or more appropriately the work-home-work journey, is also connected with their desire to lower the risk of encountering the police, who usually check documents and registration near to metro stations, and only occasionally raid the markets.

Women migrant workers change their place of work fairly easily. While remaining vendors, almost all our informants had regularly changed their places of work in favour of better conditions or better relations with the owners of the goods. They did so not just within the boundaries of one market, but between markets or retail centres. A change in place of work usually also entailed moving apartment, since the migrants tried to find accommodation close to their new work.

The area around where they live is not of great interest to them. They can find all the infrastructure they need for everyday life on the market place. That is where they usually buy food and clothes. Migrants with children are more active in navigating the area around their house. In this case, women look for nurseries, schools and surgeries nearby. They hardly explore other areas of the city. Places of recreation are 'the stuff of dreams'. Our informants dream of going to the theatre, to a concert or the disco, for a massage, or even 'just to walk around the town' (Tamara). However, migrants' life follows different dictates, and leaves no time or energy for leisure. This means that for woman migrant workers, the city is predominantly their place of work and place of abode. Recreational Petersburg is, on the other hand, an imagined city, the city of tourist brochures and 'second-hand information'. One of our informants (Olya) extolled the great number of bridges in the city. But she already knew about them prior to her move to Petersburg, and their existence remained for her 'purely theoretical', since during her five-year stay in Petersburg she had not once found the time to gaze upon them. The migrants' dominant image of the city still remains touristic:

> When I travel back home, I'm even ashamed to have nothing to tell. I live in such a city and I have seen nothing and been nowhere. (Olya)

Thus the migrant woman's city is mainly structured around two objects – 'work' and 'home'. Other places practically do not feature. For instance, we heard the expression from one of our informants who was planning on going to a pop concert for the first time in many years, that she had no 'clothes for going out in' (Olya). Such an expression basically reflects a perception of the city as a bipolar space where there is 'work and home' and 'all the rest' where the latter is sometimes generalised as 'city'.

In our informants' image of the city, there is almost no centre and periphery, no official city districts or administrative boundaries. We are accustomed to viewing city space as a map, and employ categories such as north-south and official and informal names of city districts, and we fill out this map with significant objects, uniting it into one whole. Our informants structure the city somewhat differently, and they do it 'off the map', without using our general holistic picture. This is why initially their space seemed to us to be fragmented and even broken up, not able to be pieced together cohesively. It seemed to consist of discrete parts mostly because the women rarely move around the town. They hardly use any public transport apart from the metro: Express bus services are expensive, so only those are used that are vital for travelling between home and work or to nurseries or schools. Metro is the only means of transport used more universally, although only when strictly necessary. But underground journeys do not help migrants' perceptions knit the city together. Our informants' 'Pale of Settlement' is conditioned by the harsh demands of their working conditions and their economising, for they regard each journey as costing money and risking an encounter with the police.

However, it transpired that these women's perception of the city in fact did contain a unifying dimension. Frequently changing jobs and consequently frequently 'moving home', the women moved around the city in this way, gradually navigating and appropriating it. The 'house-work' link migrates and duplicates itself through the entire territory of the city, filling in the empty space with objects significant for the women. In this, their mental structure of the city turned out to correspond to the map of the metro. When talking about places in Petersburg, about their previous work or where their friends and relatives live, our informants described these places exclusively in terms of the nearest metro station: 'My father lives at "Prospekt Veteranov"' (Rubina), or 'I used to work at "Ozerki"' (Veronika), etc. Even where migrants do not use the metro as a means of transport, it figures significantly in the way they structure space. The metro creates a holistic image of the city and is used to divide the city into districts. Its stations constitute mini-centres around which the city's space clusters. If their place of work or of abode is at some distance from a station, they nevertheless refer to the nearest to describe the location. Obviously such way of structuring space is far from unique and many locals use the same method of conceiving and ordering the city's space. But for our informants, this is the only means employed. Perhaps the development of a more complex and multi-layered system of structuring the urban space could serve as index of the migrants' integration.

The issue of social segregation, of linkage between physical and social space, is usually expected to constitute a natural part of any discussion the place of immigrants in the city. In the case of Petersburg, however, it is still too early to talk of segregation. The status of districts and the housing market are still in flux. Segregation processes in the city are to be found more on the level of blocks, houses and floors, rather than districts or neighbourhoods. A more common phenomenon is segregation between housing that looks out onto the street (front of house) and housing that looks out onto courtyards, with the former being considered much superior. Indeed, we can only talk of segregational tendencies. As described above, migrants prefer to settle in close proximity to their place of work – i.e., near the markets. They club together to rent cheap rooms and apartments in the cheapest and more downmarket areas, where no renovation has taken place and communal apartments still exist. Obviously, this strategy contributes to the formation of a certain type of social space. However, the scale of such segregation is still limited and not immediately apparent. In such districts, neighbouring blocks, neighbouring houses and neighbouring apartments can have different statuses and different states of repair. Our informants say that they do not feel any sense of belonging to such districts, any sense of being at ease and in safety. The women said that they could easily, and without any regrets, move to a new location in the case of 'career success' – that is, in the event that they found a more stable and lucrative job, and correspondingly, more comfortable living quarters.

Despite the fact that, according to the female migrant workers, there are no city districts 'where they belong', almost all of them say that they feel relatively at ease in Petersburg. In the words of A. Bikbov, 'on arrival in a strange city, or better, when navigating a differently structured space, there are many occasions for surprise, ecstasy and shock' (Bikbov 2002: 3). However, not one of our informants, all of whom previously lived in small towns or villages, remembered having such feelings. Migrants also denied experiencing any fear of the large and unknown city. For one, from their point of view, the city does not even seem that big.

Q: Did you need a lot of time to get used to the city when you arrived?

A: Why did I need to get used to it? As soon as I arrived, I found work, and also accommodation at work. I don't travel around the city. (Rubina)

Secondly, the women do not perceive their relocation as constituting migration to a different state and a change of citizenship. Petersburg is, just as in Soviet times, not perceived as being in any way a part of a foreign country. Russia 'is not Italy or Turkey', where many of their relatives and acquaintances live.

The Soviet Union might have collapsed, but you still feel yourself at home here. I am not afraid of anything here and can walk the streets safely until two in the morning if I want to. (Tamara)

**Fig. 4.2:** Veronika at her former work place, a small kiosk selling alcohol and cigarettes. Photograph of the informant, 2002.

Only once did an informant tell us of being afraid in connection with Petersburg. But this fear was not for herself, but for her children. Growth of xenophobia in Petersburg, availability of drugs and the general criminal situation in the city all comprise sources of danger (Rubina). We regard this fear not as being afraid of the city, but of general worry about the well-being and safety of the children.

Thus, the city as a localised place of practices in one way or another becomes 'home' for woman, for it is a habitable and safe space, 'their' space. For all the apparent localisation and restrictedness of their lives, our informants enjoy ease of movement around the city, they change place of work and abode, and do not get tied to one neighbourhood or district. Their conceptions of urban space fit perfectly with the idea of the modern city that has neither ends, nor a centre, nor demarcated districts. It is rather an alloy of often disassociated processes and social heterogeneity, a place where far and near intermingle, a succession of different rhythms, a place constantly spilling out in new directions (Amin and Thrift 2002).

## *The Homeland Is Where the Home Is*

In accordance with our analytical conception of the broadening space of the 'home' (housing – address – place of origin) based on our informants' own conceptions, we will here examine the conception of home as homeland. It should be noted that the word 'homeland' (in Russian, *rodina*), used in the title of this chapter, was almost never used in conversation with our informants. It is a category of elevated or official discourse, and as such not used by the migrants. Their relationship to their places of origin is more prosaic, down-to-earth and lacking any pathos and patriotic overtones. But we decided to use it because the Russian language has difficulties naming this place. The word 'homeland' is privatised by elevated discourse, and 'place of origins' – by administrative discourse. Quotidian discourse knows only the word 'home'. In this sense, when analysing the concept of our migrants' home, we should have started with homeland, place of departure, because this is what the women most frequently refer to as 'home'. However, since we started with the idea of home as a space of localised, routinised practices, place of origins is what is least likely to be understood as 'home'.

Women migrant workers' reasons for migration are predominantly economic. Migrants emigrated to earn money and provide financial support for their families – children and/or husband, parents, sometimes brothers and sisters. To start with, migrants' social ties and networks with the society they have left behind remain very strong.[10] These links are very intensive and active: migrants often phone home, write letters, pass on or send money, and visit their family whenever possible. As the duration of migration increases, with every year spent in St. Petersburg, these links weaken. The situation of migration and the distance from people with whom they used to live, forces a redefinition of the zone and degree of responsibility. As soon as possible (when there is some certainty in terms of work and housing), women migrants' children move to live with them in Petersburg. Other ties and moral and economic obligations to relatives, grow significantly weaker, or disappear altogether.

> I don't understand why I should pay for a flat when I don't live there. OK, my elderly mother lives there. But she has other children apart from me. Let them help her now! I have to live at least a bit for myself. (Olya)

Nevertheless, migrants still nurture ties with the homeland. According to informants' accounts, they are the ones to initiate contact to relatives. Obviously the reverse is made more difficult by the frequent moves of our informants, resulting in frequent changes of address, whereas addresses and telephone numbers of those in the place of origins are less likely to change. In this way, it is the migrant women who are the key to staying in touch, and they dictate the rules: the form and frequency of such relations, and whether to initiate or break such ties in the first place. They use telephone to maintain their ties to close relatives or friends left in the homeland, since it is the most accessible and direct form of monitoring and controlling the situation with their relatives.

> I phone home every evening. I hear that the children are asleep and you know that everything is OK. (Tamara)

Apart from exceptional situations, such as the death of a close relative or friend, return visits to the homeland are very rare. As a rule, they don't happen more than once every one or two years and are made during a week or two of holidays. Such trips are usually for rest and recreation. Polya sends her children home during the holidays and occasionally travels with them as well. In this way, the place of origin becomes more a zone of recreation. However, this also starts to fade:

> I travel home in the summer for two weeks to rest, but I immediately die of boredom there! There's nothing to do. Next year, if I get the money and a visa, I'll go to Bulgaria with a friend. (Olya)

Nevertheless, it is possible to talk of a sort of emotional bond to the homeland that manifests itself either in the form of nostalgic reminiscences of the past, or utopian projects of the future. In the course of our conversation with them, the women sometimes reminisced about the past, about their lives before their emigration, with regret. Veronika, for instance, told us with a note of sadness how she missed her wooden house in Moldova. According to our observations, such nostalgic touches are usually connected with their past life, but not with the actual place where they used to live.

The second form of emotional bond to the homeland is the 'myth of return'. Almost all our informants told us of their prospective move back with a large degree of doubt. We think it likely that such a myth of return is necessary to leave oneself a potential alternative to the current life. The theme of return is important more as an idea, but not as a project that they will work towards. Narratives and memories about the previous place of abode are extremely important as a point of reference for 'updating oneself'. The homeland becomes a point of departure for one's own career and development. Moreover, it is a place of confirmation of one's own success. Nostalgic longings are much less frequent as narratives of the homeland than are alarmist categories of collapse and ruin, unemployment or of boredom and nothing to do. In this way, in narratives about the place of origins, there is a distance between 'yesterday' and 'today', a break with the society they have left behind and a closer bond to the host society. However difficult life might be in Petersburg, to go back home would be interpreted as defeat. Such narratives reflect especially long-term life projects connected with Petersburg.

Thus our study shows migrants' gradual detachment from and even break with their place of origins. The homeland is more important as a point of reference, as the framework for the formation of today's identity. The fact of naming the place of origin 'home', in our view, in many ways demonstrates the very idea of home as past, superseded, having become distant and not very relevant.

## 'Home' as a Space of Social Ties

In constructing the concept of the migrants' home, social ties play a very important role. 'There they are all our friends' – Rubina said once about the shop pavilion where she worked. This important category reflects migrants' concepts of a stable and safe space where everything is comprehensible and predictable. 'One's own' space is sometimes itself accorded the status of 'home'.

> On the market we congratulate each other when there is occasion, and celebrate birthdays as if it was our home ... (Olya)

Taking into account the meaning of social ties in the construction of 'one's own' space, we decided to dedicate a section to analysing the structure of the women migrant workers as agents and social relationships between them.

Despite their relatively brief period of living in Petersburg, our informants are involved in a large number of interactions and networks. A telling manifestation of this is the large number of names mentioned and listed in almost every narrative or conversation with us on any topic, whether it was a discussion of work initiated by us or just 'something that happened.' It is not just names that were mentioned, but also the exact link – who they were and what the relationship was. Whole stories grew up around these names, such as the history of the acquaintanceship, of recent dealings, etc. The frequent mention of other people involved in the migrants' lives marks not only their extended and intensive social network, but also its great significance for them.

Who is involved in these networks? Our informants were originally the initiators of their own move to Petersburg and established themselves in the city by themselves, 'gathering' or even 'earning' networks. Relatives and people from their area, having settled in the city long before their arrival, become an important, but not a crucial resource when setting oneself up in a new place, and looking for work and accommodation. Veronika told us that her mother some years previously also came to work in Russia, and works in both Moscow and Petersburg. However, they have almost no contact to each other, since both changed address so often they finally lost each other. In this way, they chose individual life strategies, independent of each other and without affording mutual assistance. As previous studies showed, in migrants' lives, emerging social networks are not informed by shared ethnicity or kinship, they are instrumental and contextual. Ties that emerge at the place of migration, among the people in the migrants' immediate vicinity, do more for them and are more in demand (Brednikova and Pachenkov 2002: 74–81).

The main places where social ties are formed are the workplace and place of abode. The chief participants in migrants' social networks are colleagues, employers, customers and even landlords and neighbours. The women often describe their relationships with their environments in categories of kinship, emotional nearness and selfless mutual assistance.

> I've lived here three years, and I've never had an argument with Marina [the neighbour], I get on with her better than with a sister. (Veronika)

Apart from emotional support, networks also fulfil other important functions, such as integration in the host society. Networks circulate important information, exchange resources and services, etc. For example, networks help find living accommodations or work. Landlords give our informants furniture and clothes, neighbours share their domestic appliances and colleagues from the market, renting rooms in the same apartment, take on some of the housework, contribute money to the shared kitty, etc. In return, migrants can offer to keep an eye on the apartment, or offer vegetables from the market, they lend money, and help about the house, etc.

As our observations showed, women constantly work on the establishment and reproduction of social ties and networks, creating a body of reliable and mutually profitable interactions. Thus, after our acquaintanceship, it was our informants who became the initiators of meeting. They called us periodically, enquired how life was and told us about theirs, offered to meet, etc. Initially, on arriving in a new social environment, migrants have little social capital, so their work on creating social ties is purposeful and demands considerable effort and application.

Networking not only involves communicating. Our study showed the great importance of their work in creating and supporting professional and personal (moral) reputation. Women choose the behavioural strategy 'be good (kind, good-humoured) to everyone' – police, customers, employers, neighbours, etc. This emotional work helps them to 'domesticate' social space, to make it 'their own', lending life in the city and at home a degree of stability. To establish 'effective', i.e., instrumental and convenient relations with the men our informants depend on (employers, neighbours etc.), they employ 'womanly strategies' of flirting and coquettishness that allow them to balance between sexual and amicable relations and ultimately forming a circle of 'their own', 'trusted' men, on whom they can rely in case of difficulties. Frequently, women enter into relationships with men that could be called a contractual sexual partnership, when the partners are economically independent of each other, emotional entanglement is kept to a minimum, but there is mutual support and assistance.

Thus, personal reputation for migrants constitutes valuable capital that brings in regular returns. During field work, we often heard stories about how much the women's efforts to create a positive impression of themselves ('I smile at everyone') 'were working'. For instance, during the celebration of Petersburg's 300th anniversary, the police did not evict the family of one of them from the city as illegal immigrants, because the officer had a good relationship to them. Another found accommodation thanks to a customer, who recommended her as being clean and tidy; an estate agent who is the regular customer of a third migrant is now helping her find accommodation. The women love to tell stories of how customers came back to them to say how they liked their service, and how former employers phone them and offer them work, etc. 'Regular customers' are important participants in migrants' social networks. In contrast to ties to colleagues who are mostly also migrants, ties to customers are more effective in terms of integration. Such networks help find accommodation, get information about the city, etc. They attract regular customers by lowering prices, choosing the best goods. When talking to vendors at booths, we noticed that regular customers arrived at about 1 o'clock. Usually the women drew our attention to it, showing how they are appreciated by the locals around them, who regard them as 'their own'. Initially, we posed as regular customers for our informants, and it was precisely the openness and interest of our informants, their desire to chat to us that made it quite easy for us to get to know them and subsequently carry out our fieldwork.

In this way, strategic deployment of emotions and the 'commodification of feelings' become an important component of our acquaintances' economic activity and their quotidian communication, becoming a usual and even routine practice:[11]

> I always try to smile.... Everyone remembers me and says hello, even the shop vendors. My customers always come back. Recently I fell ill, and one woman came and refused to buy clothes from my replacement, saying she would wait until I was back. (Veronika)

## Conclusion

Thus the concept of home as a private space for women migrants ceases to be relevant. Their 'home' is mobile, situative and not linked to long-term perspectives and projects. Privacy breaks down and is rejected in favour of integration and economic efficiency and well-being. Under such conditions, 'home' does not denote stability and safety but functionality and convenience (cheapness, proximity to work, presence of 'one's own' circle of associates). Such a 'home' is not for returning to but for leaving. It is not where one stays after giving birth, and it is not where one 'spends time' etc. The 'home' of women labour migrants gradually broadens out spatially; its borders become unclear and are in constant flux.

For researchers of today's society of individuals, this flexible perception of space and place devalues the middle-class 'my home is my castle' ethos and actively opposes mobility to sedentariness (Bauman 2001: 35) – where the latter is the index of powerlessness and subordination, and the former the main index of privilege (Bauman: 49). The capacity to flexibly reconfigure and change one's life, to divest oneself of long-term attachments to things, to create flexible social ties and solidarity, mobility and ease in acquiring the rules of interaction – all these are key factors of contemporary social stratification, where at the top of the pyramid are those 'building' their homes by precisely these rules.

Research ascribes all these modalities to the privileged classes, the professional and political elites, whose representatives are equipped with laptops, ubiquitous Internet access, diverse means of transport and significant financial resources, allowing them to devalue place, 'play' with space and time, and enjoy 'freedom of relocation'. Migrants, on the other hand, are victimised. As a rule, they are attributed the role of 'flurrying to find a place to survive' (Bauman: 38). Our study shows that a lack of attachments to places and things is just as typical for migrants 'positioning [themselves] in a network of possibilities rather than paralyzing oneself in one particular job' (Bauman: 39) They dwell in space; however, they are not tied tightly to physical space, but control it through strategic practices and social networks they establish in their urban environment.

The women's biographies reveal scenarios of individualisation – liberation from certain social forms and certainties characteristic of modern societies. They subject the 'traditional' institutions of family and marriage to review, and form a family of convenience that dissolves on becoming inconvenient. Our informants also manage to free themselves from profession and company, decentralise the place of work (Beck 2000).

Planning, flexible rethinking of ties and change of location, openness to new economic and social opportunities characterise the behaviour of the post-modern subjects that include labour migrants. This post-modern biographical scenario of the 'independent woman' becomes possible for them precisely in the situation of migration, which would seem marked by social vulnerability, lack of resources and uncertainty. In this way, women labour migrants constitute an unexpectedly vivid example of the post-modern nomadic subject.

### Appendix: Informants

Veronika: From Moldova, thirty years old, has lived in St. Petersburg for five years; married with two children (eleven and three respectively), rents a room in a communal flat of eleven rooms, lives with husband and children. She sold vegetables on the Sytnyi market for a long period of time – and then in a booth by a metro station. For a period of some months she sold clothes at Apraksin Dvor – the largest clothes market of the city. Now she is working as dish-washer in a cheap café.

Polya: From Ukraine, has lived in St. Petersburg for ten years; thirty-five years old, divorced, two children (sixteen and thirteen respectively), sells vegetables in a booth by a metro station. She lives with her son, the elder daughter recently returned to Ukraine. Rents a two-room flat together with a Ukrainian friend who also lives with her son.

Tamara: From Georgia, eleven years in St. Petersburg; fifty to fifty-five years old, widow, two sons (thirty and seventeen years old respectively, who live in Georgia with the informant's mother) sells flowers at a metro station stall. Practices shuttle migration – lives three to four months alternatively in Georgia and in Petersburg. Works alongside her niece, a student. She currently rents a room in a three-room flat which she shares with her niece and her niece's mother.

Rubina: From Azerbaijan, nine years in St. Petersburg; approx. forty years old, married, two sons (thirteen and fourteen years old), sells vegetables in a booth by the metro, rents a room in a hostel, lives with husband and children.

Olya: From Belarus, six years in St. Petersburg, age – approx. thirty years old. Not married, no children. Sells vegetables in the Sennoi market. Rents a room in a three-room flat, lives alone.

*From the Russian by Graham Stack.*

## Notes

1. However, 15 January 2007, when we had finished the fieldwork for this story, a new migration law was passed that barred foreigners from working in petty retail. These changes are significantly altering the situation portrayed here. Now former migrant vendors lacking Russia citizenship either have to change their type of work, or find some loophole in the law, find some way of getting citizenship, or break the law.
2. One can mention here the following works on female labour migration in Russia: I. Britvina and M. Kiblitskaya, *Zhizn migrantki v monograde*, Moscow, 2004; E. Tyuryukanova and M. Malysheva, *Zhenshchina. Migratsiya. Gosudarstvo*, Moscow, 2001.
3. Projects: 'Female labour migration: a shift in gender contracts?' (funded by MacArthur Foundation, 06.2002-08.2004), 'Concept of 'Home' and practices of constructing it in migration' (situation of female migrants in St. Petersburg) (funded by Heinrich Böll Foundation, 03.2005-09.2006).
4. Shop pavilions adjacent to metro stations are roofed retail clusters containing small booths and boutiques selling cheap foodstuffs. People make purchases there on the way to or from work. Such pavilions are a more structured and controllable form of the informal market places that cropped up beside metro stations. Nevertheless, such pavilions are, after the major city markets, the largest employer of women migrants. (For a map of central St. Petersburg see fig. 2.2 ).

5. 'Sanitary day' is, as a rule, the only day in the month when markets or shop pavilions close to allow full-scale cleaning work.
6. Our informants prefer to support their children financially than emotionally or physically. Veronika, for instance, went back to work only two months after giving birth to her second child. Rubina, when she goes to work, 'used to leave my sons at home by themselves, they were six to seven years old, and they cried all day so the neighbours heard, but I had to go to work'.
7. On the construction and reproduction of the meaning of home in connection with cuisine, see, for instance, T. Döring et al (eds), *Eating Culture. The Poetics and Politics of Food*, Heidelberg, 2003; E. Petridou, 'The Taste of Home', in *Home Possessions. Material Culture behind Closed Doors*, ed D. Miller, Oxford, New York, 2001, 87–106.
8. Type of *kasha* or porridge.
9. Georgian meat dish.
10. For young women, without a family, the reason for migration might also be individual interests (not family-linked). In such a case, migration is permanent from the very beginning, and there is no shuttling to and from. However, this study does not examine such cases.
11. See A. Hochschild, 'Emotion Work, Feeling Rules, and Social Structure', *The American Journal of Sociology* 85, no.3, 551–75; A. Hochschild, *The Commercialization of Intimate Life. Notes from Home and Work*, Berkeley, Los Angeles, London, University of California Press, 2003.

## REFERENCES

Al-Ali, N. and Kh. Koser. *Transnationalism, International Migration and Home, in New Approaches to Migration? Transnational Communities and the Transformation of Home*, eds. N. Al-Ali and Kh. Koser, London, New York, Routledge, 2002.

Amin, A. and N. Thrift. *Cities: Reimagining the Urban*, Cambridge, 2002.

Bauman, Z. *The Individualized Society*, Cambridge, 2001.

Beck, U. *Oshchestvo riska. Na puti k drugomu modernu* (Risk Society), Moscow, 2000.

Berger, J. *And Our Faces, My Heart, Brief as Photos*. London, Writers & Readers, 1984.

Bikbov, A. 'Moskva/Parizh: prostranstvennye struktury i telesnye skhemy', *Logos* no. 3/4 (34) (2002): 2–17.

Brednikova, O. and O. Pachenkov. 'Etnichnost 'etnicheskoi ekonomiki' i sotsialnye seti migrantov', *Ekonomicheskaya Sotsiologiya* T.3, no. 2 (2002): 74–81.

Brednikova, O. and O. Pachenkov. "'Migrants' and 'Caucasians' in St. Petersburg: Life in Tension', *Anthropology & Archeology of Eurasia* (Armonk) 41, no. 2. Fall (2002): 43–89.

Glick Schiller, N., L. Bash and C. Blanc-Szanton (eds.) *Towards a Transnational Perspective on Migration. Race, Class, Ethnicity, and Nationalism Reconsidered.* New York: Annals of the New York Academy of Sciences, vol. 645 (1992).

Hondagneu-Sotelo, P. and E. Avila. "I'm Here, but I'm There': The Meanings of Transnational Motherhood', *Gender and Society* 11, no. 5 (1997): 548–71.

Rapport, N. and A. Dawson. 'The Topic and the Book', in *Migrants of Identity. Perceptions of Home in a World of Movement*, eds. N. Rapport and A. Dawson. Oxford, New York, 1998.

Waldinger, R. 'Immigrant Enterprise. A Critique and Reformulation', *Theory and Society* 15, no. 1/2 (1986): 249–285.

# ❧ 5 ☙

# African Communities in Moscow and St. Petersburg

*Issues of Inclusion and Exclusion*

### SVETLANA BOLTOVSKAYA

## Introduction

Racially-motivated violence against Africans and people with black skin has become a topic of discussion in both the Russian and the international press, in academic discussions and even in international monitoring (Ezhova 2002, Gaidamak 2006, Jackson 2006, Klomegah 2006, Diène 2007). Because of the number of racially-motivated attacks in Russia, it is difficult to write about African communities in Russia without focusing on the problem of racism. This, however, often results in Africans in Russia being reduced to the role of victims in public discourse, and to other aspects of African communities in Russia being neglected.

The number of Africans living in Russia is not comparable with the black population in Western countries, but most of them feel and see themselves as a part of the worldwide African diaspora(s) (Zips 2003, Fabre 2004, Mayer 2005). All Africans living in Russia regard Africa as their shared home continent, and it binds them permanently to friends and family members outside Africa and Russia. Their shared experience of life in Russia as foreign and often hostile, as well as their being pigeonholed as a group owing to their shared colour of skin, strengthens their pan-African identity ('we Africans'), solidarity and the formation of a number of interlinked communities that go beyond religious, linguistic and ethnic borders (Allina-Pisano 2007: 188).

This article describes the social practices of some Africans in Russia who are, on the one hand, marginalised in society, yet, on the other hand, involved in social organisations in Russia. It focuses on two organisations and their projects: The first is the Moscow Protestant Chaplaincy (MPC), a US church where currently 60 per cent of all members of the congregation are Africans. They are also involved in social charity projects of the MPC, such as a soup kitchen for low-income Muscovites, a parish centre, a task force on racial attacks, as project coordinators, volunteers, and participants. The other is a 'pure African' non-governmental organisation *Afrikanskoe Edinstvo* (African Union St. Petersburg[1]) founded by Africans living in St. Petersburg and *Leningradskaya Oblast'.* This organisation arranges many charitable and cultural activities for the African community, stands up for their rights and also organises many projects to fight the social exclusion of Africans in Russia and to develop racial tolerance in the city.

The choice of these organisations was determined by the fact that they are pan-African, in contrast to most other African initiatives in Russia (such as the Nigerian community in Russia, Cameroonian business community in Russia, Congolese and Somali diasporas, etc.) and secondly that they attempt to combat social exclusion of Africans dating back to Soviet times, and to integrate Africans as active participants in the public life of both cities.

## Diversity of Africans in Russia and the Problem of Exclusion

There are no exact data about how many inhabitants Moscow has: Official statistics put the number at 10.5 million officially registered in 2007; but counting so-called illegals and people living in Moscow but not registered there, the actual number of inhabitants is considerably higher. Neither are there reliable data on the number of Africans living in Moscow. Anna Brazhkina und Igor Sid, the authors of the www.africana.ru website, put the number of Africans living in Moscow at over 10,000, constituting 0.05 per cent to 0.1 per cent of the total population.[2] The activists of African Union in St. Petersburg, Aliou Tounkara and Ali Nassor, put the number of Africans living in St. Petersburg at up to 5000 (interviews 2006), making up a similar proportion of the total city population, since the total official population of St. Petersburg was 4.5 million in 2006.[3] However, Africans are far from constituting a homogenous group, comprising black people from all sub-Saharan African states speaking different African and European languages and adhering to different religions (Islam, different confessions of Christianity, traditional African religions, etc.) They are also internally differentiated by their social and legal status: Russian citizens, students, stateless persons, asylum seekers.

In Soviet times, almost all black people in Moscow and St. Petersburg were students, diplomats or state or party visitors from the pro-Soviet

African countries. Although many of them lived in the USSR for many years, they were often excluded from social life. They were neither *chuzhie* ('Others' from capitalist Western countries) nor *svoi* ('ours'). In official Soviet discourse, they were of course the 'younger siblings' of the socialist brotherhood, objects of international solidarity and comrades in the anti-imperial, anti-colonial and anti-capitalist struggle. They belonged to the socialist camp in the cold war, serving the Soviet Union's foreign policy goals and presenting an international alternative to the 'capitalist West'. Officially, the Soviet Union trained Africans to support developing countries, but these cadres were also intended to promote the Soviet Union's own political and economic interests in Africa. In the USSR, however, they were not really 'one of us', but remained foreigners, since they were neither Soviet citizens nor Russians (Allina-Pisano 2007: 188). This position as being *in-between* defined Africans as being both 'fraternal foreigners' and outsiders, and protected them in this double role from ubiquitous racism on the part of the population. It also, however, excluded them from real social integration. In the Soviet Union, private contacts between Soviet citizens and foreigners were in general frowned upon and kept under strict observation by the KGB. It was difficult, if not impossible, for a Soviet woman to marry a foreigner. The state put a large number of obstacles in the way of any such attempt. If an African man (most students were male) married a Soviet woman, it was expected that both would return to the African country of origin after finishing their studies. As a former student from Ethiopia who had studied in Moscow in the 1980s said:

> Africans are nostalgic about their university days in the Soviet Union, but to be honest, it was not all so sunny.... You were not really allowed to spend a night outside of the student dormitories. If you did, it was better to write in a report that you had been drunk and fallen asleep somewhere, e.g. under a bridge, and could not remember anything. It was important not to name any names, so that Russian friends did not get into trouble with the KGB. If you wanted to date a girl, you had to report her name to the relevant authorities [probably those responsible for supervising foreign students – S.B.], then the girl was called before the KGB a number of times, and subjected to a sort of brainwashing, and not every girl was ready after such an experience to date an African man a second time' (interview in Moscow, September 2006).

Since 1985, the social and political situation in Russia and in many Africans countries changed significantly. The African Community in big Russian cities has become more and more socially diverse during this period. Since 1991, refugees from African countries have come to Russia asking for asylum, and some of the former students have received refugee status after the political situation in their countries of origin changed dramatically.[4] Some Africans fell in love with Russian citizens, got married and stayed in Russia. But the majority of Russians are not yet ready to accept people from African origins as 'their own citizens'. The process of globalisation also changes the reasons for social exclusion of Africans. Although more and more black Russians are becoming publicly visible, mainly artists, singers and dancers on television and in the advertising industry and show business, which is a sign of globalisation in Russia, the image of Africa and Africans generated by Russian media remains negative: Africa is described as a poor, hopeless continent characterised by AIDS and hunger. The Russian inhabitants of Moscow and St. Petersburg place their cities unambiguously in the so-called 'First World' of the new global world order. Hence, Africans are confronted with many prejudices similar to those in 'western' European countries (Allina-Pisano 2007: 190). They and others from 'developing countries' are no longer 'younger siblings in the international anti-capitalist struggle', but members of the 'Third World' – i.e., migrants and perceived as a threat, forming one of the categories of social actors that make up a world city (Hannerz 1993). It is, however, primarily people from the former Soviet republics of the Caucasus and Central Asia that constitute the majority of the Russian 'Third World' population. This also makes the situation of Africans in Russia today similar to the situation of Africans in other European countries, with the exception that, in contrast to Western Europe, Russians as other post-socialist East Europeans are less accustomed to daily contact with Africans and were themselves plunged into an identity crisis in the 1990s that strengthened xenophobia and racist tendencies and offered nationalism as an alternative to the old forced socialist ideology (Kaschuba 2001: 21). Furthermore, Russian legislation with regard to foreigners is not sufficiently developed and this exacerbates the situation (Ezhova 2002).

While 'the West' has been the Soviet ideological 'alien', the post-Soviet discourses include racially oriented themes and contrast the current Russianness with 'blackness' (Caldwell 2003: 255). However, in contrast to North Africa and Western Europe, Africans are referred to in Russian usually not as *chernye* (blacks) but as *negry* or *Afrikantsy*. *Chernye* and *migranty* in contemporary Russian constitute derogatory terms mainly for people looking like they come from the Caucasus or from Central Asia, and whom the population associate with criminality, violence, illegality, and illegal work (Allina-Pisano 2007; Caldwell 2004: 261). The category *Afrikansty* connotes students living in Russia on a grant temporarily. In everyday use, the term *negry* ('negroes') is used to denote Africans, which Africans themselves find discriminatory, but most Russians regard as being more neutral than *chernye*, since, as stated, the major ethnic confrontation in large Russian cities is between the Russian population and labour migrants from the Caucasus and Central Asia. A man from West Africa, living in Moscow, said: 'It is better today to have black skin than black hair [like migrants from the Caucasus]' (Interview in Moscow, September 2006)[5]. It is still the case today that the majority of Africans are students. According to the figures of the Foreign Students' Association in Russia, in 2005 around 103,000 foreigners were studying in Russia, including around 40,000 from African countries (Kotchofa 2006). In Moscow and St. Petersburg around 80 per cent of the African community are students (interview with A. Tounkara 2006). Some receive grants from their governments or from the Russian state, others have private study contracts with Russian universities. At the Russian University of Peoples' Friendship (*RUDN – Rossiiskii Universitet Druzhby Narodov*, before 1990 called the Patrice Lumumba University), founded in 1960 to train specialists from developing countries, most of the students today are Russian citizens, with around 3,500 students from abroad, including around 1000 from Africa.[6]

Most African students regard their stay in Russia as only a stepping stone (cf. Gdaniec 2008), hoping that university study will improve their career opportunities and thus their overall life chances. Many hope later to emigrate to a third country, for instance through postgraduate study in a West European country or sometimes by marrying a citizen of a 'first world' country. This was the finding of the first and only survey of Africans in Moscow conducted by the team of africana.ru website in Moscow in 2003. A share of 5 per cent of respondents sought permanent employment in Russia and 93 per cent wanted to leave Russia forever after graduating. However, despite their plans to leave, former students constitute the majority of Africans in Russia today, 10 to 25 per cent of students stay on each year (Brazhkina 2003). Some marry Russian citizens or are employed in Russia by Western or Russian companies and thus receive a (limited) residency and work permit. Others apply for asylum or stay illegally. The legal status they have in Russia determines their life.

Two other groups of Africans worth mentioning here are diplomats and embassy staff who form a small African elite in Moscow and St. Petersburg, and refugees. The latter have been arriving since the early 1990s from African crisis regions and represent a new category of Africans that did not exist during the Soviet period. Although they are recognised as refugees by the UN, they are not recognised as such by the Russian state and are regarded as illegal, turning them into helpless victims of police and skinheads.[7]

There is also a number of black Russian families, some of whom have been living in Russia for several generations. The Golden-Khanga family is a good example: African-American Oliver Golden came to the USSR in the 1920s. His daughter Lily was born in Uzbekistan, studied and worked as scientist in Moscow and married a revolutionary from Zanzibar. Their daughter, Elena Khanga, born in Moscow, is today a well-known TV presenter and author (Golden 1994, Khanga 1992). There are other prominent Afro-Russians who have enjoyed a good career – as TV personalities, journalists, singers or actors. Present in public life and enjoying professional and social recognition, they regard themselves as role models. Grigory Syatvinda, a young journalist and TV star of Zambian-Russian origins, answered the question of how he understood his role as a Russian with black skin in an interview thus: 'I avoid politics. But I think that I am a role model not only for Russians with black skin, but also for the majority of racists whose hate comes from ignorance' (Barns 2003). Most Afro-Russians have been socialised as Russians, speak only Russian and can only identify themselves as Russian. All my interview partners with children in Russia said in autumn 2006 that they speak only Russian with their children in order to strengthen the children's Russian identity which is doubted by society.

**Fig. 5.1:** An African volunteer and a Russian client at the soup kitchen of the MPC. Photograph by the author, 2006.

# The Soup Kitchen and Task Force
# at the Moscow Protestant Chaplaincy
# as an Oasis for Africans in the Russian Capital

Religious centres where Africans take active part play an important, bonding role in the lives of Africans in large Russian cities. Moscow has six mosques and a number of Christian houses of prayer of different confessions. The Moscow Protestant Chaplaincy that runs a number of projects by and for Africans is one of these centres. The MPC is an inter-denominational, international, English-speaking Christian congregation that has ministered to the foreign community of Moscow since 1962. The Christian worship takes place every Sunday at St. Andrew's Church near Metro station *Okhotniy Ryad*. Its donors include many US Christian churches, and many other congregations and individuals around the world. Most of the financing comes from the US, and the MPC was originally intended for the English speaking community in Moscow, primarily for Americans and British citizens. Now, however, more than 60 per cent of people coming to the MPC are Africans and other blacks. Many members of staff in the MPC are also Africans. Arold Rambeloarisoa, a native from Madagascar, is the Office administrator of MPC. The most important MPC activities are the food-sharing ministry with a soup kitchen, coordinated by Kifle Salomon who is a refugee from Ethiopia, living in Moscow since 1992, the Parish Centre with Young Adults and Students Group (YAS), and the Task Force on Racial Attack and Harassment, coordinated by Rony Kumi, a former student from Ghana.

In 1991, during the collapse of the USSR, the leadership of the Moscow Protestant Chaplaincy decided to share food with the poor and sick in Moscow. This was a particularly difficult time in Russia: the galloping inflation eroded the savings and pensions of millions in Russia. The MPC decided to provide food to the poor in Moscow in two ways: through soup kitchens and food bags. The MPC had four soup kitchens in the Russian capital during the 1990s (Caldwell 2004: 256). Three soup kitchens were closed in the beginning of the new century because of financial problems of the project. Since 2006 MPC has been running just one soup kitchen (*Sotsialnaya stolovaya*) on Mosfilmovskaya street which serves up to 200 people a day, five days a week, from 10 AM to 1 PM every day. The daily meal typically consists of soup, *kasha* (buckwheat porridge), meat, salad, bread and tea.

The soup kitchen is located within the space of a private commercial cafeteria which for most part of the day is open to the general public. The ethnic origins of the people who are connected to the cafeteria, but are not part of the soup kitchen is very interesting and typical for Moscow today: The owner of the cafeteria is a Russian woman, the customers who pay for

**Fig. 5.2:** People at the soup kitchen of the MPC. Photograph by the author, 2006

meals are also Russians, the staff who work at the cafeteria (cooks, cleaning personnel, waiters for commercial clients) are so-called *gastarbaitery* (the widely-used term for labour migrants in Russia today, borrowed from the German word *Gastarbeiter,* 'guest worker'): Tajiks from the Fergana valley. The main clients of the soup kitchen are Russian elderly pensioners, invalids, single mothers and their children, and other low-income Muscovites. The soup kitchen has a list of clients – poor Muscovites – referred to the MPC by government social services administration for the neighbourhood in Moscow or by other voluntary organisations. What is not typical here are the African volunteers of the MPC that run the soup kitchen: Kifle Salomon from Ethiopia coordinates the work of his staff, speaks with clients, other African volunteers serve the food for old Russians, trying to offer a kind word along with the hot food. In principle, everybody can work as volunteer at the soup kitchen, but in 2006 I saw only one Russian volunteer, an old woman. Most volunteers are low-income too: they are themselves students or refugees or former students who have chosen to live in Russia, either because they got married to a Russian spouse or decided to stay on illegally.

A typical biography is that of a West African volunteer called Bob. Bob is married to a Russian woman he met while studying in Russia. She is living at her parents' apartment with their two children in Voronezh, south of Moscow. Although she has a job at the university, her salary is too low to provide for the family. Bob is trained as a historian, but could not find any work after graduation. He moves between Voronezh and Moscow, where he stays with African friends, and works as a car mechanic without a contract, so that he can contribute to the family budget. Regular travel on public transport is very dangerous for him, but Bob does not have any money to buy a car with. He has been attacked and injured by Russian skinheads a number of times in recent years: They broke his left leg in two places, left him with concussion and near blindness in one eye. To save money, he eats in the soup kitchen, where he also works as a volunteer in the morning. It is very important for him, as for other African volunteers, that he does not get his food for free but works as a volunteer and thus earns it. He carries a small photo album in a plastic bag with pictures of his wife and children that he likes to show. Returning to his country of origin is not an option for him, since his family would not come with him and he has almost no social contacts there to help find better work than he has in Russia. He tells passionately all he has experienced and suffered in Russia, but refuses to speak into a dictaphone, even anonymously, because he is afraid that might jeopardise his position. In answer to the question as to why he does not have a better job, he says: 'Most Russians can't bear an African who is better trained and knows more foreign languages than they do. They think he is black and has just jumped down from the palm trees, how can he speak English and French, when we don't...' I met Bob in the soup kitchen again in 2007: He looked thin and much more resigned than the year previously, and tells me that he has no work at all at the moment, now lives the whole time in Moscow, and his wife only visits occasionally.

The biography of the administrator of the food-sharing ministry, Kifle Salomon is typical too. As a young man he was sent to study chemistry in the USSR by the Ethiopian government. In 1987 he started studying at the University of Baku, Azerbaijan. After the collapse of the USSR, and because of the war between Armenia and Azerbaijan, he continued his studies in Moscow at the University of Peoples' Friendship. Then he was taken ill and could not study any more. At the same time the political regime changed in Ethiopia and Kifle asked for asylum in Russia in 1993. He is today still waiting for a decision of the Russian government, meaning he has no legal status in Russia. During his time in Moscow, he has been beaten by skinheads five times.

Since 1992, directly after his relocation to Moscow, he started to work for the food-sharing ministry of the MPC and especially for the soup kitchen. He motivated his social work at the MPC with his Christian religion and his personal destiny, saying:

> I believe in socialism, but I'm Christian. There are old Russian people who come to us. We, foreigners, have also different thinking about these people. One time some young people, who were drunk, said to me: Why do you give food to them, they were communists and it is their own problem that they are poor now. But I sympathise with these old people. I also suffered in my life. I understand them, they are educated people, they did a lot for their country, but the state abandoned them.... We have the same destiny, the only difference between us is age, they have their last days of their lives now, they are alone, they need communication and contact to other people, somebody must console them. They come here not only for food; they need contact with other people (interview in Moscow, 2006).

Twice a month the Moscow Protestant Chaplaincy distributes 200 bags of groceries. The average bag contains a frozen chicken, rice, sugar, and cooking oil. The recipients of the food bags are primarily refugees and foreign students. This practice was started in the years after the break-up of the Soviet Union characterised by economic hardship. The Russian state stopped paying grants to African students and the remaining stipends lost their value in the high inflation of those years. In addition, wars and regime changes in many African countries prevented graduate students from returning to their home countries. Instead, they decided to stay as refugees. On 11 September 2007, I witnessed the distribution of the food bags to refugees. At 1 PM, after the soup kitchen closed, refugees from many Moscow districts and satellite towns came to the cafeteria. They included an Afghani single mother and her 14-year-old son, who collected food bags for themselves and three other children, a woman from Mozambique, who also collected a number of food bags, and a number of fathers of families from Iraq, Afghanistan, Angola, etc. Although most of them have already lived here for over ten years, they have neither refugee status nor work permit. Most of them knew each other and swapped news in French, Russian and English. Kifle Salomon and Rony Kumi drove a car laden with groceries from the market into the yard of the cafeteria. Together they unloaded the boxes with groceries from the car quickly, and its owner, an Azerbaijani, drove it back. An employee from Ghana speaking English and Russian, checked the refugees' names on a list and collected their signatures, after which the groceries were sorted into bags. While this was going on, the white American minister, Father Bob, talked to refugees who were there for the first time and needed help. A sick old African man had come on crutches and asked for medical assistance, since he had no health insurance. Finally, the Ethiopian staff members were congratulated on the new millennium, since the year 2000 according to the Ethiopian calendar was due to be celebrated on the following day.

Melissa Caldwell, an American anthropologist who did her fieldwork at this soup kitchen between 1997 and 2002 wrote that when the kitchen first opened in the early 1990s, many Muscovite recipients approached African volunteers with a mixture of curiosity and suspicion, and some clients even refused to accept meals from black volunteers. The situation was so acute that the white American minister finally issued an ultimatum: either recipients would accept food from black volunteers or they would not be served (Caldwell 2004: 262f). When I visited the soup kitchen in 2006 the situation had changed. In no other places in Moscow did I see such 'good-heartiness' and hear so many warm words from white Russians addressed to Africans. The soup kitchen was a place where people come together not only to share a meal but also to have social contacts, to discuss the local news, their health and the stories of their lives with each other. It is one of a few places in Moscow that is free from racial discrimination. African volunteers and co-ordinators are the only and very important social contact for many elderly without families, they and Africans know each other for long time.

Other projects at the MPC linked to Africans are the Parish Centre and Task Force on Racial Attacks, starting their work every day in the afternoon, when the soup kitchen is closed. The Task Force on Racial Attacks and Harassment was established by MPC in April 2001. The reason for it was a tragic occurrence: skinheads attacked a church member on a Sunday morning in April, just steps away from the St. Andrew's Church at Metro *Okhotny Ryad*. They beat him and knocked him over the head with a beer bottle. At that time, the congregation and the city were awash with reports of acts of violence against black people. Members of the congregation who had suffered attacks included diplomats, students, and refugees from Africa and Asia. Although the rise of such attacks was publicly known among the foreign community of Moscow, the police, other government officials, and the media made no mention of this growing problem. In response to this widespread silence, the Task Force was born.

The goals of the Task Force are: 1) to gather evidence and data regarding racial attacks and harassment, thus demonstrating the reality of the problem; 2) distribute this evidence and other supporting information to embassies, human rights groups, Russian government officials, and the media; and 3) provide spiritual, pastoral, and emergency care to the victims of these attacks. According to the MPC web site the Task Force members have documented more than eighty cases of harassment, violence, or unlawful police detention based on race, collecting evidence and compiling reports. In the spring of 2002, Task Force members interviewed 180 members of the African community in Moscow on a range of issues to assess their perceptions and experiences as black people living in Moscow and in 2003 they made public the rise of racist violence in Russia[8].

Task Force members also travelled to the southern Russian city of Voronezh in April 2004 to help foreign students establish a community of support for victims of racist violence in their city. They encourage all black people to be very careful in Moscow: on the web page of the MPC black people can read safety tips compiled by African members of MPC. The members of the Task Force also organise workshops for newly arrived students from African countries who do not speak Russian yet and constitute an easy target for skinheads.

In January 2002, MPC opened a Parish Centre to house their expanding ministry with African refugees and students, where also the Task Force office is based now. On the list of the Parish Centre in 2006 were approximately 140–150 refugees, more than 100 of them Africans. The Centre also houses a growing library of English-language textbooks and six computers with Internet access, as well as a reading room for Africans to gather in peace and security, only among other black people (when I visited the Parish Centre on a Friday afternoon in September 2006, I was the only white person there). Here students and refugees can do online research and communicate with their friends and families in and outside of Russia. Some refugees speak only English or French when they come to Russia. Volunteers, who are African students in Moscow, teach them Russian and also give lessons in English. Most participants who join these classes are Africans, but also refugees from Afghanistan or Chechnya or other former Soviet republics. A few students of English classes are Russians.

## Africans in St. Petersburg and the African Union

St. Petersburg is sometimes called the 'Capital of Russian Fascism' by the media and among the population owing to the large number of racially motivated murders. Although there are half as many Africans living in St. Petersburg as in Moscow, there are more African activities than in Moscow. In St. Petersburg there are not only African shops and bars but also African exhibitions and companies run by Africans. Here most Africans are organised in an NGO called African Union (*Afrikanskoe Edinstvo*).

I got to know the representatives of the African Union at a demonstration in front of Finlyandsky railway station on 1 October 2006. The murder of an Indian medical student, Nitesh Kumar Singh, in September 2006 was

**Fig. 5.3:** The president of the African Union, A. Tounkara, at the protest demonstration in St. Petersburg, 1 October 2006. Photograph by the author.

the sad occasion for the demonstration. Around 500 foreign students along with a small number of Russians chanted in both Russian and English 'We want justice', closely flanked by the police, who argued with foreign and Russian journalists about audio and video recordings. Members of the African Union had organised the demonstration and afterwards we went to the organisation's centre. Interestingly, it is located in the former cinema Maxim situated by the Metro station *Chernaya Rechka*, the spot where in 1837 the famous Russian poet Alexander Pushkin, great-grandson of the African Abraham Hannibal[9], was fatally wounded in a duel with d'Anthès.

The initiators and co-ordinators of the African Union are Aliou Tounkara, a businessman, and the journalist and university lecturer Ali Nassor from Zanzibar. In 2007, the board also included Desiré Deffo, a businessman from Cameroon, and Valence Maniragena, a university lecturer from Rwanda. Their biographies demonstrate how biographies of Africans living in Russia can have things in common and yet differ markedly. All four studied in their youth in Leningrad or St. Petersburg, and have lived there on and off for a total of fifteen to twenty-five years, and they are or were married to Russian women with whom they have children and are almost all Russian citizens.

Aliou Tounkara, President of the African Union, came to Leningrad in 1982 with a state grant from the Mali government, studied at the Polytechnical University in Leningrad, where he experienced Perestroika and the political and economic liberalisation of the country, which also made it possible for him to marry his Russian girlfriend in 1989 after graduating, stay in the Soviet Union and establish his first company in computers. During the 1990s, Aliou experienced all the highs and lows of those times. Initially his computer business flourished and Aliou was even involved in foreign trade between Africa and Russia, until the Soviet Union collapsed and tractors which he had bought in the USSR and sent to Dakar via the Baltic, suddenly vanished in the newly independent Estonia. Once during the 1990s, Aliou Tounkara even returned disappointed to Mali, where, however, he discovered that after so many years he had become 'Russian'. After a number of months, he decided to return to St. Petersburg and he completed a second degree in economics and environmental protection, but then opened some bars in the city and also a large African disco in the former cinema Maxim, which later became the offices of the African Union.

Ali Nassor, from Zanzibar, came to the USSR in 1986 'at the peak of Perestroika', as he says. He studied journalism at Leningrad State University, married in 1992 and has a son. Since 2004, he has worked for the *St. Petersburg Times* and the BBC, and taught African languages at the state university.

Valence Maniragena, from Rwanda, studied at the Leningrad University for Engineering and Technology (LITI) and after graduating in 1991 returned to Rwanda with his wife and child. Then the civil war erupted and they fled first to Zaire, then to Russia. Since they lacked registration in St. Petersburg, they went to live in the small village Novosokol'niki near Pskov, more than 460 km from St. Petersburg. On the same day that his second son was born in 1998, Valence's mother and sister were shot in Rwanda. Today, Valence, who has since acquired Russian citizenship, teaches computer science at his alma mater. Apart from his involvement with the African Union, he runs an aid organisation, *Ichumbi* ('Asylum'), which was first established for Rwandan refugees, but now aids refugees from a number of African countries (Racheva 2006).

These people joined up and founded the African Union (AU) in September 1999, and later registered it with the state authorities as an NGO for St. Petersburg and *Leningrad Oblast* (Region). Today it has 400 members[10]. The main goals and tasks of the AU fall into three categories: 1) defending the rights and interests of Africans and their family members; 2) integrating Africans, especially refugees, in Russian society, and 3) presenting and spreading African culture in St. Petersburg. It is intended to be an official representative of the African community for all state authorities and other social institutions. Membership IDs issued by the African

Union are even recognised by the St. Petersburg Interior Ministry, 'since they know that we have information about our people and that they can phone us when anything happens to any particular African' (interview with Tounkara 2006). The success of this official recognition by state authorities has, however, a double-edged effect. On the one hand, almost all Africans in St. Petersburg think they are automatically members of the organisation and therefore their rights must be defended by the AU. On the other hand, many of them do not pay any fees and do not want membership IDs, since they earn little money and also understandably do not want to pass on information about themselves to state authorities. At the same time, precisely those Africans who have no papers in Russia at all appreciate the IDs of AU, their only means to prove their identity. This is vitally important for them, since the Russian police can detain anyone who lacks ID papers. As Aliou Tounkara reports: 'Fewer than one hundred Africans in St. Petersburg possess Russian citizenship. Seventy per cent of Africans have been living here more than ten years, but have no registration. Many do not manage to switch from one status (on arrival) to residency status. They have families here, work here, but have no papers. People used to simply be arrested in such a case. Today, thankfully, they are at least not sent to prison any more' (interview 2006).

The African Union is a member of St. Petersburg's House of Nationalities (*Dom Natsional'nostei*[11]) and works together with NGOs, international human rights organisations and religious institutions such as Civil Control (*Grazhdanskii Kontrol*), the Red Cross, Caritas Russia, etc. The AU provides these organisations with information and advice relating to Africans in Russia, and tries with their assistance to organise help for Africans and their families. For example, the AU has an agreement with the Red Cross regarding medical treatment for Africans who have no health insurance. 'We have sick people who get no help from the state and have no health insurance. One of them has been housebound for three years, since he cannot walk any more. Another is trying to convalesce but is in constant pain since skinheads attacked him and smashed his eye and all his teeth. He is no longer fit to work...', Aliou Tounkara told me in St. Petersburg in October 2006.

Representatives of the AU often work at St. Petersburg's state migration service as translators and assist African asylum seekers during the asylum hearings. Aliou Tounkara mentions two types of asylum seekers: the former students and the so-called 'transits'. The 'transits' arrive in Russia as tourists, 'then discard their passports, invent a biography, file a claim for asylum and then the whole procedure starts. But those who have lived here all their life, they are ashamed to go to the migration service, and to invent a story suitable to obtain asylum, and the longer someone lives without papers, the worse things become for him: The family breaks down, and eventually he ends up on the streets like a homeless person.' For such people, Aliou Tounkara keeps a couple of beds in the cellar ('that is of course not hygienic, but better than nothing') so that they can spend the night here in an emergency. Then he sends them to the Red Cross. In addition, the AU assists single mothers of Afro-Russian children and organises childrens' events 'for our children and also for children who have been left by African fathers, to create a family atmosphere.'

Ali Nassor relates: 'Very few know about African people here. They are Russians in all aspects, in everything, they only have dark skin, but society doesn't recognise the African community living a Russian life just as Russians' (interview with Nassor 2006). Aliou Tounkara is of the same opinion:

> Our people here live badly. It is seldom that someone works according to his qualifications. Even if they have Russian citizenship, people work as doorkeepers, guards or waiters... They work at filling stations, wash cars... People always regard us as foreigners. But our work has helped create a good relationship to the municipal authorities and police. They understand: We are normal people and it is possible to work with us. We have written a number of petitions to the municipal authorities and the governor due to our concern about systematic attacks based on racial motives. Previously, it was the case that if a black man walked along the street, the police would stop him, take all his money (*'ochistit"*), and then skinheads... In 2001, we went to the police academy, and gave talks about Africans to more than a thousand future policemen. All of this was voluntary. They asked questions, sometimes stupid questions, but we anticipated this. That is very important – a simple contact: A black man stands before them on the podium, gives a lecture, speaks Russian. Merely seeing that makes a difference for them. (interview with Tounkara 2006).

Between 2005 and 2006, African Union worked together with the government-funded pro-Putin youth movement *Nashi* ('Ours') and this became one of their most important projects in the media. '*Nashi* came to us themselves and suggested a joint project, since they have a lot of money. We held five hundred talks at different schools, all of them theatrical, with drums, in African costume. *Nashi* paid our travel expenses, we did everything voluntarily. Most of the children responded well. The teachers also realised how useful our activity was. Africans also understood what we were doing: After each meeting they saw how people started talking to them' (interview with Tounkara).

Another success of African Union was in organising an official city celebration of Africa Day on May 25, including funding from the municipal authorities. In addition, AU representatives have participated in a number of different radio and TV programmes, conferences and seminars for human rights, and always underlined that they understood themselves as being members of Russian society. 'That is often the simple principle of participation, not to be from outside, but instead to be a fully fledged participant and member of society', says Aliou Tounkara.

## Conclusion

The MPC is a Christian English-language charitable organisation, whereas the African Union is a pan-African NGO, but both play important roles for the African communities:

1. In a situation where most Africans avoid public spaces such as bars, discos and restaurants for financial reasons and safety considerations, and thus are almost completely excluded from city life, both organisations create 'third places' or 'great good places', as Ray Oldenburg calls them (Oldenburg 1991)[12]. The term denotes tolerant places where Africans can gather and communicate in a relaxed and safe atmosphere free of charge or at least without requiring large expenditures. Oldenburg writes that these 'gathering places' play an important role in the continuation of the community, because in contrast to 'first places (home)' and 'second places (work)' they create informal, free and easy communication between people. For the many members of the MPC and the AU who lack permanent accommodation and employment, the value of such places is enormous.

2. Social exclusion does not just limit the financial position of the affected, but primarily injures their social interaction and psychological and emotional health. The MPC gives Africans the chance to integrate themselves in the social life of the city by helping other marginalised social groups in Moscow (pensioners, refugees, single mothers). This provides them with recognition, material and moral support, and thus strengthens their self-esteem. Mutual prejudices between volunteers and recipients are also reduced, and new social contacts and relations emerge. The African Union also tries to integrate its members in St. Petersburg society by organising cultural events in their club or in state organisations, where Africans and Russians can communicate and thus dispel their prejudices. The public position and behavioural strategies of community members aim to demonstrate tolerance in an intolerant society (Ezhova 2002).

3. In addition, the representatives of both organisations conduct public relations work with city authorities as well as with Russian and

international media to publicise the life of Africans in Russia, dispel prejudice and improve their position. The anti-racist activities of both organisations, in collaboration with other Russian NGOs, has already brought some real results. The situation with racism and xenophobia in Russia was the subject of a session of the Human Rights Council of the UN in 2006 and 2007 (Diène 2007). Russian courts have held trials of racist attackers and taken into account racist motives in their sentencing (Kozhevnikova 2007). Some state programmes have now been launched to increase tolerance in society. Everywhere in Moscow and in some places in St. Petersburg in 2007 I saw large posters showing the face of an African footballer and the slogan 'No to racism, Yes to the game' ('*Net – rasizmu, Da – igre*').

Both organisations' projects continue: The MPC Africans were very proud in September 2007 to be able to open a second soup kitchen in Moscow and in September 2009 they published a new study on racism. African Union lost use of the Maxim cinema building, and the new premises in a meeting hall on Nevsky Prospekt could only be used for a short while. Thus, in 2009, the Union only organised a number of exhibitions and is currently looking for a new centre. In the words of Aliou Tounkara and Desiré Deffo, 'We don't want to leave here. This is our home'(Kostyukovsky 2005; interview with A. Tounkara).

### NOTES

1. The organisation's Russian name is *Afrikanskoe Edinstvo*, which is translated into English by its activists as 'African Union of St. Petersburg and Leningrad Region' (interviews with A. Tounkara and Ali Nassor, St. Petersburg 2006).
2. See the official Internet site of the Moscow administration, http://www.mos.ru/wps/portal.
3. See the official Internet site of the St. Petersburg administration, http://gov.spb.ru/people.
4. This affects people from Somalia, Rwanda, Sierra Leone and many African countries where armed conflicts took place in the 1990s; the former students had to stay in Russia after their studies or flew back to Russia from their home countries. See also the case of Valence Maniragena from Rwanda in the section 'Africans in St. Petersburg and the 'African Union''.
5. To illustrate the fact that 'black' and 'African' in contemporary Russian are not identical: An Afro-Russian friend told me in 2007 that a white Russian friend had been murdered in a taxi. With reference to the murderer she said with disgust 'It was the blacks!' When she noticed my surprise, she corrected herself and said 'I mean, Caucasians' (since most taxi drivers in St. Petersburg are in fact migrants from the Caucasus).

6. According to the official website of the university: http://www.rudn.ru/?pagec
=13, 09.07.07.

7. The sociologists Lubov' Ezhova and Sergei Damberg studied application of the
Russian asylum and citizenship laws and interviewed fourteen experts and sixteen Africans (Ezhova 2002). This is one of the few studies in Russia on racism
and discriminatory administrative practice.

8. Amnesty International incorporated Task Force data and reporting into
its March 2003 publication, 'Dokumenty', the centerpiece of Amnesty International's year-long focus on racism in Russia. In January 2003 a Dutch television journalist interviewed Task Force members for a story on racism. An
April 2003 *Moscow Times* newspaper article highlighted the plight facing African refugees seeking asylum in Moscow. Interviews with Task Force members and victims of violence were published in the *New York Times, Financial
Times,* and Toronto. The US State Department cited Task Force data in its
2003 Human Rights Report for Russia.

9. Abraham Petrovich Hannibal (approx. 1696–1781), kidnapped by Ottoman
Turks from Africa as a child, came to the court of Peter the Great in 1704.
Hannibal grew up in close proximity to the Tsar, became his personal secretary
and assistant, studied in France, fought in the Franco-Spanish war and became
one of Russia's first enlightenment scholars, translating books on mathematics
and fortifications into Russian and training military engineers. He rose to the
rank of full general in the army, became governor of the engineering corps
and a Knight of the Order of Alexander Nevsky, raising him to the aristocracy
(Blakely 1986; Gnammankou 1998).

10. These and following facts and quotes come from extensive interviews with
Aliou Tunkara, St. Petersburg, 1 October 2006; with Ali Nassor, 2 October 2006
and a number of conversations in September 2007. An interview with Aliou
Tounkara and Desiré Deffo was also printed in the newspaper '*Argumenty i
Fakty*' (Kostyukovsky 2005).

11. The term *natsional'nost'* in Russian denotes not nationality or citizenship, but
ethnicity. *St. Petersburg Dom Natsional'nostei* is a state institution that the
city authorities created to facilitate cooperation with ethnic communities in
St. Petersburg. The official Internet site is http://www.kvs.spb.ru/ru/activity/
national/nation_house/.

12. In his book *The Great Good Place* (1991), Oldenburg demonstrates why the
gathering places are essential to community and public life. He argues that
bars, coffee shops, and other 'third places' (in contrast to the first and second
places of home and work), are central to local democracy and community vitality. By exploring how these places work and what roles they serve, Oldenburg offers place-making tools and insight for individuals and communities
everywhere.

## References

Allina-Pisano, Jessica and Eric Allina-Pisano. "Friendship of Peoples' after the Fall:
Violence and Pan-African Community in Post-Soviet Moscow', in *Africa in*

*Russia, Russia in Africa: Three Centuries of Encounters*, ed. Maxim Matuse-vich, New York, 2007, 175–98.

Amnesty International, 'Russian Federation: Racism and Xenophobia Rife in Rus-sian Society', press release, 4 May 2006, http://web.amnesty.org/library/Index/ENGEUR460182006?open&of=ENG-RUS (accessed 20.01.2008).

Barns, Hugh. 'Black People in Russia Are Afraid of Militia and Skinheads', 2003, http://moscow.hrights.ru/etnic/data/etnic_28_11_2003-3.html (accessed 20.01.2008).

Blakely, Allison. *Russia and the Negro: Blacks in Russian History and Thought*. Wash-ington, D.C., 1986

Brazhkina, Anna. 'Ubili negra, ubili ... stikhiinaya ksenofobiya ili rasistskoe ob-shchestvo? (The Negro was killed, was killed ... Spontaneous xenophobia or racist society?)', Soobshchenie, 2003, http://www.soob.ru/n/2003/7-8/practics/7 (accessed 20.01.2008).

Caldwell, Melissa L. 'Race and Social Relations: Crossing Borders in a Moscow Food Aid Program', in *Social Networks in Movement: Time, Interaction and Interethnic Spaces in Central Eastern Europe*, eds. David Torsello and Melinda Pappová, Šamorín, 2003, 255–73, www.vmek.oszk.hu/01800/01847/01847.pdf (accessed 31.01.2008).

Diène, Doudou. Implementation of General Assembly Resolution 60/251 of 15 March 2006 Entitled 'Human Rights Council', Report of the Special Rapporteur on contemporary forms of racism, racial discrimination, xenophobia and re-lated intolerance, Addendum: Mission to the Russian Federation, 2007, http://ohchr.org/english/bodies/hrcouncil/docs/4session/A-HRC-4-19-Add3.pdf (accessed 10.10.2007).

Ezhova, Lubov' and Sergei Damberg. 'African refugees and asylum seekers in St. Petersburg and in North-Western Russia, 2002', http://www.cisr.ru/complete_etnos.html (accessed 12.04.2006).

Fabre, Geneviève and Klaus Benesch. *African Diasporas in the New and Old Worlds*, Amsterdam, 2004.

Gaidamak, Andrei. 'Tsentry vrazhdy v Rossii (Centers of hate in Russia)', *Novaya Afrika* (New Africa), no. 1(2006), 26–29.

Gdaniec, Cordula. "Ordinary Young Hooligans' or Moscow Geographies of Fear: Spatial Practices in and around the Peoples' Friendship University of Russia', in *Hierarchy and Power in the History of Civilizations. Cultural Dimensions*, eds L. Grinin and A. Korotayer, Moscow, 2008, 3–15.

Gnammankou, Dieudonné. *Abraham Hannibal: L'aieul noir de Pouchkine*. Paris, Dakar, 1998.

Golden, Lily. *My Long Journey Home*, Chicago, 1994.

Hannerz, Ulf. 'The Cultural Role of World Cities', in *Humanising the City? Social Contexts of Urban Life at the Turn of the Millenium*, eds. A. P. Cohen and K. Fukui, Edinburgh, 1993, 67–84.

Jackson, Patrick. 'Living with race hate in Russia', *BBC News* website, Moscow, 2006, http://news.bbc.co.uk/2/hi/europe/4737468.stm (accessed 09.07.07).

Kaschuba, Wolfgang. 'Geschichtspolitik und Identitätspolitik. Nationale und eth-nische Diskurse im Vergleich', in *Inszenierungen des Nationalen*, eds. Beate Binder and W. Kaschuba, Köln, 2001, 19–42.

Khanga, Yelena and Susan Jacoby. *Soul to Soul: The Story of a Black Russian American Family 1865–1992*, New York, 1992.

Klomegah, Kester. 'Living with Race Hate in Russia', *The Voice* 7, no. 76 (May 2006), 62–63.

Kotchofa, A. G. 'Tezisy vystupleniya prezidenta Assotsiatsii inostrannykh studentov v Rossii' (Theses of the report of the president of Foreign Students' Association), Moscow, 2006 (unpublished).

Kostyukovsky, Artem. 'Zharkie lyudi severnoi stolitsy (Hot people of the Northern capital)', *Argumenty i Fakty*, no. 11(604), 16.03.2005, www.aif.ru/online/spb/604/06 (accessed 12.02.2008).

Kozhevnikova, Galina. 'Prestupleniya est' – statistiki net (There are crimes, but no statistics)', *Novaya Gazeta*, 30.08.2007, http://www.ng.ru/politics/2007-08-30/3-kartblansh.html (accessed 20.01.2008).

Mayer, Ruth. *Diaspora: Eine kritische Begriffsbestimmung*, Bielefeld, 2005.

Oldenburg, Ray. *The Great Good Place*, New York, 1991.

Racheva, Elena. 'V snegakh Pskovskoi oblasti raskinulas' nebol'shaya Ruanda (In the snows of Pskov Region there is a little Rwanda)', *Novaya Gazeta*, no. 3(2003), 25, http://2006.novayagazeta.ru/nomer/2006/03n/n03n-s25.shtml (accessed 10.02.2008).

Zips, Werner. *Afrikanische Diaspora: Out of Africa Into New Worlds*, Münster, 2003.

### Newspapers, magazines and websites

*Africana* www.africana.ru

*African Union* www.africa.smolny.nw.ru/Petersburg/African_Union/

*Association of African Students at University for People's Friendship* www.africana.ru/assafstu/index.htm

*The Moscow Protestant Chaplaincy* www.moscowprotestantchaplaincy.org

*My Africa Magazine* www.myafrica.ru

*New Africa Magazine* www.newafrica.ru

*Nigerian Community in Russia* www.nigeriancommunity.ru

*The People's Friendship University* www.rudn.ru

## ⁖ 6 ⁖

# The Construction of 'Marginality' and 'Normality'

### In Search of a Collective Identity
### Among Youth Cultural Scenes in Sochi

IRINA KOSTERINA and ULIA ANDREEVA

## Introduction

In contemporary youth subcultures, street groups have special significance. On the one hand, such groups are far from new, and by comparison with the weakly structured and little-studied Internet community they are more comprehensible and accessible, i.e., more publicly visible. At the same time, city streets constitute a site *intrinsically suited to youth* where control over youth practices by adults is weak, and where juveniles do not just spend time, but socialise, communicate, grow up. It is possible to identify an enormous number both of general city spaces (courtyards, staircases, parks, central squares) and local places specific to individual cities, the location of which is known, as a rule, only to insiders of the respective milieu. For instance, it is sufficient to recall St. Petersburg's legendary Saigon club where members of 'informal' structures from all over the USSR gathered. In the Soviet Union, young people who did not participate in the activities of 'formal' youth structures (Komsomol, circles and sections) and even resisted them, orienting themselves towards 'Western' subcultural movements, were called 'informals'. The important thing about this category was that, in informal groups, young people escaped from the control of 'adults' and the state. Such places were important because it was possible to find there people of similar cultural persuasion and be accepted by the regulars. The phrase 'street youth' in Soviet times had negative connotations as it was associated first and foremost with neighbourhood gangs of youths, homeless children – i.e., deprived and 'socially dangerous' people. The polar opposite were 'domesticated' adolescents who spent their spare time under the supervision of adults

This category, without doubt, was connected with the predominance of the 'public sphere' and public spaces, including in youth leisure activities. Young people's appropriation of new urban spaces was perceived as a protest against the norms and demands of official culture. It was no coincidence that in the 1960s and 1970s, *druzhinniki* (voluntary assistants to the police) patrolled the streets, bestowed with powers to check and apply some punitive measures to anyone they perceived to be spending their free time or be dressed contrary to the established order. Gradually, young people were abandoning school clubs, music schools and sports sections, and starting to fight for territory and authority. Subcultural groups claimed specific locations for themselves. In every more or less large town, places appeared where hippies, punks, rappers, skaters, rock fans, etc., hung out. Such locations usually comprised public squares, parks, cafés, sport facilities, separate courtyards or even porches. Cultural identity became 'open to view', public and demonstrative.

Today, street youth primarily means people engaged in urban sports and urban activities such as graffiti spraying – i.e., boys and girls sharing completely legitimate and socially approved activities. In the Russian tradition of studying and describing different types of youth culture, it is worth noting that, in contrast to the British tradition, Russia has up till now lacked an understanding of 'subcultures' in the classic sense. Now, on the wave of post-subculture theory inspired by the work of D. Muggleton, there is an active search for new terms denoting solidarity among young people (Muggleton 2000). In the context of our article, we will employ the terms 'youth cultures' and 'youth groups', by which we understand 'imagined communities' based on ideas of general cultural solidarity.

Cultural group identities are considerably more important for adolescents than for adults, since adolescence is a period of searching for oneself, one's individuality, one's own style of life, self-definitions and self-descriptions. That is why such mechanisms of identification such as solidarity, feelings of belonging to a specific group and of distance to 'Others' and 'outsiders' are particularly strong during this period. Adolescents are constantly constructing borders and rules of existence for their communities, searching for the basis of solidarity. In our article, we will focus on different types of differentiation of youth groups and styles in the city of Sochi, and also examine the case of a specific group, or rather a specific location – squares in the town centre – which have served for some years now as a meeting place for sports-oriented youth and simply informal, unconventional adolescents.

The empirical basis for this article comprises material collated by the Centre for Youth Studies of the *Region* independent research institute conducted over the period 2004–07 in Sochi, employing the methods of biographical interview and participant observation. The methodological framework is extremely important when studying youth identities, since only qualitative methods allow us to see and partly understand the different meanings which adolescents apply to their world, and also to understand their means of constructing group identity. The use of biographical interviews allows us to tap self-presentation and the basis of collective identities, and to identify the logic and argumentation of someone claiming membership in a certain milieu. Participant observation aids understanding of important aspects of interaction which are not articulated by informants, and also to identify gaps between declared and real principles and practices.[1]

## The Case of Sochi

Sochi is Russia's most popular resort town, visited by thousands of tourists from Russia and abroad every year.The city's touristic role will increase still because of the decision reached in 2007 to award the 2014 Winter Olympics to Sochi. This event will serve as a powerful impulse for the economic, social and cultural development of the city, bringing billions of dollars in investment. Last but not least, Sochi is special because of geographical factors: it is Russia's southernmost point, bordering with Abkhasia – a disputed territory claiming independence from Georgia. It boasts a good climate with mild winters which is the exception rather than the rule in Russia. In addition, Sochi is Russia's longest city, stretching 145 km along the Black Sea coast from Lazarevsky to Adler, and comprising a multitude of small resorts, the largest of which is known as Bolshoi Sochi (large Sochi). Contemporary Sochi is a multiethnic city, where Russians live together side by side with representatives of the numerous peoples of the Caucasus, especially Armenians. This has led in recent years to interethnic tensions, since disputes over whether it is a Russian or Caucasian city spill over into violent incidents and also prompt attempts at regulation by the state.

In our article, all these factors are significant, but primarily the fact that Sochi is a resort town: locals perceive there being only two seasons, summer (resort season) and winter; it is the only city in Russia where you can conduct leisure activities outside all year round, and the 'resort town' atmosphere creates a specific, 'relaxed', easy-going way of life for young people. For adolescents, this means that summer is the time to hang out with friends, go from party to party, and meet new people who bring new ideas, music, and fashion to the town. During this time, the whole city turns into one single *tusovka*[2] based on clubs and beach parties, cafés and restaurants, cinema and musical festivals. The general practice among youth is to 'live for show', i.e., to show off how fashionable, how hip, one is. Foreigners and Muscovites vacationing in Sochi become an object of admiration and imitation. They are regarded as incorporating a certain standard of style, innovation, and are bearers of 'progessivity'. Local youth actively appropriate this important cultural channel, and appropriate information about new and fashionable brands, books and music, ways of appearing and clothing, slang and fresh ideas. Winter leisure time differs significantly, since communication usually does not go beyond the boundaries of one's own group, or rather those who remain in the group, since the composition and boundaries of groups change significantly from summer to winter. As a rule, in winter groups change their preferred hang-outs, and often only the most committed and interested people comprising the core of the group remain active. Sochi's climate means that leisure time can be spent outdoors almost any time of year, so that street groups meet here a lot more often than in other Russian cities. In many ways this factor influences the very character of adolescent groups. Groups that prefer to be closed and isolated from the external world look for special places available only to those in the know, such as individual courtyards, spots on the coastal promenade, in the park, etc. Those groups which actively appropriate urban space (with sport, graffiti, as musicians or members of subcultures) try, on the other hand, to stand out and display themselves publicly. The boundaries of such groups are more porous, and their structure and membership less obvious. To a certain extent, such groups form one single urban *tusovka*, but on the level of microgroups there are specific spots perceived as frequented by adolescents or even as 'belonging' to individual groups of adolescents. For example, there are places such as 'the wall' (a memorial wall in memory of the rock star Viktor Tsoi) where punks, heavy metal fans, and, now, football fans meet; McDonalds, where scooter and moped riders meet; and park benches on the city outskirts where anime fans meet. These are the most 'steady' places, having existed already for a number of years, whereas every year new places and new 'roaming' *tusovki* appear .

The Fun Box is an area in the centre of Sochi on Ostrovsky Square. The name derives from a special ramp used for skateboard jumping. In Sochi, the Fun Box is a place for skateboarding, inline skating, riding BMX bikes and also just a youth hangout. Kids hang out here from morning to late at night, and when it is warm they can even sleep here. Sochi's youth regard this place as being the most 'subcultural' place in the town, a place where unconventional, interesting people meet. The area is small, about 20m by 15m, with a special surface and equipped with ramps and other facilities

**Fig. 6.1:** Competition for the best skater and rollerblader at the Fun Box. Photograph I. Kosterina, 2007.

for skateboarding, skating and biking. At the edge of the Fun Box zone are park benches where the regular boys and girls change, leave their things, sit, chat and spend time. The majority of kids here regard themselves (or are regarded) as belonging to a specific subculture (skaters, rappers, break-dancers, graffiti artists) or in general to unconventional, non-conformist youth. They are all marked by an aversion towards mainstream 'pop' culture and a tolerant (or even approving) relationship to alcohol and drugs.

For instance, the geographical centre of the 'Fun Box' subculture is the square in the centre of Sochi where rollerbladers, skateboarders and BMXers gather. The square has been set up specially for rollerblading and skateboarding. Young people have now been gathering at this location for around eight years. In 2003, an initiative group took it upon themselves to install the first facilities for skateboarding. Hostile youth groups (*gopniki*[3] and skinheads) have on a number of occasions damaged the facilities, which was facilitated in part by their poor quality. As a result, the young people turned to the city administration with the request to help them equip the facilities more professionally: to install a special surface instead of asphalt and paving unsuited to skateboarding, and also to install ramps, rails and other skateboarding equipment. Now the Youth Committee of the Sochi municipal administration works together with the kids from the Fun Box and holds events there, such as graffiti, skateboarding, and BMX competitions. Some of the kids are sceptical regarding such events, considering them an attempt by the administration to take control of the location. In connection with the Winter Olympics 2014, there are rumours that the Fun Box will be moved to a different area of town.

The Fun Box is a sort of business card for Sochi's youth culture, since this spot is perceived as the most exotic in terms of a concentration of unconventional, non-conformist local youth. Our informants constantly referred us to this spot as proof of Sochi's 'subculturedness'. The Fun Box is truly one of Sochi's oldest *tusovki*, and has its own history, myths, rules, personalities and most importantly, a cultural identity uniting its people. It is located on Ostrovsky Ploshchad (square) near the Stero cinema. About eight years ago, kids started to meet here for rollerblading and skateboarding. Its proximity to the town's main attractions (coastal promenade, shopping centres, concert halls) together with its distance from adults' attention were the key reasons for choosing this spot. The Fun Box immediately became a noticeable feature of the city's cultural landscape: If, previously, individual representatives of youth subcultures or simply colourful, stylish teenagers trying to stand out from the crowd were an isolated and thus not so noticeable phenomenon, the Fun Box *tusovka*, uniting the city's extreme sports crowd with others seeking alternatives to the mainstream, immediately revealed itself to be a new cultural phenomenon.

## 'Marginals' in the City Centre

The city centre constitutes a space stretching between the 'Riviera' beach, Theatre Square, the coastal embankment and the train station. Most cafés, nightclubs, discos, cinemas, concert halls and shopping centres are to be found here. Its key locations include the municipal administration, the hotel 'Moskva', McDonalds, the 'Festival' concert hall and the port. The main street – *Kurortnyi Prospekt* – stretching through the whole city centre – runs parallel to the coastal embankment. This not very large territory is inhabited by a number of different youth groups, which both co-exist and compete among themselves. For our article, the key idea will be that of the Fun Box youth's self-portrayal as 'marginals', i.e., non-conformist youth. These characteristics are crucial to the group identity as opposed to the surrounding 'grey mass'. The words 'marginal' and 'informal' are synonymous with the desire for oneself and one's companions to stand out, and underscore individuality.[4] Violation of conventional rules, a challenge to social norms and morals, justifying and consciously constructing and underlining one's own non-conventionality is the ideological backbone upon which the collective identity of the Fun Box is constructed. The division between normal (mainstream) and progressive (subcultural) strategies in youth styles has been described by Hilary Pilkington (Pilkington 2002). 'Normal' in this case means the usual, uninteresting strategy predominant in most Russian cities, whereas representatives of the progressive strategy are regarded by the 'conventional majority' as marginals. Correspondingly, adherents of the marginal life style (mostly associated with a specific subculture) are subject to attacks, and sometimes even to violence on the part of the 'normal majority' who aspire to the role of producer, supporter and enforcer of basic norms and rules of youth culture. Many informants remark on the negative connotation of the terms 'marginal' and 'informal' yet consciously use these terms to demonstrate that they do not care about public opinion (of the passive majority), underscoring their non-conformism, and that they are 'outside the system.'

> I am a marginal, the word sounds insulting, but if you look closely, why is it insulting? Because it is not similar to the words we are told are 'good.' There are people who are rich in spirit, who are a prism on the world, but nobody understands them, because they do not look further than the surface. There are conventional people, uninteresting, and even if they say something interesting, hundred to one it's not them, they've just heard it somewhere. It's difficult to be a person who draws on magic. Marginals are people different from the grey mass, to be a marginal now does not mean to be good or bad, happy or sad, to believe in magic or in the TV. To be a marginal means not to be afraid to be yourself and not to hide your inner world. (Anya (f), 21, former member of Fun Box *tusovka*)

This girl's quote is revealing because she argues that being marginal is equivalent to being a hero, a revolutionary, a dissident. This entails a conscious opposition of oneself to the 'crowd', the silent majority, without hope of understanding and recognition, with risks ensuing for one's own well-being and comfortable existence. It entails opposition to a soulless system, even its destruction through the very fact of one's own existence. It is no coincidence that many 'informals' like the film *Matrix*, which depicts a totalitarian society that seeks to stamp out individuality and turn people into slaves or other objects of control. This is why it is better from the informals' point of view to be rejected by this system than to be a cogwheel in it, and it is why they want to stand out from the 'grey mass' even by assigning themselves a negative identity, such as 'degenerates' and 'junkies', which are sometimes used with reference to the Fun Box *tusovka*.

I hang out with people whom ignorant people call informals. I don't regard them as informals, nor me myself. I regard them as people who frequent the Fun Box, who spend their free time there. I find it interesting hanging out with them, because all these people are quite interesting. They are all different, all of them from different parts of the city, each has their own life, each their own way of thinking. The label 'informal', as ignorant people explained it to me, includes all people who are different from others. If you put on something which isn't quite correct, or say something that you shouldn't. *I understand by informal a person with his or her own world view, completely different from others.* In Sochi I personally know not more than five such people. All the rest are just simply people, completely normal. For some reason informal is equated with the word 'degenerate'. (Masha, (f), 16, '*lavochker*')[5]

The important thing in this quotation is that the negative label applies to outsiders, whom the girl calls 'ignorant people', i.e., those who do not understand the essence, and do not share the common practices, so that she believes them unqualified to judge about the cultural allegiances of the scene. This is why the girl is keen on 'justifying herself', rejecting the term 'informals' for her and her group. At the same time, we see that in her interpretation, the term takes on a positive connotation and even a certain exclusivity. For the lack of any other term, she uses it to denote the specialness, individuality of people with whom she hangs out at the Fun Box. In this way, the 'right of the speaker' applies here: Only bearers of the culture have the right to assign themselves to any particular culture or style, outsiders are not able to judge, since they lack the competence. Besides, among the Fun Box *tusovka,* there is an openly expressed dislike of any labels, which are regarded as a feature of a totalitarian culture.

In the understanding of the young people, the words 'marginal' and 'informal' are close in meaning to 'non-conformist', as someone not accepting of the rules of the system. In the words of D. Muggleton, non-conformists constitute 'a heterogeneous minority, opposed to the homogenous majority' (mainstream), i.e., an attempt to go one's own way, shrugging off the dominant culture and its institutions and also 'normal' youth (Muggleton 2000). The marginal identity imparts the illusion of freedom, the right to behave and look different, and the violation of general rules becomes the group's main rule. In the words of informants, any display of individuality and difference to others is welcomed by the Fun Box, the key attitude is 'not to be like all the rest'. The Fun Box provides a unique chance to reveal oneself, to discover in oneself an independent, interesting personality. But it is very important that all these extravagant ideas can be recognised and approved by the scene. In order to belong to the scene, one must first and foremost set oneself apart from the conventional community, prove that one is different from them, and thus that one's place is at the Fun Box:

> It's a group of friends, in my opinion, it seemed, that I was free there, that I can say what I want, think what I want to think, wear what I want and do what I want. That I'm not the same as all the others in my class. Not like other girls who are interested in other things, and I thought I was interested in my life, I learn something new, read unusual books, I watch films, I get stoned there, I open new doors in my soul. (Anya, (f) 21, former member of Fun Box *tusovka*)

For Slavik, another informant, the word 'informal' is synonymous with the terms 'youth' and 'adolescence' and thus is opposed to the world of adults – i.e., the period when a person loses certain positive qualities, appreciated in the scene, when a person loses his or her individuality:

> Earlier he was involved in the informal culture, then he became more civil, more adult, more manly, in general he became a normal, conventional person. Basically a normal person. A conventional, normal person with common sense, and that's all. (Slavik, (m) 20, musician, BMXer)

It is interesting that the informant focuses attention on such characteristics as usual, normal, common sense and considers these not as positive characteristics but rather as a loss. In this way he justifies his own 'nonconformism', presenting it like a quality peculiar to youth.

In contrast, another young man (not a member of the Fun Box *tusovka*, but more mainstream) is afraid of losing his 'normality' and repeatedly underscores in the interview that he is 'the same as all, usual, normal' in opposition to the 'informals' of the Fun Box. For him, to be informal is a legitimate life strategy only if you do something legitimate or even useful, and, importantly, something in agreement with one's own world of values, culture and aesthetics and not in contravention of social norms.

> Interviewer: How do you relate to informals?
>
> Informant: It depends. I relate neutrally to the more neutral ones, and negatively to the more negative ones. The neutral ones are the ones who were at the skate park (Fun Box). The lads skate and skate, and this is fine, they don't harm anyone. I get on with my life. That's how I relate to them, normally, they are doing sport and that's good. There are different groups. Some do sport, and it makes no difference whether blades, skateboards or bikes. And there are also freaks. And rockers. Recently I started watching

people into rock. Those clips, like Marilyn Manson, complete rubbish. (Pasha, (m) 22)

Recently the word 'informal' has accumulated such a number of interpretations and connotations that young people themselves have started to avoid it. For instance, a skateboarder said that he has encountered the word 'informal' in Sochi in the meaning of 'person with non-traditional sexual orientation / gay', therefore although previously considering himself 'informal', he now rejects the term. Other negative expressions used in relation to the kids from the Fun Box (and occasionally by themselves) include 'junkies' and 'druggies'. In as much as drug usage is a permissible and widespread practice here, the young people from the Fun Box call themselves junkies as a joke, boasting of their experience with drugs. It is interesting that drug use is becoming an important part of non-conformist group identity. The generality of such experience (in comparison with its absence among 'normal youth'), its illegality, risks and exotic character, draws a line marking off the 'correct' domesticated children from the 'disobedient' street kids.

## The Fun Box as Social Space

Gender plays an important role at the Fun Box. Girls do not count as having equal rights in the *tusovka;* they are allowed to hang out here, but they are not taken seriously. Since there are no girls who skate among the microgroups of rollerbladists and skateboardists, and the boys themselves claim that extreme sport is a male thing – i.e., connected with pain, injuries, risk and physical stamina – it is reckoned that girls just 'play' at being skaters but are not the real thing. For the skaters of the Fun Box, skating is in general a male brotherhood and in their opinion the most serious come here not to chat up girls but to skate; everything else is just idle distraction. Girls consider themselves full-fledged participants in the *tusovka.* They successfully create their own space within the general *tusovka,* and many of them achieve authority in the community by other means – by, for example, their ability to spray graffiti, their membership in a rock band, or their particular personal qualities, all of which can inspire pleasure and respect among the others. An example of the 'acceptance' of a girl and of her winning a high status are the extent to which she is not regarded as a sexual object but as a full-fledged member of the *tusovka,* a professional, or just a 'good person'.

Girls can come and sit with their friends on the bench, chat and have fun. They do not regard the Fun Box exclusively as a place for skateboarding or skating. For them, it is simply a place for young people to hang out. They can regard themselves as being full-fledged members of the group,

**Fig 6.2:** 'Lavochkery' at the Fun Box: Punk girls and transvestite boy. Photograph U. Andreeva, 2006.

although the boys do not regard them as such. Sometimes the girls can join up with the boys when they drink beer. It is notable that while sport 'divides' the boys from the girls, alcohol and drugs tend to unite them. In as much as the basic authority in the *tusovka* belongs to the boys (who are also in the majority), it is they who decide on the group rules and control the interrelationship. This results in girls often being marginalised and pushed to the edge of the group.

Ethnicity, too, plays an important role in the Fun Box. It is important to note here that *Krasnodar Krai,* including Sochi, is one of the poorest areas of Russia, where there is clearly a tense, even openly hostile, situation between different ethnic groups. In public discourse the idea is widespread that the lawful 'masters' of the land are the Russians and Cossacks, meaning that the state should be there to defend their interests only. The politics of the *Krasnodar Krai* administration regarding the overall non-Russian population and illegal migrants in particular, is characterised by active utilisation of patriotic (pro-Slavic) ideas. Because Krasnodar is a border region, and there are also large numbers of migrants who have arrived in Sochi over the last decades and now constitute real competition to the locals, the ethnic Russian population feels itself threatened, vulnerable and undefended. This means that there is not just a political, but a ubiquitous and quotidian conflict between Russians and Caucasians. Under these conditions, young people's cultural and social experience prompts them to construct their own youth discourse, to support practices that express their relationship to the ethnic situation in the town. This relationship is characterised by demonstrative intolerance towards representatives of other ethnicities.

> Just go to the square [points to the square in front of city hall] at 4–6 o'clock, and look to see who comes out of the doors, who gathers there, and you'll immediately understand – they're all Armenians. (Sasha, (m) 21)

Xenophobic stereotypes reproduced in the youth milieu facilitate hierarchisation and marking of 'good' and 'bad', 'normal', 'peaceful' and 'criminal', 'wild', 'aggressive' ethnicities. In this connection, the Fun Box is marked as a place free from other ethnicities, apart from the Russian one, if only on a symbolic plane. It is notable that 'Russian' does not denote necessarily Russian ethnicity. It can cover Ukrainians, Jews, Cossacks and even people with Armenian, Abkhazian or Georgian roots. The main thing is that the person should regard himself as Russian and should not be obviously 'Caucasian' in appearance. Appearance and clothes are the primary reasons for marginalisation named by young people. In particular, attempts by Caucasians to be and look subcultural are mocked as fake, as cheap kitsch, an imitation of 'true' subculture, indicating a lack of subcultural feel and taste, and displaying glaring mistakes in the use of visual elements – clothes, haircuts, etc. The following factors attract special criticism: tracksuits and fashionable boots among Armenian boys, vulgar clothes and make-up among Armenian girls. Adhering to the dichotomy between 'progressive' and 'normal' youth strategies, the Fun Box crowd tend to talk of Caucasians' lack of progressiveness and their conservatism. A second vector is to refer to young Caucasians as *gopniki* who might beat up, insult or humiliate the 'Russian' youths of the Fun Box.

As was already noted, Sochi is a city where youth groups are divided along ethnic lines and the cultural characteristics assigned to ethnicities. Armenian, Georgian and Abkhazian youths are marginalised by the Fun Boxers as backward, non-progressive, conservative and limited in terms of self-expression and behaviour. For instance, Sochi's *gopniki*, in the opinion of Fun Boxers, are usually Armenians. They are said to exhibit aggressive behaviour, and lack the cultural capital that could be a resource within the *tusovka*. The stereotype of the *gopnik* Armenian as 'Other' is one of the most powerful myths constructing Fun Box identity. Here again we see that this cultural non-acceptance is based on a refusal to accept anyone who seems 'usual' or part of the 'system', together with a fear of losing one's own 'uniqueness' and 'difference'.

Regarding the principles of Fun Box group identity, cultural codes and general practices play an important role in unifying different people into one *tusovka*. What qualities does someone need to really belong to the group? One of the most obvious markers of youth identity is appearance: haircut, clothes, piercings, tattoos, etc. The Fun Box crowd wear original, unconventional (not fashionable) clothes that mark adherence to a certain lifestyle or subculture. Clothes are the simplest code in terms of marking those who belong and those who do not, since brands, accessories and attributes serve to place people in one or another category.

> For me, clothes mean a lot. I am not obsessed with clothes, but its important to me how I look, where I buy things. I don't care what I eat, but I spend a lot of money on clothes. I economise, but I buy for instance a new T-shirt or jeans from Extra. I even have a rebate card for Extra. And if I see someone who buys clothes on the open-air market or from a kiosk or in tracksuit and trainers, then of course, you need to talk, to have a look at the person, but the first impression will be the clothes. (Stas, (m) 18, skater)

Clothes not only have a functional role in the *tusovka* but serve as a marker of either 'positive', progressive, unconventional and 'negative' or conservative, limited people. The clearest example is the contrast between the clothes of informals and *gopniki*, between which there is an ideological and cultural 'enmity'. Informals are ascribed the quality of 'unconventional' appearance and regard this positively, whereas *gopniki* are ascribed the qualities of conformity, absence of taste, conservatism. Appearance plays the role of cultural capital: if you lack any knowledge, information or abilities specific to the group, then your exterior image can help you find a place: You look like you belong or have the courage to do something outrageous, risky, which others would not dare to do. The Fun Box crowd use youth brands (Extra, Camelot, Converse) and also sports brands (Nike, Finn Flare) as the easiest was to signify one's membership in the group's culture. Another way of standing out from the crowd is to wear (i.e., apply to one's body) something that others definitely will not have and that is impossible to imitate, which explains the attraction of hand-made clothes, accessories, original haircuts and the inventive use of cosmetics. Jeans torn by hand, sports shoes emblazoned by marker pens, bleached T-shirts or ones with cool words, sweaters with holes – the main thing is that everything should be individually produced. At the same time, there are unwritten rules about which cultural symbols are in and which are to be avoided. Punks (or rockers) and *gopniki* are polar opposites. The latter are excessively conformist, lacking imagination and taste, while the aesthetic of the former is rejected as unhygienic and overdone with respect to black and subcultural attributes. But these are examples of stylistic antagonism, and the Fun Box crowd do not like either *gopniki* or punks.

Haircut is another external marker, including length and colour, headware (genuine hip hop headware or just baseball caps and bandanas). Many of the boys in the Fun Box crowd have long or uneven hair, and many of the girls have brightly dyed hair. Among physical manifestations, flesh tunnels in the ears, piercing of eyebrows, of lower lip or tongue, numerous rings and rods in the ears, finger rings, necklaces and ribbons are most popular among the Fun Box crowd. However, all these exotic attributes are often only important when joining the group, and later lose their relevance, since someone who already belongs to the group no longer requires this subcultural resource.

> For instance, there's Julia. Now she's so arrogant, loves smart shoes and all that. She used to be such a daring girl. She pierced her lip, tongue, ears here, and brows here. She took it all off and now walks around the Fun Box as if everyone knows her – Yulka, Oh Yulka has come. (Masha, (f) 16, former rollerblader, now sprays graffiti, *lavochker*)

This indicates that if you already belong, or have somehow earned the trust of the group, you can look however you want to look. Sometimes, however, Fun Boxers make excuses for people who appear 'too normal' or even 'vulgar' along the lines of 'he might look like a *gopnik*, but he is actually a good guy (one of us)'. The code of appearances, having considerable importance in distinguishing 'those belonging' from 'outsiders' and expressing cultural identity, is only important as a 'membership card' or a resource to join the group.

At the same time, unconventional appearances are often the factor that most irritates 'conservative' youth (especially aggressive young men), sparking conflicts and fights. Informants often say that they have to stand up for their right to look different from others during clashes with *gopniki*, skinheads or simply more grown up and stronger youths, who criticise their long hair, torn jeans and piercings. This chapter will only touch on the topic of cultural clashes between youth groups. These entail attempts to establish a pecking order between groups and to define 'masculinity'.

Other important indicators of belonging to the Fun Box clique are the use of slang, 'cool' phrases and a special intonation when talking. Some of their lexicon is shared with other youth groups and some lifted from Internet lexicons, such as udaff.com and bashorg.ru, or from popular TV shows such as Comedy Club. Some comes from 'junkie' slang. Their talk also features a large number of anglicisms and terms denoting different stunts, feats or accessories for rollerblading, skateboarding and BMXing. For outsiders,

**Fig 6.3:** Masha 'Jenny' spraying in a competition. Photograph I. Kosterina, 2007.

their language can be very opaque. Many of the kids are known by nick-names, as is common among skaters, rappers and sprayers. Nicknames also serve as a password. If you come to the Fun Box and ask for Jenny instead of Masha, it means you are 'in the know'.

Those who come to the Fun Box specifically to practice their rollerblad-ing, skateboarding or biking skills, have greater authority in the *tusovka*. The core of the group comprises these people who regularly come and maintain social contacts. The 'regulars' fall into different categories: Those who skate or bike, and those who do not. The latter are referred to as *lav-ochkery* or *skameikery* (bench-sitters), since they sit on the benches around the square:

> Interviewer: Who belongs to your group?
>
> Informant: In general, all those who skate and bike hang out together, they are all friends. Others who join us, some of them are simply acquain-tances, the *lavochkery* sit there and watch, and some come from the uni-versity as well. So it basically all works out. There are also people who play in groups (meaning musicians), even some visitors from other towns (Zhenya, (m) 18, skater)

The large group of skaters and bikers contains microgroups based on what equipment they use as well as on other characteristics. These include friendships, shared place of study or living, previous shared communicative or cultural practices. Wheel skills, however, are a priority factor in belonging to the Fun Box *tusovka* because a person who displays them must be respected and treated as equal.

> Interviewer: Are you one single group or are there divisions relating to whether you are on blades, boards or bikes?
>
> Informant: Generally, we all belong to the same *tusovka*, but here, locally, everyone has their own people. Among all these skaters and rollerbladers there are four people I am close to, and the others constitute a general *tusovka*. That means, basically we are all together in the one place, so a rollerblader will never tell a skateboarder where and how he has to skate, along the lines 'Don't skate there on the ramp, we're there'. Everything's OK, we're all one *tusovka*, but there are local groups. (Zhenya, (m)18, skater)

Regarding structure and hierarchy in the group, there is a core comprising several of the most authoritative members. Authority can be defined by feats and professionalism in boarding or skating – i.e., the group's 'subcultural capital' – as well as in communicational skills, access to resources (music, sports inventory, computers, drugs), social networks and simply experience in life. According to Sara Thornton, 'subcultural capital confers status on its owner in the eyes of the relevant beholder' (Thornton 1997).

Attempts to assert territorial claims, or separatism, on grounds of different sports activities (which the young people perceive as cultural differences) occur often.

> Regarding communication with each other. Yes, they communicate, but now it is like this: There sits Roka, graffiti artist, I sit there, Erik the BMXer there, and then the skaters. The rollerbladers basically do not, they always sit in a separate group and only say hello. They do say hello, but they go to their own group which also includes BMXers and skaters. But why do they sit with them? Because they used to be good friends, before they split up into groups according to sports.
>
> Interviewer: And why do the rollerbladers sit separately in the first place? Is it a way of segregating themselves?
>
> Informant: It's not interesting for them. No, they don't set themselves off, we can sit there, there would be nothing unusual about that, just that they sit on their ramp, do their stunts, no one hinders them, they don't trouble

anyone [...]. They sit there and drink their beer. (Masha, (f) 16, former rollerblader, now graffiti artist, *lavochker*)

These statements reveal a number of rules and methods of differentiation between rollerbladers and skateboarders. According to Masha, rollerbladers are 'they', 'Others' who are different from the rest. She ascribes to them the initiative in splitting from the general amicable *tusovka* and positioning themselves in a separate space (they sit on a ledge, a structure used predominantly by rollerbladers). In her opinion, they have formed their own group, with their own practices and own interests. This indicates that among those skating and rollerblading, polite harmony and neutrality reign, but there is no wish to associate more closely. Nevertheless, the BMXers, the newest arrivals at the Fun Box, are in the least favourable position: Because the area was created for skaterboarders and rollerbladers, these two groups retain (and assert) rights of ownership to the area, laying down the rules and priorities. That is why, when speaking of BMXers, our informants call them 'they' in contrast to the 'we' that refers to skateboarders and rollerbladers.

> We often send the BMXers a bit further from the ramp, when they slide they spoil the marble ledges and because of this they often have to move to other ledges nobody is using. They, generally speaking, understand this, there are no particular conflicts. (Zhenya, (m) 18, skater)

Another example of the 'right of the oldest' is the way the *tusovka* refused to acknowledge a group of moped riders and even pushed them out of the Fun Box. This subculture is one of Sochi's newest, and so they, regarding themselves as 'informals', arrived at the Fun Box, where they, however, met with a fairly cold reception. The Fun Box scene perceived the moped riders as arrogant (mopeds are expensive), posers (they stand around more than they ride) and even hostile elements – girls perceive them as an object of sexual expansion (being more grown up than the boys from the Fun Box, the moped riders come here to check out the local girls). In their stories of the appropriation of the area by different youth groups, the history of the Fun Box gets mythologised and idealised, and this case is presented as a violation and even erosion of important collective norms by 'adolescents' or newcomers who are perceived as being bearers of quite other values.

This shows that such an important resource as 'ability to ride' does not always constitute a basis for group solidarity. This makes it more important to demarcate the borders of the community. It is important to define the composition of the 'imagined community', i.e., who the members are, what the cultural and ideological core is, who stands at the periphery. It is also important to understand the borders of this community, who can and who cannot join it, who can belong and who can never belong.

Apart from the basic core of people who regularly use the Fun Box, skateboarders and rollerbladers who irregularly frequent it and regular *lavochkery* also belong. The latter are regarded as an essential part of the group, and many of them have their own specific role and enjoy high status in the group. It is important that such a person possess some sort of 'cultural values': the ability to do something else well (for example, to play a musical instrument, break-dance, spray graffiti). Then there are no questions asked about belonging to the *tusovka*. The arrival of new people in the *tusovka* is an important indicator of its openness and its limits. Many current regulars at the Fun Box present the process of joining the crowd as easy, and they talk of there being an absence of any hostility, or caution on the part of the 'seniors', and underscore their openness and hospitality:

> I just moved from a different town, and there I had started with all this and I wanted to start skating in another city. In Moscow, through which I travelled on the way here, I bought myself a skateboard. I arrived here and asked where it was possible to skate. I came to the Fun Box and got to know some of the kids. There you can just go up to the people skating, get to know them without any problems, the skating scene is remarkable, no one tells you straight off to get out, they don't say we don't like you. *Everything is fine, everyone here is hospitable – here's a new boy, let me introduce him.* And that's all. That's how I joined the group. (Zhenya, (m) 18, skater)

In this example, the whole process of entering the group is described step by step (I learnt about this place and the crowd, I talked to the people, and was accepted and became one of them), and usually presented using the words 'simple' and 'normal'. The first case underscores the ease and simplicity with which a new person joins the group, the second the normalcy of this process. The important thing here is that the boy already has an important resource or marker of collective identity – his skateboard and ability to skateboard. Many kids use this resource to join the group, but having won their place, they stop practising the sport. Nevertheless, when necessary they are always able to refer to their experience.

On the other hand, the story of how the *lavochkery* (benchers) girls join, reveals a different aspect of collective identity, showing that a person who has no connection to the sports, can never wholly belong to the *tusovka*.

> I was in the tenth class, my best friend left Sochi, and I started to look for new friends. I knew a girl who loved the band SPLIN, and that was

the first step towards friendship. We started to hang out together ... and then she invited me along to her group of friends (Fun Box). For a long time I did not want to go, because I was shy and nervous, but the desire to find something new was stronger. And then there I encountered the world I had seen in films about youth, especially non-Soviet youth. I can't say that *everyone was delighted to see me*, there was no aggression, but their world was surprising in that everyone was on my wavelength. Everyone was initially surprising and unusual, but soon everyone in one way or another shared themselves, and revealed their true nature: whether traitor, sycophant, arrogant idiot, for want of any other words, *I did not fuse with them* as I talked mostly with Marina (or SPLIN, as they called her) who had taken me there. (Ksyusha, (f) 17, *lavochker*)

She acutely senses her lack of belonging to the general *tusovka*, which is for her a new and alluring place she never met with in her daily life. In her words, this group is a model of 'Western' adolescent groups that she had only ever seen in films. That is why she does not see here the conventional forms of interaction, she perceives an exotic culture instead of real people. Her own experience consisted only of homely schoolgirl adolescence, which is why the kids who spent their leisure time on the streets seemed to her to be free, unique and 'different'. This is the reason why she perceives herself to be 'different' from them, and gradually starts to feel disappointment, finding in them signs of the 'conventionality', banality and triviality of human behaviour.

To indicate similarities and shared interests, many from the Fun Box use the expression 'to be on the same wavelength' – meaning to share the fundamentals of collective identity, concerning daily cultural practices: To listen to the same music, watch the same films and TV programmes, belong to the same groups and even 'wish for the same'. At the same time, it means to share values, a world view, to have the same ideas about what is 'permitted' and what is not acceptable. The group presents itself as open, heterogeneous, amicable, and comprising different variations in terms of lifestyle and position. These qualities – openness and friendliness – are important for the construction of collective identity, since in the process of narration they are opposed to the closedness, conservatism and hostility of other groups or generalised 'Others'.

## Conclusions

Constructing collective identities requires not only a shared basis, but also construction of the figures of 'the Other' and 'foreign', in relationship to which (and even in opposition to which) collective identity is activated. Regarding the Fun Box newcomers, 'Others' include especially *lavochkery*, and other people who just come by irregularly and are not well known. 'Territorial rights' are another source of power:

> Are there any benches at the Fun Box that are reserved for you to sit on?
>
> Informant: Sometimes I arrive and am annoyed to see there is nowhere to sit. I want to skateboard, but there is nowhere to put my cases. I just go up to the people sitting there, these youngsters, and say: Have you gone crazy there? They just came over. I say it like I'm joking, they all know me, but they bunch up anyway. And that's what all of us do, because in the final analysis it is true that they come here just to loiter and laugh at everything. Their old places were beside the park, there by the steps somewhere, that was where they hung out, and then one day they decided that they could just come over to the benches. Perhaps they grew up. But how could they have grown up in their sense of where they should hang out, but not grow up in their sense of how to behave. (Zhenya, (m) 18, skater)

It is the older adolescents who have been hanging out there for the longest time who try to hierarchise relations and establish rules. 'Youngsters' are a widespread figure of 'the Other' differing not only by age, but by values, behaviour, and, more importantly, lack of knowledge of, and failure to observe, group norms. The basic arguments supporting their rights are

- age (we – adults, they – youngsters),
- practices or object of interest (we 'skate', i.e., we have business here; they just hang around, hang out)
- legitimate behaviour and observation of the 'rules', subordination (skaters have the right to come and lay their things on the benches; 'youngsters joke around', i.e., do not respect the 'masters' of the place', get cheeky, i.e., cease to observe the rules, spread litter)
- expansion to foreign territory (they had their own places but now are claiming ours).

In this way, the 'old' members of the *tusovka* try to control the relations within the group, assuming authority and applying sanctions to violators. Such sanctions include refusing to accept someone in the group by restricting information about the Fun Box people themselves, their practices, and refusing to communicate with newcomers, their 'marginalisation' in the eyes of other members of the *tusovka*. The rules are treated as an a priori traditional code that has to be obeyed. It is revealed in rituals, especially in the ritual of 'joining' the group and the rituals of 'saying hello'.

It used to be like that. You don't have any rights, not regarding sitting at the Fun Box, but to draw attention to yourself and assert yourself relative to others, until you know people here, and don't simply come and sit around. If you want to sit, sit, but don't get in anyone's way. If people want to get to know you, they will come up to you. If someone wants to introduce themselves, they will come up and say: 'My name is ..., hi, and you're new here? We haven't seen you before', and that sort of thing. But now people just come up to you without being asked. Perhaps you don't want to say hello, or get to know this person? (Masha, (f) 16, former rollerblader, now graffiti sprayer, *lavochker*)

Of course, a large number of these rules relate to the *lavochkery*, because, as we already mentioned, skating automatically gives you the right to be accepted, if only temporarily. And, for instance, a skateboarder arriving from a different town has a lot more rights than a local *lavochker*. The older regulars at the Fun Box thus claim the right to initiate introductions (and thus include someone new in the *tusovka*). *Lavochkery*, sensing this discrimination, also declare their rights to the Fun Box with reference to the length of time they have frequented the area, various 'feats' they have performed, such as staying out nights at the Fun Box or risky adventures, and even involvement in the story of key personalities, authorities and legends of the Fun Box.

Another example of construction of the *tusovka's* borders and rules is the hierarchisation along the principles of real / not real (*nastoyashchii/ nenastoyashchii*), ours / not ours (*nash/ ne nash*). The discussion about the 'authenticity' of youth cultures is still of relevance in adolescent circles. This explains why identity is constructed, as a rule, in terms of either 'genuine subculture' or (local) group identity but not in terms of a subculture per se. The Fun Box crowd argue that they are not a subculture, but that among the *tusovka* there are 'genuine' representatives of subcultures (rappers, emotionals or emo music people, break-dancers). They construct other rappers, emos and break-dancers (not from the Fun Box) as inauthentic, pretentious, stupid, posers, along with Sochi's other subcultures, mentioned as being hostile to the Fun Box, such as punks, goths, football fans, neo-Nazis.

The main reason for marginalisation at the Fun Box is lack of cultural capital as a resource for communication in the *tusovka*. Cultural capital can derive from a specific unique skill, ability or experience. For instance, there was a case of an Armenian boy being accepted as 'one of us' because he was a virtuoso skateboarder. Construction of territorial borders is the most effective and the toughest Fun Box strategy as far as asserting its 'unique' cultural identity goes. Because this is what in the final analysis gets converted into authority. The appropriation and enclosure of the Fun Box territory is clear proof of the 'power of owning'. In this way, the difficulties of youth self-identification, practices, norms and personalities create independent 'informal' youth communities where the very declaration of one's own or another's marginality becomes a relevant, valuable and fashionable resource, securing one's own uniqueness, specialness and progressivity.

*From the Russian by Graham Stack.*

## NOTES

1. 'Everyday but not normal: Using drugs and youth cultural' practices in contemporary Russia' (ESRC, 2001–04, No. R000239439, project leader: Hilary Pilkington). 'Everyday Xenophobia: From passive dislike to aggressive action' (Mini-project within the framework of RIME, 2005–06 B7-701/2002/03 1843(RX154), project leader Elena Omel'chenko. 'Youth subcultural activities', grant from Warwick University (within the framework of EU project SAL (2006–07), FP 6-2004-029013, project leaders E. Omel'chenko, H. Pilkington).

2. *Tusovka* – a term denoting the group of 'one's own', united by general cultural practices, world view or leisure activities. The term emerged in Russia at the end of the 1980s. It is close to the terms *kompaniya* and *subkultura*. The original meaning denoted an authentic cultural youth group at the core of which was a style, usually alternative to the mainstream. Not all members of a *tusovka* are necessarily personally acquainted, but they gather in a place that is reserved for this *tusovka*. This is how Hilary Pilkington describes the term: 'The word *tusovka* has been part of Russian youth slang since the 1960s but its origin is unclear. Common-sense interpretations trace it to the word *tasovka* from the verb *tasovat'* meaning 'to shuffle', as in 'to shuffle cards'. *Tasovat'* itself, according to Dal', stems from the French verb *tasser* which, in its reflexive form, means 'to huddle together'. This is close to the current, slang usage of *tusovat'sia* as 'to gather', 'to get together' (H. Pilkington, *Russia's Youth and its Culture: A Nation's Constructors and Constructed.* London and New York, Routledge, 1994, p. 226).

3. *Gopniki* – a collective term for young people demonstrating the following characteristics: 1) Extremely aggressive behaviour, on which norms and practices are based; moral code supporting hierarchic relations, similar to the criminal milieu; practice of street robbery, when *gopniki* beat up their victims and take mobile phones, money, clothes or use threats to force their rendition. Sometimes *gopniki* have connections to organised crime or street gangs. 2) Bad taste – wearing clothing that instantly marks them as being 'one of them': often cheap clothes with imitation brands (for instance Chinese imitation D&G), no holistic style (e.g., leather boots and sports trousers). 3) Low cultural level – they listen to primitive pop music, pepper their speech with obscenities and prison jargon, have a low intellectual level and low level of education. The term

is not usually used by the group to characterise itself. In this article, the group is defined by its opposition to the group of 'informals', featuring as a 'primitive' non-progressive youth group. It is also worth mentioning that each region has its own marker of what constitutes *gopniki*. For instance, in Sochi ethnicity is a marker of being *gopniki* ('Here *gopniki* are mostly Armenians' – male, 18, Sochi), followed by aggressive behaviour and then dress. In central regions, by comparison, physical appearance (black hood, tracksuit from the market or dark leather jacket with loose track suit trousers or jeans) is the first marker. In the Russian context, the term *gopniki* has symbolic significance since it reflects the cultural polarity between 'progressive', subcultural youth and their conservative, mainstream counterparts.

4. We use the word 'marginal' not in its sociological sense but as a youth expression with a different sense which we will explain here.

5. *Lavochker* (bencher) denotes someone who comes to the Fun Box not for skateboarding, skating or BMXing but just to hang out, spend time, sitting on a bench and chatting with the kids.

### REFERENCES

Anderson, Benedict. *Voobrazhaemye soobshchestva. Razmyshleniya ob istokakh i rasprostranenii natsionalizma* (Imagined Communities: Reflections on the origin and spread of nationalism), Russian translation V. G. Nikolaeva, Inst. of Sociology, Russian Academy of Sciences, Moscow Higher School of Social and Economic Sciences, Centre of Fundamental Sociology, Moscow, 2001.

Muggleton, David. *Inside Subculture. The Postmodern Meaning of Style*, Oxford, 2000.

Muggleton, David. 'Legitimating Subcultural Authenticity – Ideologies of Similarity and Difference', in *Youth – Similarities, Differences, Inequalities*, University of Joensuu, Report of the Karelian Institute, 2005.

Pilkington, Hilary, et al. *Looking West? Cultural Globalization and Russian Youth Cultures*. University Park, PA, 2002.

Thornton, Sarah. 'The Social Logic of Subcultural Capital', in *The Subcultures Reader*, eds K. Gelder and S. Thornton, London, 1997, 200–09.

## ⁝⧉ 7 ⧉⁝

# 'You Know What Kind of Place This Is, Don't You?'

## *An Exploration of Lesbian Spaces In Moscow*

### KATJA SARAJEVA

### Introduction

The aim of this chapter is to explore the spatial practices of sexual minorities in Moscow and how negotiations between public and private aspects of space make it possible for gays and lesbians to create their own spaces within the city. In the first part of the chapter I will describe two very different meeting places for lesbians in Moscow. The first is a public space, a park-like section on the Boulevard Ring, and the second is a private apartment that occasionally functions as a library. These spaces incorporate varying degrees of privacy and public-ness that enable different degrees of visibility and accessibility to people from outside the subculture.[1] In the second part of the chapter I will compare these semi-public spaces with the openly political claim to public space that was made by the organisers of Moscow Pride Festival in 2006. The presence of gays and lesbians in the streets was announced and publicised within a framework of human rights and democracy, which set in motion a public discussion of legitimate use of public space both within the subculture as well as the national and international media. Here both the controversy around the event in the media and the event itself reveal assumptions about visibility, access and legitimate claim to the streets of the city.

### City Space in Moscow

The architecture in Moscow has a striking tendency to be monumental. Whether in the city or in the dormitory districts on the outskirts of the city, everything is large-scale – the buildings are tall, major thoroughfares tend to be eight-lane highways and much of the Stalinist architecture is not only built to express the grandeur of Soviet power but also effectively dwarfs the individual. In between the big *prospekts* and the Stalinist skyscrapers, however, there are alleys and courtyards that form the intimate, yet public, counter-side to the monumental architecture. One has only to take a few steps beyond the big street to find oneself in a completely different environment. And these are the spaces that people take pride in knowing. On a stroll along the embankment of the Moskva River a friend told me that when he lived in the centre as a child, he walked to and from school *only* through the courtyards. He took great pride in knowing the city so well that he could make his way through the labyrinths of backyards, only occasionally, if ever, stepping onto the streets. Since then, these spaces have changed considerably as residents have invested in gates and other security measures to provide a safer environment for themselves. As a result, many courtyards are closed off, thus restricting not only passage but also views for the pedestrians.

Public space in Moscow is, like all other spaces, raced, gendered and sexed (Bell and Valentine 1995). People of a non-Russian appearance run a greater risk of being stopped in the street by the police, asked for documents and detained than a person passing for an ethnic Russian. During the past few years there has been an escalation of xenophobic violence in Russia, targeting primarily exchange students and migrant workers but affecting all people who can be categorised as 'black'.[2] The possibility of violence that most probably will remain unpunished is a discourse that communicates who is allowed to be someplace and move from one place to another. It cautions people against moving through certain spaces, indicating that they do not 'have a right' to walk the streets. The sexual order of public space is strictly heterosexual. This is signified not only by the omnipresence of heterosexual couples but also by the conspicuousness of homosexual and lesbian ones. 'Only through repetition of hegemonic heterosexual scripts (...) does space (become and) remain straight' (Bell and Valentine 1995: 19). These structures of exclusion force people to negotiate their routes and spatial habits as well as monitor their behaviour, and in the case of sexual minorities this also includes passing. While a woman cannot pass for a man and a 'black' cannot pass as white, homosexual men and women can, and often do, pass as straight. A reversal of this is to publicly display or mark homosexuality and in such a way dispute the heterosexist assumptions about space. Making homosexuality visible in public space is one of the main political motivations behind pride parades and similar manifestations. A pride parade is an explicit challenge to the heteronormative structuring of space, making explicit what is usually hidden, ignored or repressed.

The geography of the lesbian subculture in Moscow consists of many different types of places that range from secret clubs to open-air meeting spaces. A lesbian woman becomes doubly marginalised in public space, excluded both on the grounds of gender and sexuality as different structures of exclusion and invisibility interlace and build upon each other. The marginalisation of women thus continues within the spaces of homosexual subculture where clubs and venues are predominantly oriented towards gays rather than lesbians and outnumber the lesbian or even mixed venues (Cieri 2003; Casey 2004). The most common way to maintain this segregation is to double the entrance fee for women. The gay clubs are populated by gay men and to a certain extent their heterosexual womenfriends which tends to make lesbians invisible even within homosexual spaces (Casey 2004; Binnie and Skeggs 2004). During my fieldwork there were two 'stable' clubs that catered to a lesbian public. One of these was the bar/café 12 Volt, run by the 'lesbian of the nation' Evgenia Debryanskaya. Debryanskaya was an integral member in the Russian movement for gay and lesbian rights in the early 1990s and was a highly visible activist and organiser throughout the larger part of the decade until she 'retired' to devote herself to her bar/café business at 12 Volt, though she still is regularly invited to talk shows as the 'grande dame' of gay and lesbian activism in Russia.[3] Another club that is frequented by lesbians is the nightclub Udar. It is hidden away in the sports complex *Olimpiiskii,* and on Friday and Saturday nights it holds 'women's nights'. While these events are listed in the gay and lesbian press, in *Time Out* Moscow in the gay section, and on relevant Internet sites, the fact that on Fridays and Saturdays Udar functions as a lesbian club is conspicuously absent from the club's homepage as well as from the sign at the club's entrance.

Beside the openly gay and lesbian venues, Moscow nightlife offers a multitude of different clubs, bars and restaurants, some of which are considered to be unofficially gay friendly. Maki Kafe is a restaurant/café that belongs to the former category, at least during the central part of my fieldwork. Natasha, who introduced me to this place, explained its popularity by its location. 'It's just a five minute walk from the (gay/lesbian) bars 12 Volt and 911 which have a tendency to become crowded quite early in the evening, so people who can't find a place there come here, it's sort of half way. It is also a very nice café'. Sometimes the establishment is considered gay and lesbian friendly simply because a large part of the clientele is recognised as gay or lesbian or because a part of the staff is suspected to be gay. It was not unusual for groups or networks of friends to patronise a particular bar or café if there was 'one of our own' on the staff. Sometimes such patronage results in attracting a wider group than the immediate circle of friends and acquaintances. One such cluster of friends came to an agreement with the owners of the restaurant Yakitoria to hold a 'girls' night', advertising the event on the internet and giving out flyers to friends. Many of the lesbian cafés and clubs that were available during my fieldwork were this kind of 'one night of the week' arrangements. The art café TemAtik, for instance, was housed in an art gallery. Dyke Café moved several times between different locations, and the club Pink Fly had yet to secure a venue but promised on its homepage that it was one of the oldest lesbian clubs in Moscow. There is also a tradition of 'closed clubs', either where a circle of friends regularly rent an entire restaurant for an evening or where there is a restaurant that is run as a closed establishment. Nevertheless, there are spaces within the city that are not dependent on purchasing power or connections. I will shortly outline the characteristics of two such spaces in terms of the physical space, access/visibility and social interaction. By this I mean what they look like, how one usually finds out about them and what usually goes on there. The places represent small enclaves within the cityscape where lesbians can feel that they are not the wrong gender or sexuality.

## The Pushka

Moscow has developed in stages that form concentric circles around the medieval core of the city – the Kremlin and *Kitai Gorod*. This is enclosed by the Boulevard Ring, a semicircle of boulevards with a wide swath of green, trees and benches down the middle. Pushka is the nickname of a particular part of the Boulevard Ring. It specifically refers to the square around the statue of the poet Sergey Esenin just a few minutes' walk from the metro station *Pushkinskaya*. The boulevard is lined with benches and the square itself has benches on all sides with the statue of the poet in the centre. There are people of all ages, though mostly young, sitting on the benches – drinking, talking, resting or waiting for someone. Weather permitting, people also sit on the grass. Within the subculture it is primarily the square around Esenin that is recognised as a lesbian space in Moscow. Different youth cultures and subcultural networks establish spatial anchoring in the city (Pilkington 1994). And as a public space it is, of course, frequented not only by lesbians. In general, there are many different types of people on the boulevard – people just passing through or taking a stroll, ice-cream and beer vendors in the summer, destitute pensioners looking through the rubbish bins for empty bottles or cans, the occasional punk or vagrant asking for change or begging for a cigarette. Almost always there are men playing chess at one or several of the benches. And, of course, there are tourists; usually in small groups, betraying their tourist status by stopping to take a picture of the bronze statue in the centre of the little square.

**Fig. 7.1:** The Pushka on Tverskoi Bul'var, on a rainy summer day, too wet for a crowd. Photograph by the author, 2005.

All the people who pass by or stay on the square can be divided into two categories: 1) those who are oblivious to the specific subcultural meaning of the space, to whom this is just another part of the Boulevard Ring with yet another statue of a great Russian poet, and another mass of people simply hanging out; 2) then there are those who know about this place, who are able to discern between the different kinds of people there or the different activities that are going on. Thus not all of the people who happen to be near the Esenin monument at a given moment are actually at the Pushka. They may not even be aware of the fact that this is a place with a specific social meaning. This 'mistake' is facilitated by the fact that to the unknowing or the 'untrained' eye, the crowd may appear mixed. Some of the girls at the Pushka dress and behave like one would expect teenage boys and are easily mistaken for such. Something that goes on in a public space is not necessarily visible to all the individuals in this space. This creates a space within the space, which could also be conceived as a parallel space. The relationship between knowledge and ignorance creates a splitting of the same physical space into several spaces and places. As Stephen Hodge points out '[p]laces are more than locations on maps (...) they are cultural creations with varying meanings to the different people who experience them' (Hodge as quoted in Markwell 2002: 88). Here the ignorance serves as a buffer that can provide a certain level of privacy not to mention safety, as increased homophobic violence has been linked to visibility (Corteen 2002: 260). Invisibility and ignorance are often the prerequisite for safety and the closet then becomes more than a site of oppression (Seidman, Meeks and Traschen 1999). Women in the know might make veiled allusions to the place in communication with newcomers. As I was sitting at the Pushka one day waiting for some friends to finally show up, a girl sat down next to me and struck up a random conversation. We talked about the weather and how nice it is to spend time outside in the summertime. Then she made a slight pause, looked me over and said with a glimmer in her eye, 'You know what kind of place this is, don't you?' This was both a cue that she has recognised me as someone who can be in the know and a way to check whether she was right or not. But it also left the possibility open that I am not willing to admit that I know or that I am just a random visitor to the park and thus not actually at the Pushka.

## Public and Private Space

Privacy in a public space can be juxtaposed with a lack of privacy at home that gays and lesbians sometimes experience as a result of the surveillance by other household members. 'Coming out' and 'being out' at home is a process that in many cases has to be done in stages and repeated over and over (Holliday 1999; Valentine, Skelton and Butler 2003).[4] Hiding one's sexuality from some, if not all, family members turns the private space that is assumed to be offstage into a place where a certain amount of self-restraint needs to be exercised, almost reversing the relationship between public and private space (Johnson and Valentine 1995: 100ff). The equation made between private space and safety has been harshly criticised by feminist geographers (e.g., Bell and Valentine 1995), who point out that being at home far from always means being safe. Private space in no way guarantees privacy, just as visibility is not guaranteed in public. The relationship between the two is more complex and intertwined. The non-private aspect of domestic space has been widely recognised in literature on Soviet society (Boym 1994; Kharkhordin 1999; Tuller 1996). Irrespective of social status, people sought to create actual private spaces among friends that were vigilantly guarded (Tuller 1996; Kharkhordin 1999; Yourchak 2006; Pesmen 2000). According to Oswald and Voronkov, this collective privacy suggests that 'clear-cut borderlines, especially dichotomous space models ascribing every social phenomenon either to a public or a private sphere seem to be of little use for understanding communication in Soviet society' (Oswald and Voronkov 2004: 111). I would like to carry that model into the post-Soviet era and suggest that the hard divide must be drawn between a state/official public sphere and a private public sphere, and that the latter shares a rather permeable border with the sphere of the intimate private (Oswald and Voronkov 2004: 111).

To give an idea of how people who spend time at the Pushka manipulate the public and private aspects of space it is necessary to provide a brief glimpse into the different opinions regarding this space and what goes on there. There are two different views of the Pushka. Most often it is met with ridicule and disdain, described as 'the lowest of the low', a place for girls who are either too young to go anywhere or people who have not 'made anything of themselves'. This is a stereotype of girls who are considered to be interested only in drinking, fighting and being rowdy. Because of the close connection made between the place and the people who spend time there, Pushka can mean the place, a type of person and a form of interaction. For those who avoid it, the Pushka is 'a disgrace' because of the type of women who go there. Viewed another way, the women who go to the Pushka are a particular kind of people because they go to the Pushka. These judgements of spaces and places reveal the values attached to them, how spaces are understood, related to each other and experienced. They are also a reflection of what is appropriate behaviour in public space.

The Pushka is often described as 'one of the worst places to be', both because of the place itself and because of what goes on there. As a physical space it is open to everyone and is, therefore, by definition not exclusive. Both within mainstream culture and subculture there is an implicit hierarchy of spaces – be it clubs, restaurants or other places. Here, I see the hierarchy of spaces in terms of how accessible they are – the more exclusive the club or restaurant, the more difficult is it to get into. Access is regulated not only by financial means such as entrance fees and prices but also by membership requirements and making certain establishments completely secret, where one can come by invitation only. Following this logic, the least valued spaces are those of easiest access or places that are passed through, such as parks or railroad stations. People there are seen to be on their way to somewhere else and thus actually nowhere. To see the Pushka as a place of transition, a space to move through and move on from makes it also a liminal place, a dangerous place. This has a great influence on the (self-)perception of people who spend a lot of time there. Their preference for the Pushka is often perceived as simply the result of their not being able to move on, for they cannot gain access to any other spaces. 'Pushka is a place all of us have been to, but most people move on as soon as they can. To something better' (Jana, age 35). People who spend time at the Pushka are characterised as failures because they are *still* there.[5] The observations above are opinions of the Pushka from the outside, expressed by two lesbians, the first of whom has never frequented it and the other who used to but no longer does. Those who used to go there tend to say that 'in my time things were different. We just sat there, talked, maybe with a guitar, today everything has changed'. Some state that they left because the place changed, others because they outgrew it or settled down with a partner. Insiders, on the other hand, paint a different picture. People who spend a lot of time at the Pushka are well aware of the reputation it has within the subculture. There is an internal mythology, a set of stories that underscore the positive experiences of the place, that present the Pushka as a place of freedom and inclusion. One of my informants, who has spent three or four years on the Pushka, recounted an incident where a girl had spent most of the evening sitting on a bench waiting for a date that never showed up. At the end of the night she was almost crying and, feeling sorry for her, the girls invited her into the group and made her feel welcome. The physical openness of the space is equated with social openness, something that allows anyone and everyone to meet and spend time together. 'It is a place without hierarchies and money doesn't matter. That's why it's good. There are places like that in every city' (Olga, age 49). These stories of openness and hospitality create a positive counter-image of the Pushka that is maintained by those who spend time there.

But my own experiences have contradicted these stories of immediate inclusion. First of all, people who come to the Pushka most commonly come to see someone they already know or have made plans to meet. It is possible to come on your own and 'be open to suggestions', as it were, and it is true that people will come up and sit next to you and talk to you for a while, but you will not become a member of a group. A certain distance is maintained towards newcomers, which becomes obvious only after a while. There is a polish of openness that covers, if not a hostile, then at least a somewhat cautious stance. Irina who had spent some time there when she was younger and occasionally still does so, told me that 'the Pushka is an open place, but if you come alone, you'll leave alone' (Irina, age 29). The more I visited the place, the more I noticed that people will greet you and talk to you a little but they keep their distance. One explanation given by regulars is simply that not all people who come there have the appropriate 'egalitarian outlook'. 'Anyone can come to the Pushka, but not all can stay, it will not accept just anyone. A person who is very keen to show off or to establish their superiority will not be long-lived' (Sasha, age 23, a frequent visitor to the Pushka since she was 17). While reserve towards newcomers was explained as a reluctance to include those who are keen to show off or try to create hierarchies, and in this way supported the internal image of the Pushka as an egalitarian place, this behaviour was simultaneously a way to close off the social space. Seemingly a paradox, this is a space where everyone can come but far from everyone can make it 'in' or stay, which in a way reverses the 'all access' aspect of the place. By being cautious or conservative in their interaction, girls who spend time at the Pushka can create a more private sphere within the public space. The line between public and private space, or perhaps within a public private space, is continuously constructed by the social interactions that go on in that space. This 'public private' sphere (a private realm in public) is a reversal of the 'private-public' sphere described by Oswald and Voronkov (2007).

The same physical space not only is perceived differently but actually becomes several different social spaces depending on who you are and your level of access (see also Andreeva and Kosterina this volume). The creation and negotiation of spaces is of course a continual process where 'places are never complete, finished or bounded but are always becoming – in process' (Cresswell 2004: 37). What kind of space a person is in depends on his or her relationship to the space and the people around him/her. To a great extent it was the ignorance of the wider public that allowed the Pushka to be a lesbian space, and this ignorance was seldom disrupted by the girls themselves. If a stranger attempted to join a group, most often that would be a man, he was politely turned away, with the explanation 'we have our own private party here, please go somewhere else'. Sometimes this was done less politely but the space was never singled out explicitly as a lesbian space.[6] The 'live and let live' mentality reigns as long as people do not have to take a stand or openly face alternative lifestyle choices.

The partial visibility, access and the internal division of the Pushka underscore the different layers present and the social construction of space. Rather than being a meeting place for all, the Pushka is a space of overlapping and at times parallel spaces, parallel almost in the mathematical definition of the term, planes that never intersect. To those who feel at home, the Pushka is a big living room, a place of familiar interaction with friends. To many other lesbians, who know of the place but do not spend time there, the space is a marginal one, a place to pass through and then avoid if possible, where girls who are considered to be nobodies hang out in a place that is nowhere.[7] Even passers-by who recognise what kind of place this is, along with casual visitors, do not gain access; and, in practice, the space becomes a public private one within a public space. To those simply passing by, it is an open space, a thoroughfare, a space to be crossed from point A to point B. For those who come here regularly, it is seen as a private space that is guarded if not by physical barriers like walls and doors then by rather rigorous social exclusion.

## The Archive

Once a week a private apartment on the north-eastern outskirts of Moscow, also known as the Archive, opens its doors to visitors, who can find or discuss interesting reading matter, preferably on the subject of gay and lesbian culture or written by a gay or lesbian author. It is called the Archive because it hosts a unique collection of the early Russian gay publications from the 1990s along with a smaller amount of imported gay and lesbian magazines and newspaper clippings from the mainstream Russian press. There is a reference library as well as a collection of gay and lesbian fiction and non-fiction within a lending library. It is advertised in magazines and on the Internet and is renowned among social scientists abroad who are researching the lesbian and gay scenes in Russia and among Western LGBT activists. Although about 130 people hold library cards, on a regular day one can expect between five and fifteen visitors. There are people who come here just for the books or the magazines, but they are in the minority. Most people come here to socialise, and then the Archive turns into a typical Russian kitchen with a lot of heated discussions and gossip. Visitors move between the tea, biscuits and cigarettes in the kitchen and the books and magazines in the living room. In comparison with the Pushka, the Archive is perceived by its visitors as a private space that, for a short period of time, functions as a 'private-public' space (Oswald and Voronkov 2007). It retains some of its 'private' qualities in combination with 'public' aspects.

The dynamic variation in the private-public realm within the apartment itself can illustrate the shifts between public and private aspects of space. Often it is the living room, with the books and magazines, that becomes the public gathering place. Most people behave as they would in a library, quietly looking through the shelves, or flicking through a magazine. Sometimes discussions erupt or there is a commotion when a lot of people arrive at once or there is a long-absent guest, but most of the time the place is still and quiet. To have some privacy people do what they usually do in these situations, they go to the kitchen. The phrase 'let's have some tea' could accurately be translated into 'let's talk'. But sooner or later almost everyone ends up in the kitchen, and the more private space has to be found somewhere else. But, as a private space that allows information exchange on a topic that was almost completely silenced in the Soviet era (Kon 1995; Essig 1999) the kitchen of the Archive can function very well as a metaphor for the Archive itself. During Soviet times, kitchens were the places where people could meet and informally discuss issues that they could not discuss openly in public (Boym 1994; Yourchak 2006). It was a private-public sphere where social life went largely unimpeded by state powers 'regulated by informal norms of everyday life' (Oswald and Voronkov 2004: 106). But unlike Soviet kitchens, the Archive is advertised and available to people who are not part of a limited social network. There are a handful of small adverts on some internet sites and a regular note in the small but stable publication *Ostrov*. The most common way to find out about the Archive is to be told about it and/or brought there by someone.[8] But despite its scant

**Fig. 7.2:** The kind of apartment complex in which the Archive is housed. Photograph by the author, 2008.

advertising, it is relatively famous abroad – at least among social scientists and activists. During my fifteen months of fieldwork in Moscow beginning in February 2005, I met six academics from the US, the UK and Italy at the Archive.

Just as people during Soviet times were aware that there were private spaces serving as meeting places, the knowledge of the Archive is not restricted to the lesbian subculture. According to Elena Grigorievna, her neighbours in the building are aware that the apartment functions as a meeting place, and that it attracts people of a certain interest though it remains unclear exactly of what kind. An anecdote that I have heard her recount on several different occasions illustrates the question of whether the neighbours know that her apartment doubles as a library. Two girls had made their way to the Archive. They had found the building and the right stairway, punched in the right code for the intercom but they did not know which floor they had to go to. Another resident of the building, who waited for the elevator with them, overheard their conversation, looked up and down at them. At this point in the story, Elena Grigorievna usually mimics the slightly condescending gaze, and then says curtly 'you'll need the eighth floor'. When asked whether the neighbours have had any complaints, Elena Griegorievna calmly responds 'what would they have to complain about? There is never any ruckus or noise. People who come here are calm and civilised, thank God, though there is no way to guarantee that of course. But when people come here, they are well aware that they are guests in my house, my home, and they behave accordingly'. Once again, it is the 'live and let live' mentality that provides the safety of the lesbian space. Even if people know or suspect that something is going on, there is no need to get involved since nothing is stated explicitly.

But the adverts both online and in the press made the Archive a place known not only in Moscow but also in the Russian regions and one of *the* gay/lesbian spaces to visit when in the capital. The Pushka is not held in such renown, being infamous rather than famous; but it, too, is occasionally visited by people almost as a tourist attraction. Lena, a woman who had recently moved to Moscow from Astrakhan in southern Russia, was expecting visitors and decided to take them to Udar and to the Pushka, 'so that they will have seen what it is like' she said, smiling broadly. Another one of my informants, Helga (age 35) said: 'I would never go there to spend any time, to sit and drink, that is not interesting for me. But if I am taking a walk in the city with my girlfriend and we are nearby ... then sure, why not? We will walk by. And in a way it is nice. Even if they are very different [the girls at the Pushka] they are one of us. We will be seen as a couple and not as just two women walking hand in hand'. The Pushka is an example of 'how lesbians produce place in the city to be visible to each other' (Podmore 2001: 348; on visibility see also Cieri 2003; Eves 2004). Giorgi has discussed gay tourism not only in terms of seeing but also in terms of being seen, places where you will be visible and recognised. '[Y]ou'll see' and 'you'll be seen' – that is the tacit promise and the contract between the gay guidebooks and their readers' (Giorgi 2002: 65). Visibility is not simply to be seen, it is also a question of by whom you are being seen. Different sites in the city offer possibilities to be out in a way that is not allowed at home or at work. While moving through the city one can come out just by moving through the right places and being recognised, by belonging to that place. Visibility thus becomes an experience that is also connected to movement (Giorgi 2002: 66; Kaur Puar, Rushbrook and Stein 2003: 386). Both when it comes to the Pushka and the Archive the lesbian spaces are kept hidden from mainstream society irrespective of whether they are in public or in private. The Pushka blends in with the general culture of parks in Russia, while maintaining more or less strict boundaries between in-group and out-group. The Archive as a place of access and knowledge is restricted to begin with, but accepted and tolerated because it is not explicitly announced. Both these spaces exist parallel with the spaces they look like to the unknowing public, a park and a private apartment, and can therefore be ignored. Discretion, or perhaps ignorance or secrecy, depending on your perspective, separates different subcultures from each other and from mainstream culture. It creates multiple dimensions of city spaces that coexist side by side, sometimes even simultaneously within the same physical space, as is the case of the Pushka.

Most gay and lesbian meeting places throughout the city exist thanks to the fact that they are not announced anywhere. This tacit agreement of silence was ruptured when in July 2005 Nikolai Alekseev announced plans to organise a gay pride parade through the streets of Moscow. The parade was to be the festive pinnacle of Moscow Pride Festival '06, which also included a cultural program with lectures and seminars by invited guests. Plans to hold a parade not only brought up the issue of gay rights but also highlighted the question of who had the right to be visible in public space, thus questioning the national image of Russia, which is a very sensitive issue. While people are willing to overlook what goes on in a park or a private apartment, judgments take on a different tone as soon as claims are made explicitly.

## Moscow Pride 2006

While Russia is keen to maintain and strengthen its position as a powerful nation on the world political scene, and Moscow is occasionally promoted as a capital on par with London and New York, this is not done by way of underlining diversity.[9] Both in theoretical explorations of world cities and in journalistic and tourist accounts, one of the markers of a world city is cultural and ethnic diversity that exists within its borders and continually flows through it. A minority populace that is becoming increasingly recognised within this idea of diversity is that of gays and lesbians. Gay culture in

the form of nightclubs, gay and lesbian parts of town and especially different forms of parades and festivals are becoming a weighty argument on the
global and national tourist market, adding a multicultural and cosmopolitan flavour to the cities (Markwell 2002; Rushbrook 2002; Binnie and Skeggs
2004; Waitt 2005; Puar 2002a, 2002b). Gay pride parades, Europride, Mardi
Gras and similar festivals have become something of a global franchise and
an annual rite of gay culture (Johnston 2005; Puar 2002a, 2002b). This kind
of advertising is aimed primarily at gays and lesbians but also reaches a part
of the majority that is interested in cultivating an image of being 'chic and
open-minded' or simply enjoys the spectacle of the 'sexually Other'.

The presence of sexual minorities on the streets of Moscow became a national, even international, issue when on 27 July 2005 Nikolai Alekseev and
Evgenia Debryanskaya announced their plans to organise a pride parade
in Moscow the following year.[10] While Evgenia Debryanskaya was a well
established name in the gay and lesbian rights activism in Russia, having
participated in the movement since its inception in the early 1990s, Nikolai
Alekseev was almost entirely unknown, both within the subculture and to
the mainstream public. With a degree in law from MGU (Moscow State
University), Alekseev's only contribution to the gay and lesbian subculture
were two volumes on same-sex marriage. The parade was to be held the following year on 27 May, which would mark the 13th anniversary of the repeal
of Article 121, and thus a commemoration of the day that homosexuality
was decriminalised in the Russian Federation. The following day the may-
or's office released a statement that such a parade would not be allowed.
Quite soon a number of religious leaders of various persuasions followed
suit and spoke out against the event. Simultaneously, a controversy erupted
within the gay and lesbian community of Moscow. Many of the local activists in the gay and lesbian subculture voiced criticism against the plans.
There were three main concerns: first, what was the event meant to achieve
for gays and lesbians; second, how safe would it be for the participants; and
third, what was the motivation of the organiser. Many considered that a
march through the streets of Moscow modelled on pride parades in western Europe and the US was both unsafe and provocative. The gay activists
interviewed by *gay.ru* voiced opinions ranging from outright fear to very
cautious optimism.[11] It was argued that no amount of wishful thinking or
references to the constitution by the main organisers would change the fact
that in some respects Russia is not anything like western Europe or North
America. Too little time had passed since decriminalisation, and the views
of people on sexual minorities were still too negative. The Russian populace was seen as too prejudiced to be trusted in order *not* to react violently.
Even if the city authorities, against all odds, were to allow the parade and
thus at least nominally promise protection, many gays and lesbians did not

consider this to be an actual guarantee that the state, i.e., police, would intervene on behalf of the participants. And finally, the entire announcement was seen as a personal PR campaign by the main organiser, Nikolai Alekseev who until then had been an unknown figure. The controversy died down after a few weeks and there was little news of the parade. The issue resurfaced in the media in late April 2006 when right-wing fascist groups had sent threats to the organisers of another festival, Rainbow Without Boundaries, that was to be held a few weeks before Moscow Pride.[12] The threats spread to other venues when several gay clubs were picketed by skinheads and women in headscarves holding candles and icons.[13] A small art café for women was burnt down and the Rainbow Without Boundaries Festival was ultimately cancelled.

The violence and threats against gay and lesbian establishments during the months that preceded the event did not considerably change what people said about Moscow Pride, though they did bolster the conspiracy theories. Alekseev was no longer someone who was organizing a gay pride parade in his quest for fame and fortune but he was increasingly portrayed as a pawn in a bigger scheme, though it was never specified who was pulling the strings. In some cases it was Western gay activists, en masse, who imperialistically wanted to spread 'their' gay culture worldwide and had found a fool they could pay to do it in Russia. The other, far more common scenario was that the Russian government was behind both the parade as well as the inevitable violence against it. The scheme was either a diversion, so that the 'people' did not pay attention to government business elsewhere, or simply a demonstration of power. Gays and lesbians would march in the streets, be beaten down by fascists or the police and the general public would not consider them victims since they had no business flaunting their perversion in the public space. In his comment on the plans to hold a pride parade, Igor Kon describes the use of homophobia as an instrument against democratic transformation.[14] Both the use of force by the state and/or the unwillingness of the state to prevent violence would be perceived as justified (Richardson and Hazel 1999) – at the expense of gays and lesbians who would end up either in hospitals or in cemeteries.

These speculations and discussions reaffirmed that what is in the West considered to be a public space is in Russia one that essentially does not belong to the public but rather to the state. This is supported by Oswald and Voronkov, who place the crucial spatial divide in Soviet and post-Soviet Russia between the 'official-public' sphere and the 'private-public' sphere rather than between public and private as is customary in the West (Oswald and Voronkov 2004). What is considered to be the private sphere in the West would correspond to a more intimate sphere which is not sharply divided from the private-public sphere.

The tradition of public manifestations differs markedly if one compares Russia to the United States, where the pride parade originated. During Soviet times, celebrations in public space were minutely orchestrated manifestations where participation was obligatory and the object of celebration was ultimately the Soviet state, be it in the guise of the First of May celebrations or the October Revolution (Lane 1981). Soviet-ness was the identity to be celebrated; ethnic and religious minorities re-allocated their specific place within the Soviet state, both geographically and within the hierarchy of nationality, whereby the ethnic identity was always subordinated to the Soviet identity (Hirsch 2005). To single out one minority to march down the streets of Moscow and celebrate their uniqueness is highly incongruent with the Russian (Soviet) tradition of public celebrations. Seen in the context of other parades and celebrations, the pride parade would be of equal importance as the celebration of the 1$^{st}$ and the 9$^{th}$ of May, the International Day of the Worker and The Day of Victory respectively, celebrations that to a very high degree link to fundamental features of Soviet ideology.

As discussions of the parade continued, on the Internet, at café tables, in clubs and at home, the fears became more or less articulated. First of all, the parade had yet to be banned or allowed, and that would be known only shortly before the date of the parade. But if the parade were to proceed, the main fear was not so much that the state would beat down the demonstration, but rather that the counter protesters would not be hindered from harming the participants. A common tactic of the Soviet state, utilised both during revolutionary times (Courtois et al 1997) and as a control mechanism in Soviet society (Kharkhordin 1999), was to pit different groups against each other and manipulate the population to monitor and exert violence against unwanted elements or groups within itself. In the end everything depended upon the benevolence of the state, something that could not be counted on due to the constantly shifting political agendas of city politics and the unknown forces that were assumed to be constantly at play. Both Aleskeev and Debryanskaya emphasised that the Russian leaders would be forced to allow the parade in order to save face in the international arena.[15] Others recognised the fact that the condemnations of Western leaders and LGBT rights organisations did not hold any actual force in Russia, neither in terms of jurisdiction nor physical protection.

## The 'Parade'

Most of the programme of the Moscow Pride Festival was held in a five-star hotel with tight security. Policemen were stationed outside, and men in suits with walkie-talkies were pacing the lobby. Of the perhaps fifty participants, no more than fifteen were Russians, the organisers included. As many had expected, the municipality did not grant permission to hold the parade, with the motivation that they would not be able to guarantee the safety of the participants. The organisers had filed a petition to overrule the decision of the municipality at the district court of the city area. The day before the parade the district court confirmed its ruling to uphold the decision of the mayor's office, in effect disallowing the march for the second time. The organisers were now facing the choice of either cancelling the parade or holding it, irrespective of the ruling of the court, i.e. illegally. This question was hotly debated among the participants of the Moscow Pride Festival the day before the set date, but the final decision was made public only at the press conference on the day of the parade. The decision to keep the plans secret were motivated in part by the illegal character of the march, if it were decided to hold one, but also by the fact that on many different neo-Nazi forums, people had been rallied to gather for a march on the very same day, in protest against the gay parade. This secrecy resulted in the paradoxical situation that the people for whom the parade was to be held knew neither where the parade was going to be nor whether it was going to take place at all.

At the press conference it was announced that instead of holding a march/parade through the city, the participants were invited to join the organisers of the festival in laying flowers at the Tomb of the Unknown Soldier by the Kremlin walls as a sign of protest against fascism and the proliferation of neo-Nazi organisations. Alekseev emphasised that this would be an individual decision and the public ritual was no longer presented as demonstration for gay rights but as a number of individuals protesting against the increasing fascist tendencies in Russia today. Alekseev attempted to re-frame the march, removing it from the context of minority rights and democracy into the context of commemoration of the fight against fascism and Russia's victory in the Great Patriotic War. This last-minute re-framing of the parade did not reach any further than the press conference. All of the participants at the conference proceeded as if the parade was to go on as announced though under a different form. All of the reports on the subsequent events in central Moscow, both on national and international news, referred to the events as the Moscow Pride that was banned.

The footage in TV reports was dominated by shots of a variety of different groups holding icons or crosses, women in headscarves holding candles and singing orthodox hymns, young male anti-gay protesters being hauled away and stowed onto buses by the riot police OMON, Alekseev in front of the cameras and the German politician Volker Beck being punched in the face during a scuffle. CNN juxtaposed these scenes with colourful footage of pride parades in Western cities as a reminder of the ideal that had been strived for but was not being achieved, namely, a colourful carnival with rainbow flags, balloons and music. The footage was taken from different gay pride marches around the world. Even though the Russian footage was an edited version of the most violent and spectacular events, when compared to the real-time events, the footage is accurate on one point – the almost absolute invisibility of the people for whom this event was organised

Fig. 7.3: On the sidelines of the 'parade'. Photograph by the author, 2006.

in the first place: Russian gays and lesbians and their supporters. Those visible were foreign visitors, anti-gay protestors (orthodox Christian groups and right-wing extremists) and the riot police. The only identifiable gays and lesbians were the organisers and the visitors from abroad.

## Witnessing or Participating

During that day I met a few friends and acquaintances who had, just like me, come to see what was going on, to document rather than to participate. Gays and lesbians who had come to see the parade or to participate wore no distinguishing symbols. And the protestors against the parade could only be identified if they held an icon or communicated their standpoint in some other way. But most had arrived without any visible markers whatsoever, and thus there were no lines between participants and bystanders, sympathisers and protesters. In this case there was no clear line between participation and witnessing. The fact that there was no established marching route, no demarcations between the parade and the crowd, no banners, no flags and thus no sideline made the (organisation of the) event even more disorienting. People moved in all directions, back and forth, and at times their movement was blocked by riot police. Even in 'successful' parades the distinction between participant and observer is elusive, since a bystander can easily step onto the street and join the procession or, inversely, step off and become a bystander.[16] But even though the line between audience and participant is fluid in those events too, a more or less clear demarcation between participants and bystanders is created by the fact that an actual flow of people who parade moves along an established route which is sometimes marked off by fences (Johnston 2005).

There is yet another way in which all those present turned from (passive) witnesses to (active) participants. Any kind of show requires both a performer and a spectator to complete the performance. Irrespective of the mindset of the crowd, amicable bystanders or irate protestors, the people around the parade were an integral part of the parade itself. In this way, ironically enough, all of the people who showed up to prevent and protest against the parade became participants. But different people played different roles and used the streets and the media for staging their own particular agendas. Once again the same space was split into different, almost parallel planes. The anti-gay protestors saw the streets as something that needed protection; their moral indignation and outcry was what was standing between debauchery and the holy soil of Russia. For the riot police this was an ordinary working day, maintaining order and keeping apart groups of people who should be kept apart. The journalists were also working hard, establishing where the action was and how to get the best footage.

The foreign gay activists were frantically documenting events, witnessing and taking a stand for the rights of Russian gays and lesbians to walk freely in the street without fear. The Russian gays and lesbians, on the other hand, as well as the majority of the protesters, had come to witness and document what was happening.

During the events of 27 May in central Moscow, two different imaginings of the city collided head on. The organisers of the parade, the visiting activists, and the few local gays and lesbians who supported the parade, constructed an idea of Moscow as a metropolis that could join the league of world cities that annually hold pride celebrations: London, New York, Rome, Amsterdam and many other centres famous for a cosmopolitan lifestyle, cultural diversity and being at the 'cutting edge of modernity'. The promotion of a pride parade was indirectly a promotion of identity politics, tolerance and celebration of cultural diversity and the right of gays and lesbians to be visible in public space. Needless to say, this ideal of Moscow was not shared by the people who spoke out against the parade. There were people among the opponents to the parade who shared some of the ideals of the organisers, in theory, but not in this particular time and place. Even though one should fight for the rights of gays and lesbians, they stressed that Russia was not ready for such a public display. The religious and right-wing protesters envisaged Moscow as a city of religion, tradition and (a)sexual purity, making Russia the keeper of spiritual values rather than a worldly centre. During the 'parade' itself Russian gays and lesbians remained largely incognito.[17] Not counting the very public figures of Alekseev and Debryanskaya, the only other participants who could be recognised as gay were the foreign activists and politicians who had joined the event which, ironically, in a strange way validated the statement that homosexuality is not Russian but imported from the West, since no Russian gays or lesbians were immediately recognisable. The gay and lesbian population in Moscow proved unwilling to embrace this tradition of public celebration, in this way underlining that this practice is not a part of Russian homosexual culture. This can be extended to Russian culture in general, where what is considered as a public space in the West is regarded in Russia as a space that is primarily the stage of the state, the 'official public' sphere. To voice private and intimate matters in the 'official public' space is the same as to welcome the attention of state structures to one's private life. Throughout Soviet history people have been striving to minimise the presence of the state in the private sphere and in personal matters, both in regard to the public private sphere of friends or the more intimate private sphere of family and loved ones. Added to this in this case was the fact that the topic of concern was the rights of homosexuals, a highly controversial topic both within the government and among the general population, where homophobia is the rule rather than the exception. To attract the attention of the state to such a topic appeared even more dubious.

## Aftermath

When I came to the Archive the following Thursday, it was unusually crowded considering the summery weather, and people apparently felt the need to discuss the recent events. Tatiana, in her early twenties, studying to become a journalist, had visited several pride parades in Europe and defended the event and the organisers. She stressed the importance to fight for gay and lesbian rights with all means possible. A woman in her mid-thirties simply noted that Alekseev had a right to 'do his own thing' even though she had no intention of participating. Most people who had been to the event said they had gone there as witnesses, to see what would happen, and did not consider themselves participants in a march for gay and lesbian rights. The proprietess of the Archive, Elena Grigorievna, was pleased to have so many people there and to have such lively discussions. Her own opinion in this debate was more critical: 'Of course that kind of activism is needed and very important. But the parade is one day, and then it's over. It is the less glamorous and radical places that welcome people the rest of the year that are really important. Those are the places that really change people's lives'. This was partially supported by a French gay activist who had participated both in the festival and the 'parade', who told the gathering in the Archive that most of his gay and lesbian friends in France were deeply disinterested in gay and lesbian politics, especially in the form of parades and demonstrations. They were quite content living their lives, calmly and without publicity or overzealous political activism.

## Conclusions

The presence of gays and lesbians in Moscow seems to function only through ignorance on the part of the majority population, i.e., by way of an active or passive invisibility of gays and lesbians. But this shying away from public visibility is a part of the minimisation of contact with official structures that became a part of everyday life during Soviet times.[18] Therefore, the claim to visibility and recognition made by the organisers of the 'parade' was a provocation both to the conservative mainstream society and to the local lesbian and gay community. Very few among the gay and lesbian subculture supported the plans to openly march through the street and claim their fundamental democratic rights in this way. While both Debryanskaya and Alekseev, as well as the foreign visitors to the festival, were quick to chalk it up to simple fear, few of the opponents to the march perceived the parade as a practical way to increase tolerance towards homosexuals in Russian society. Most saw it as a provocation and an unnecessarily aggressive tactic that would force things upon people that they were not ready for (Brickell 2000).

While the attempt to place Moscow on the map as a large multicultural city that hosts a pride parade failed, it definitely demonstrated the official position of the municipality and the Russian state towards sexual minorities, and to a certain extent the diversity of the public space in general. The streets of Moscow were defended against an 'alien' sexuality through a performance of the city space in terms of tradition, religion and nationality. At the same time, what was not visible, in neither the national nor the international media, was the profound ambiguity that the parade evoked among gays and lesbians in the city. To assume that fear was the fundamental emotion behind any negative reaction against the parade is to place Russian gay and lesbian subculture on the path established in the West which inevitably leads to a public celebration of sexual identity. The spaces for lesbians in Moscow are, to a great extent, dependent on their inconspicuousness, and sometimes even invisibility. While there is a 'Gay&Lesbi' section in the Moscow edition of *Time Out* consisting of a small feature article about an event and followed by a listing of the gay and lesbian venues, most spaces of diversity exist even if they are not advertised in *Time Out* or function as a major tourist attraction on a national level, as would be the case with the Mardi Gras in Sydney, say, or the pride parades in London and San Francisco. For many Russian gays and lesbians, what is acceptable abroad may be far from desirable at home. A large part of the criticism against Moscow Pride from within the gay and lesbian community was the concern that it will bring unwanted attention to the places that do exist and jeopardise the already established clubs and meeting places around town as well as increase the visibility of individual gays and lesbians who would become more vulnerable to homophobic violence. The pride parade attempted to break down the barrier between the 'public private' sphere, where people can be left to their own devices as long as they behave discretely, and the official public sphere, which is ruled by official ideology. It was an unveiling of private behaviour in the public sphere which disrupted the balance between the visible and invisible that makes it possible for gays and lesbians to gather in the streets and other places.

### NOTES

1. Many gays and lesbians are well aware that there are others like them, both in Russia and in other parts of the world, in this way constituting an imagi-

ned community based on sexual preference (Anderson). But belonging to an imagined community of lesbians does not automatically inspire social interaction. In many cases the commonality in one characteristic is cancelled out by dissimilarities in others, most importantly class, age or education. The lesbian subculture in Moscow is comprised of networks of people who create spaces, both physical and virtual, where they can meet and socialise as lesbians. A subculture therefore carries 'the simultaneous emphasis on cultural distinctiveness and relational anchorage' (Hannerz 1992: 71). But as there is a great variation in other social factors, the lesbian subculture is heterogeneous and multifaceted, overlapping both with other subcultures and incorporating cultural flows from mainstream society (Hannerz 1992: 72).

2.  In Russia 'black' (*chernye*) is used in reference to people from the Caucasus while people of African descent are called *negry*, 'negroes' (see Boltovskaya and Kosygina in this volume).

3.  In July 2005 she returned to gay and lesbian rights politics as she joined Nikolai Alekseev as one of the organisers of Moscow Pride Festival.

4.  'Coming out' is a well established description of disclosing or informing people around you of your sexual orientation. 'Coming out of the closet' is an old expression that did not refer to sexuality as such but is now widely used specifically for that meaning (Lazerson 1981).

5.  All names, except when just first or last names are stated, have been changed.

6.  Knowledge of subcultural spaces like the Pushka among the wider population can have consequences. In the summer of 2007 I heard that religious groups had begun targeting the stretch of the Boulevard Ring near the metro station *Kitai Gorod*, the cruising spot for male homosexuals, handing out leaflets about sin and saving your soul. Though this may seem a comical exercise, if the municipality suddenly decided to care about the Boulevard Ring and ventures on a crusade to 'clean up' this space, all of the groups would find themselves placeless, because the city space would be too clean for hanging out – a gentrification of park space so to speak. The gay cruising spots that were located outside the Bolshoi Theatre until the mid-1990s had to move due to reconstruction.

7.  Here there are apparent similarities with Turner's conceptualisation of liminality as a space where change occurs, a space where one is no one and outside of society, therefore a threat (Turner 1965).

8.  Ostrov is a small lesbian/feminist journal that features mainly poetry and prose but also interviews and reviews.

9.  Moscow has the largest concentration of capital and investment in Russia. The city attracts large numbers of migrants from the Russian regions, and holds the economic and social potential to become a global city (Beaverstock as quoted in Brade and Rudolph 2003: 78).

10.  Nikolai Alekseev had until 2005 been unknown to the wider public as a gay activist, he has received a degree in law at MGU and written two books on same sex marriage. Until June 2005 he had not gained any notoriety as an activist or organiser. Evgenia Debryanskaya, on the other hand, is a veteran in the gay and

lesbian activism in Russia. She was one of the central figures during the early 1990s when the Russian gay and lesbian activism was just beginning to get organised, with much financial and other assistance from the West. Since then she has moved away from activism and into business. She is the owner of the café 12 Volt in central Moscow, but she remains the number-one out lesbian of the nation and is regularly invited to television shows.

11. A few reactions were presented two days after the announcement http://www .gay.ru/news/rainbow/2005/07/29f.htm (Russian only), see also http://gay.ru/ english/communty/news/2005-10-29.htm for comments by Igor Kon.

12. Interestingly enough, both Suvorova and Zuyev, the organisers of the Rainbow Without Borders Festival, had been very critical of the plans to hold a pride parade, but considered their own festival fundamentally different since it was to be held indoors and could in no way be considered a provocation.

13. According to Russian Orthodox tradition women cover their heads when entering a church. This custom also has roots that are not strictly religious. In peasant Russia rules of propriety demanded that married women cover their hair. The headscarf is thus not only a religious sign but also a sign of traditional Russian womanhood.

14. In the country there are influential political powers that are using homophobia as an instrument in the fight against a democratic transformation and for the return to totalitarianism. Even if you exclude the possibility of excesses and violent actions from the direction of the fascist organisations, which only need a reason for violence, the inescapable reaction to gay pride is that those suffering from homophobia will increase in number. Igor Kon http://gay.ru/ english/communty/news/2005-10-29.htm

15. Communicated in interviews with Debryanskaya and Alekseev in 2005.

16. This of course depends on whether you have dressed up for the parade or not. It is difficult to become a simple bystander if the only thing you are wearing is a thong and a feather boa.

17. This to the great disappointment of some of the protesters. On several occasions I overheard people grumbling 'where the fuck are the fucking *pederasty*?'

18. To willingly expose yourself to state structures is still perceived as a way to set yourself up for trouble and is a deeply counter-intuitive tactic in everyday life in Russia today.

## LITERATURE

Binnie, J. and B. Skeggs. 'Cosmopolitan Knowledge and the Production and Consumption of Sexualized Space: Manchester Gay Village', *Sociological Review* 52, no. 1 (2004): 39–61.

Bell, D. and G. Valentine. 'Introduction: Orientations', in *Mapping Desire, Geographies of Sexualities*, eds D. Bell and G. Valentine, London, 1995, 1–27.

Brickell, C. 'Heroes and Invaders: Gay and Lesbian Pride Parades and the Public/ Private Distinction in New Zealand Media Accounts', *Gender, Place and Culture* 7, no. 2 (2000): 163–78.

Butler, R., T. Skelton and G. Valentine. 'Coming out and Outcomes: Negotiating Lesbian and Gay Identities with and in the Family', *Environment and Planning D: Society and Space* 21 (2003): 479–99.

Casey, M. 'De-dyking Queer Space(s): Heterosexual Female Visibility in Gay and Lesbian Spaces', *Sexualities* 7 no. 4 (2004): 446–61.

Cieri, M. 'Between Being and Looking Queer Tourism Promotion and Lesbian Social Space in Greater Philadelphia', *ACME: An International E-Journal for Critical Geographers* 2, no. 2 (2003): 147–66.

Corteen, K. 'Lesbian Safety Talk: Problematizing Definitions and Experiences of Violence, Sexuality and Space', *Sexualities* 5, no. 3 (2002): 259–80.

Courtois, S. et al. 'Kommunismens svarta bok', *Bokförlaget* DN, 1997.

Eves, A. 'Queer Theory, Butch/Femme Identities and Lesbian Space', *Sexualities* 7, no. 4 (2004): 480–96.

Giorgi, G. 'Madrid en Tránsito, Travelers, Visibility, and Gay Identity', *GLQ* 8, no. 1–2 (2002): 57–79.

Hirsch, F. *Empire of Nations: Ethnographic Knowledge and the Making of the Soviet Union*, Ithaca, NY, 2005.

Holliday, R. 'The Comfort of Identity', *Sexualities* 2, no. 4 (1999): 475–91.

Johnston, L. *Queering Tourism: Paradoxical Performances at Gay Pride Parades*, London, 2005.

Johnston, L. and G. Valentine. 'Wherever I Lay my Girlfriend is my home', in *Mapping Desire Geographies of Sexualities*, eds D. Bell and G. Valentine, London, 1995, 99–114.

Kon, I. *The Sexual Revolution in Russia*, New York, 1995.

Puar, J. K., D. Rushbrook and L. Schein, 'Guest Editorial', *Environment and Planning D: Society and Space* 21 (2003): 383–7.

Kharkhordin, O. *The Collective and the Individual in Russia*, Berkeley, 1999.

Lane, C. *The Rites of Rulers: Ritual in Industrial Society: The Soviet Case*, Cambridge, 1981.

Lazerson, B. H. 'In and Out of the Closet', *American Speech* 54, no. 4 (1981): 274–7.

Markwell, K. 'Mardi Gras Tourism and Construction of Sidney as an International Gay and Lesbian City', *GLQ: A Journal of Lesbian and Gay Studies* 8, no. 1–2 (2002): 81–99.

Oswald, I. and V. Voronkov, 'The 'Public-Private' Sphere in Soviet and Post-Soviet Society Perception and Dynamics of 'Public' and 'Private' in Contemporary Russia', *European Societies* 6, no. 1 (2004): 97–117.

Pesmen, D. *Russia and Soul: An Exploration*, Ithaca, NY, 2000.

Pilkington, H. *Russia's Youth and It's Culture: A Nation's Constructors and Constructed*, London, New York, 1994.

Podmore, J. A. 'Lesbians in the Crowd: Gender, Sexuality and Visibility Along Montréal's Boul. St-Laurent', *Gender, Place and Culture* 8, no. 4 (2001): 333–5.

Richardson, D. and M. Hazel. 'Deserving victims? Sexual Status and the Social Construction of Violence', *Sociological Review* 47, no. 2 (1999): 308–31.

Rushbrook, D. 'Cities, Queer Space and the Cosmopolitan Tourist', *GLQ* 8, no. 1–2 (2002): 183–206.

Seidman, S., C. Meeks, and F.Traschen. 'Beyond the Closet? The Changing Social Meaning of Homosexuality in the United States', *Sexualitites* 2, no. 1 (1999): 9–34.

Tuller, D. *Cracks in the Iron Closet. Travels in Gay and Lesbian Russia*, Boston, 1996.

Turner, V. *The Ritual Process – Structure and Anti-Structure*, New York, 1995 [1965].

Waitt, G. 'The Sydney 2002 Gay Games and Querying Australian National Space', *Environment and Planning D: Society and Space* 23 (2005): 435–52.

Yourchak, S. *Everything Was Forever, Until It Was No More: The Last Soviet Generation*, Princeton, NJ, 2006.

## ❖ 8 ❖

# Begging as Economic Practice

## *Urban Niches in Central St. Petersburg*

### MARIA SCATTONE

### Introduction

One of St. Petersburg's most conspicuous features today is the intensity of
commercial activity in public spaces. Small shops and kiosks are ubiquitous, and open round the clock. New shopping centres replete with Swiss
bakeries and French perfume shops have opened downtown. Megamalls
are being built on the outskirts. Huge advertising boards invite the public
to an 'unforgettable' trade fair, to the 'mall of their dreams', to a 'top class'
jeweller or furrier, or to a restaurant or casino. At entrances to metro stations and in street underpasses, every few metres pedestrians pass flyer
distributors, street vendors, street musicians and beggars, who are part of
the inventory of the city's outdoors. Begging was criminalised until 1991,
but in the last fifteen years it has become part of the repertoire of informal
economic practices characterising the public space of most post-Soviet cities. This chapter will examine the practice of begging by asking how beggars have appropriated urban space. Which urban spaces are allocated to
them and what influence do the different sorts of urban spaces have on
begging practices?

I will do this with reference to empirical data collected during field research between 1998 and 2002 in the milieu of Petersburg's beggars. The
research method used was participant observation. Participant observation is a research process where the social researcher observes a culture or
subculture directly and immediately, discussing what he or she sees with
bearers of the culture. I made the acquaintance of a number of individuals
who lived by begging, and accompanied them at their place of work and on
their paths through the city. I wrote up all my observations and the conversations I had with them in my field research diary, which I use as a source
for this chapter.

My first informant was Anna Alexandrovna, who, as she termed it, 'worked' in a pedestrian underpass crossing under Nevsky Prospekt, Petersburg's famous high street (see fig. 8.1). She stood there with her little dog Krosha (Crumb) and asked passers-by for money. My second case study was a group of church beggars. They also provided me with a glimpse of their world. They collected alms on the steps of the Kazan Cathedral, one of Petersburg's main churches. These city spaces – the pedestrian underpass and the church steps – constitute two contrasting cases. The underpass is a part of public urban space where behavioural rules do not require any special knowledge. The main rule is that of 'civil inattention' (Goffman 1963). The underpass was built as a transit space, thus bereft of any reason to dally. It was so dimly lit when I conducted my field research that it was almost dark, and there were no benches on which one could sit. The street underpass was a 'non-place' in the sense of Marc Augé: It was constructed for a certain purpose – getting from one side of the road to the other, and entering the metro, and its use was sign-posted as 'Way to metro station ...' or 'Exit to the Passazh shopping centre' (Augé 1995). The church, on the other hand, is a place with highly specific rules for all who enter it. It is a place that 'is completed through the word, through the allusive exchange of a few passwords between speakers who are conniving in private complicity' (Augé 1995: 77). A place, according to Augé, is characterised by 'identity, relation and history'(Augé 1995: 77). The priests and beggars, tourists and pilgrims, church employees and church visitors all know their own position with respect to each other and to the church, and know how they are meant to behave. There is an institutionalised hierarchy respected by all and strictly obeyed.

But these are not the only features making these spaces useful for analysing begging practices in public space. These places are also multifunctional. The pedestrian underpass is no longer solely a space of transit but also a niche for street vendors, artists and beggars. The church is not only one of the most famous sights in Petersburg and one of the city's most beautiful architectural ensembles. It is not only a place of prayer for the faithful but also attracts many tourists and sightseers. Both the pedestrian underpass and the church play host to a large number of social practices that add meanings to these spaces. This juxtaposition of contrasting social practices at the same place is a result of the socio-economic and political transformation that took place in Russia over the course of the last two decades. New social institutions have emerged, relationships, hierarchies and communicative forms, that create new social practices and lend new or additional social meanings to specific places. Places take on a complex structure expanding the behavioural strategies they make available. The question in this context is how these two spaces, having such contrasting significance and structure, respectively influence practices of begging, or even inspire completely new practices.

I define begging here as a 'street-level economic activity'. I refer here to the concept of the British social researcher Hartley Dean and his colleagues, who regard the spreading or rather the re-emergence of begging in the West today as a result of the failure of state social policies. They regard begging as 'street-level economic activity' alongside prostitution, drug trade, street vendors, people selling newspapers for the homeless, etc. The spread of the street-level economy reflects fundamental changes taking place in the economy and with respect to the role of the welfare state (Dean 1999: 1). Since the flourishing of begging in the post-Soviet space is closely connected with the root-and-branch restructuring of the socio-political and economic order, I believe this concept is applicable to understanding the phenomenon of begging in today's Russia. Following Hartley and his colleagues, I employ the term 'street-level economic activity' to denote the broad spectrum of informal economic activities unfolding in public spaces not originally intended for economic activity: on streets and in squares, in underpasses leading from one metro station to another, in open areas surrounding metro and train stations, etc. In my chapter, I describe the informal, non-criminal sector of the street-level economy such as begging, selling, and performing, and omit the criminal sector such as drug dealing and prostitution.

## Nevsky Prospekt

Both places where I conducted field research are located on Nevsky Prospekt, or Nevsky, as the city's inhabitants call it for short. This street is one of the most striking and one of the oldest in the city. Both in Tsarist Russia as well as in the Soviet era and right up to the present, the most expensive and luxurious shops and restaurants, the most famous libraries and museums, and the most important churches have been located on Nevsky. This was where the most important city events took and take place – from public festivals to demonstrations. The street was and is a place where people go simply to stroll, to see others and be seen. A large amount of renovation work was performed in the run-up to the city's 300th anniversary in 2003, but the back-courts remained largely untouched. The surrounding streets were restored to former glory and some transformed into Western-style pedestrian zones. Only a few, however, became popular as urban spaces; others remained bereft of life. The Prospekt's façade now looks smart and modern after years of restoration work, scaffolding and dug-up pavements.

Currently the city centre – especially Nevsky Prospekt – is a place where rich and poor, past and present confront each other. Nevsky unites features of the former Soviet Leningrad with those of a Western European city. On one hand, the district is still home to many poor people living in *kommunalki*[1]. On the other hand, the city centre is gradually transforming into a new centre similar to that in Western cities, 'where employment and non-residential land use are concentrated, and where the distribution of all sorts of goods and services takes place' (Hamm und Neumann 1996: 248). Long-standing inhabitants of this area of town – mostly older generations who survive on a pension of 3000 rubles (less than €100 per month) – glance in the shop windows as they pass by. The 'poor' are excluded from the boom times on Nevsky and do their shopping instead at open air markets far from the centre or in cheap chain stores located on side streets. 'People who cannot afford the expensive boutiques and have neither time nor money for restaurants and entertainment, will only occasionally visit the city centre ... unless to beg for crumbs from the richly laden table' (Hamm and Neumann 1996: 248–49).

In the period of my field work, there were more beggars on Nevsky Prospect than there are today (2009). At that time they were arrayed every three hundred meters on alternating street sides. A large number of beggars gathered in the two pedestrian underpasses under the Prospekt: between the Gostinny Dvor and Passazh shopping centres, and between Gostinny Dvor and Mikhailovskaya street. Not only beggars but also other participants in street-level economy, such as street musicians and street vendors, also descend from the Prospekt to the underpasses. Above ground, on Nevsky, the scene of representative public life, such a concentration of street life would be conspicuous and attract the attention of the police. But underground they are 'out of sight, out of mind'. These underpasses provide a niche for society's margins, the poor and the subcultures. This is where a whole spectrum of alternative economies and lifestyles thickens into a second hidden level of Nevsky's public space. The beggars line up at intervals of two or three meters; the street vendors, usually old men and women, stand side by side selling a whole range of wares, like at a Russian village market. They sell home-made articles, such as oven cloths, embroidered handkerchiefs and knitted socks. Old women sell colourful hand-knitted tea-cosy hats and plastic bags with fashion emblems. The men sell craft work such as wooden mats for teapots and wooden spoons. From home-made marmalade to marinated cucumbers and even pets, the variety of small articles on sale is endless. Street musicians perform all sorts of different music: from the dawn chorus of a 'Babushka choir' singing Russian folk songs with gusto, to the afternoon song of the 'Red Indians' and then the evening's hippies with their glass beads, singing the Beatles.

These two levels can be interpreted differently. From the perspective of historical change from one social form to another, the appropriation of public space would seem to constitute a loosening of public order. In Soviet times, public space was strictly regimented and social phenomena that could have cast an unflattering light on the regime were excluded. In this context, socially weak groups and alternative cultures and lifestyles now have better access to public space. On the other hand, this opening of urban space took place in a time of dramatic social upheaval, and displays the increasing cleavage in society. The population of the underpasses exhibit their poverty openly, and do not experience their presence there as an expression of freedom but rather as a necessity to survive in the face of social deprivation. The concept of 'contested spaces' (Low and Lawrence-Zuñiga 2003: 18) would seem to match this situation. I will use this concept to provide a framework for answering the following questions: What form do social conflicts take in social/physical space? How is the space reorganised and structured? The 'downward' displacement of informal economic practices on Nevsky Prospekt to the pedestrian underpasses can be seen as an expression of 'contested spaces'. Since marginals cannot escape the realities of social control in the urban space, they descend to the underpasses to attract less attention from the police. I refer to such public enclaves of the poor in the middle of Petersburg's representative public space as spaces of compromise. The compromise is achieved between those involved in street-level economy and the city powers, by means of bribing policemen, as direct representatives of power structures, or through 'normed' and 'conventional' behaviour when selling, begging or playing music. In the following section I will describe specific examples of how such a space of compromise is organised by the participants and how they are organised by it.

## In the Pedestrian Underpass

In December 2006, I met Anna Alexandrovna, whom I had known since 1998, at the historical Gostinny Dvor shopping arcades on Sadovaya street. She stood beside her dog that was dressed up as a doll, and with a box for donations, just as she had when I first made her acquaintance when conducting field work. She had earned her and her family's daily bread in this way for over 15 years. Immediately on first seeing her, I realised she was a potential informant. I had been looking for informants among people collecting money on the streets for a few days. I had seen many people begging, but had lacked the courage to go up and talk to them. However, this woman looked more approachable, since she did not bear any marks of extreme poverty. She was a sprightly woman about sixty-five years old who looked like the many passers-by of the same age. Her clothes were typical of her generation: somewhat old-fashioned, but practical – a warm dark-coloured overcoat and a neat light-coloured fur hat. She wore lipstick. The only discrepancy in this picture of respectability was the white Pomeranian lap dog standing on its hind legs and sporting a knitted dress and a lace bonnet. A KLIM powdered milk can, of the sort imported to Russia as food aid at the start of the 1990s, stood before him. Passers-by threw coins into this receptacle.

I got to know her in the pedestrian underpass between Gostinny Dvor and Mikhailovskaya street. This underpass also serves as a lower level entry to the metro station Nevsky Prospekt. However, this entry was being renovated at this time and the underpass thus lost a lot of its significance. It was very empty, and Anna Alexandrovna was very conspicuous there with her dog. Her body language, posture and the distance she cultivated to others made it clear that she was attempting to construct her relationship to others as one of mutual equality. She did not hold out her hand, lower her eyes or stare into space, as other beggars often did. She stood straight and proud, quietly watching the passers-by. She never sat down during work. This was her way of controlling social distance, which in physical space corresponds to hierarchies such as 'up' and 'down'. Anna Alexandrovna did not put her collection tin in front of her, but in front of her dog, and thus

**Fig. 8.1:** Anna Alexandrovna wanted to present her dog Krosha as main protagonist. Photograph by the author, 1998.

indicated that it was not she, but the dog that was begging. She did not perform any actions. She only stood there, and smiled and nodded in response to contributions. Her appearance with the dressed-up dog could be regarded less as begging and more as a small street-circus performance. She staged herself in a way that tried to avoid the social stigmas connected with begging.

The following winter she worked in a different pedestrian underpass under Nevsky, the one communicating between the two shopping centres Gostinny Dvor and Passazh. This underpass was always busy with people. Here Anna Alexandrovna shared the space with other street musicians and beggars, who also worked there. To avoid competition and conflict, the people working the underpasses co-ordinated their daily routine with each other. Anna Alexandrovna arrived every day at 2 PM at her place, which she referred to as her 'rightful place', and stayed until around 5 PM. Krosha in all his finery jumped down from the shopping trolley he was transported on, and the shift began. It was routine shift work. 'Shift' is not meant metaphorically. Anna Alexandrovna regarded her performance as constituting a real job and called it 'work'. It was very important for her not to be regarded as a beggar. She drew a clear boundary between herself and the underpass's beggars, and pointed this out to me time after time. She only entertained 'friendly relations' with a certain 'Elena Ivanovna' (an elderly woman who sold home-made clay figures) and with the saxophonist 'who plays here now and again'. She underscored that she only had contact to people who actually worked there, i.e., with street vendors and musicians. She excluded beggars from her circle of communication. They angered her and she angered them: 'The beggars insult me when I stand near to them. They don't get anything at all, if I stand close to them.' Anna Alexandrovna wanted to portray herself as a street artist, and her performance was successful, in as much as passers-by, with whom I often talked briefly, out of politeness or respect referred to it as work.

Anna Alexandrovna was a pensioner who had worked as teacher. Her permanent place of residence was the region around Moscow (*Podmoskov'e*) where she lived from spring to winter. In winter she moved to her family in Petersburg. The whole family was employed in the street-level economy. Her son-in-law was a professional painter and exhibited his pictures in the open air for tourists. This segment of the informal street economy is officially recognised to the extent that it is allowed to take place in the city centre where the tourists flock. Such open-air exhibitions and galleries often occupy fenced-off areas and their organisers pay rent to the city authorities. In the professional world of artists, however, working on the street and selling paintings outside is regarded as humiliating. Anna Alexandrovna's daughter sketched portraits of passers-by for small sums. She was not a trained painter and her motto was 'the main thing is that the customer likes the portrait.' Even the youngest granddaughter played viola on the streets, but only in the summer when she visited her grandmother. In this way, the whole family was involved in different capacities in the hierarchic structure of the street economy. Only Anna Alexandrovna, however, generated a steady income. This meant she regarded herself as the family's only reliable source of income. The money she earned with her dog was not spent only on food. Anna Alexandrovna was the family's accountant. She divided up the family's money for fixed costs such as metro and sustenance during the day. She paid for extra tutoring for her granddaughter, who studied at a distinguished music school, or bought her a new concert dress.

Anna Alexandrovna put all her effort into helping her family get out of poverty. Day after day, she and her dog joined the other vendors and beggars in the underpass under Nevsky Prospect. She exposed herself to certain dangers in doing so. Working in the street-level economy entails exhibiting oneself and risking recognition from undesirable quarters. Being 'seen' means jeopardising and possibly irrevocably losing one's social status. I once witnessed how Anna Alexandrovna once stepped in front of her dog and turned to face the wall when she saw friends of the family approaching in the underpass. She was strictly opposed to her granddaughter playing as street musician in Petersburg: 'I don't allow Mila to work here! Why should she? This is where she lives. And this is where she goes to school. She knows people here. They might see her. Her teachers know that she sometimes plays on the Arbat. But here it's impossible.' The anonymity and the 'civil inattention' 'protecting' the individual in the world of the city only partially applies to people who work in the street-level economy. Some exhibit themselves deliberately and distance themselves from their social loss of status by saying, 'I've stopped caring.'

Working conditions in the underpass depend on a number of factors. This small informal street market emerged as an unwritten agreement between rich and poor, between strong and weak. Such unwritten agreements between participants in the street economy and, for instance, the police, the direct representatives of the city authorities, can be changed, reinterpreted or terminated at any time. The 'work permit' can depend on a number of factors: From the mood of the police patrol, from personnel changes in the police and sometimes from their readiness to take money from the vendors.[2] For instance, once two policemen on patrol passed by. One said to Anna Alexandrovna, pointing to the dog: 'It can't sit like that for three weeks on end! It'll catch a cold!' But the police were not always so engaging. Another day I saw how the 'grandmothers' hid their wares when the police arrived, to blend in with the pedestrians. Anna Alexandrovna's Pomeranian jumped in her shopping trolley, Anna Alexandrovna hid the collecting box and affected the air of an old woman simply waiting for someone. She only needed a few seconds to transform herself from someone asking for money on the street into an inconspicuous pedestrian.

In describing Anna Alexandrovna, I am not suggesting that all 'begging people' in the underpass present themselves as 'working artists'. I want to show how poor and marginalised people can assert individuality and character in the city centre. The inherent lack of character of a space of transit affords people the chance to recreate their identity. They are active subjects in the construction of their relations, but 'when individuals come together, they engender the social and organize places' (Augé 1995: 111). A place emerges where none existed previously. Such compromise spaces have no fixed borders, they are situational and mobile.

In the pedestrian underpass, begging is only one part of the broad spectrum of informal economic practices. Beggars are tolerated alongside the other participants in the street-level economy, but somewhat more niggardly. People who portray themselves as beggars utilise specific props and a specific body language: An outstretched hand, signs requesting help, etc. Nevertheless, their appearance is not allowed to exceed certain limits.

The compromise spaces I have described are gradually being eliminated by the city authorities. Previously exclusively used as transit spaces, they are now being formally leased to small vendors by the city authorities. They put up booths selling books, CDs and DVDs along the walls of the underpass previously used by street vendors and beggars. This means they occupy the beggars' space and commercialise a space that was hitherto officially non-commercial. The beggars are gradually disappearing from the pedestrian underpasses and indeed from the city centre, which is meant to become again a site for the urban flaneur. Beggars and street vendors are now on a hunt for new locations – in railway stations, shopping centres and markets.

## Kazan Cathedral

Nevertheless, some places for beggars do remain in the city centre. One such place is the steps of Orthodox churches. Many beggars include the churches in their daily or weekly schedule, so that church steps or porches can be regarded as part of the territory of the street-level economy. While beggars are only tolerated alongside other street economy actors in the underpasses, the churches expressly permit begging but exclude other informal economic activities such as street trading or street art.

Despite decades of official atheism, the tradition of begging for alms on church steps has survived. Begging on church steps is an institutionalised and systematic act performed at a specified place – the papert' (church steps or porch)[3]. Beggars and benefactors form a 'setting' for specific activities to be performed at specific times. 'A setting comprises a milieu with an ongoing system of activities, where the milieu and the activities are linked by rules as to what is appropriate and expected in the setting.... Settings are connected in varying and complex ways not only in space, ... but also in time' (Rapoport 1994: 461–62). Churchgoers almost automatically give alms to the waiting beggars after attending mass. The prime positions on the papert' seem to be those closest to the church entrance. Churchgoers, when exiting, usually start handing out alms to the first beggar, and by the time they reach the last one, they may well have nothing left except apologies. The beggars thank the donors in a traditional fashion: they cross themselves and utter a blessing such as 'Spasi vas Bog' (May God Be With You). With this degree of ritualisation, the beggars' self-presentation is often unimportant.[4] The beggars in front of the church include both women and men, both old, sick and disabled people as well as alcoholics and homeless children. In front of the church, they are not required to explain their personal situation or provide any official confirmation. The beggars do not use cardboard signs explaining their plight or display medical certificates, as beggars in 'profane' city spaces often do.

**Fig. 8.2:** In front of the entrance to Kazan Cathedral. Photograph by the author, 2006.

I made the acquaintance of some beggars at Kazan Cathedral on Nevsky Prospekt. This cathedral is one of Petersburg's most famous sights, and is reminiscent of St. Peter's in Rome. Until the revolution in 1917, it was one of Russia's most important Orthodox churches. At the start of the 1930s, the cathedral was closed, and in 1932 it was reopened as the Museum of the History of Religion and Atheism. Since 1991, church services have been conducted in the cathedral, although the building officially remained a state museum until 2001. The museum name has been removed from the entrance, and the altar and iconostasis re-installed. Along with the tourists came black-robed priests, churchgoers, pilgrims – and beggars. The multi-layered significance of this place as church, former museum and architectural jewel expands the usage options and times. Early in the morning, the faithful attend the church service. Tourists often come outside of church services. It could be said that beggars here have a well-paid full-time job. They come in the morning and stay until evening because the setting exercises an influence on them all. The worshippers throw a couple of rubles in the beggars' receptacles, and tourists often also make donations, even in foreign currencies.

On a cold March morning, I arrived at the church at half past nine and saw two women sitting on a bench[5] of the small, dimly lit vestibule of the church. One of the women was obviously an alcoholic, who was unwashed and smelt of urine and looked sick. Although Zinaida was only forty-nine, with her shrivelled face and toothless mouth she looked as if she was in her seventies. She wore a thin green raincoat that did not suit the cold weather at all. The church vestibule where she begged was unheated. On her head she wore a dirty green scarf with red flowers embroidered with golden threads from which the grey and untidy hair sprouted. The second woman – Valentina – was her polar opposite – a small, plump old woman with a clean and tranquil face. She was always dressed neatly and warmly. In her blue *vatnik*[6], which was tied round with a large woollen shawl, and with her black headscarf, she looked dapper in comparison to Zinaida.

Both women were homeless and completely dependent on the alms that they collected at the church. Zinaida who used to work as a teacher trainer, lost her apartment in the mid-1990s. This was the time when a free property market emerged in Russia. In the transitional period, the free market in conjunction with a legal vacuum meant that many people fell victim to property sharks. People signed documents to sell their apartments, without ever receiving the promised money. When Zinaida lost her apartment, she dropped to the lowest rank of society as a homeless person. In order to survive, she collected glass bottles, worked a whole summer for a farmer who, according to her account, exploited her and other homeless people almost as slaves, and she collected wild berries in the forests which she sold in the city, until one day another homeless person brought her to the Kazan Cathedral. Valentina's story remained unknown to me. At the start she did not trust me and refused to talk to me. Zinaida told me that Valentina had been defrauded of her apartment by relatives.

Zinaida called herself and Valentina the only 'genuine beggars' and claimed that the other beggars – during the period of my fieldwork there were nine regulars – were fraudsters (*moshenniki*), i.e., they were not homeless, received a pension, state benefits and had families who could support them, but still went to the cathedral to beg. I doubt, however, that Zinaida was seriously outraged about her colleagues' dishonesty. She was more intent on reducing competition, and cloaked this desire in moral categories by dismissing the other beggars' right to enjoy the protection of church and church steps. The beggars' main problem at Kazan Cathedral was that so many people laid claim to such a small space. Their 'working conditions' were difficult because up to nine people bunched together in this small space and they all avidly kept track of who had got how much. My informant said it was not possible to expel her competitors physically. This motivated her to invent an imaginary category for her colleagues on the church steps by calling them 'pretend beggars' who had no right to enjoy the church's protection.

Some begging practices were more successful than those of others. On the church steps, the place of begging, it is allowed to draw attention to oneself and make oneself heard. It is not customary to keep quiet as it is elsewhere. It is legitimate to be loud and to beg insistently. There were a couple of beggars whom Zinaida and Valentina particularly did not like – a blind man and the woman who accompanied him. They came to the cathedral in the afternoon, after having collected alms in other locations. They took up position directly beside the doors and addressed the church visitors loudly and incessantly. 'Alms for a blind man! Alms for a blind man!' They attracted so much attention, that my informants were unable to compete with them. This aggrieved Zinaida and Valentina so much that they often simply left. At any other place, this type of begging might be interpreted as 'aggressive begging'.

Once, Zinaida was not content to simply imagine the expulsion of fraudsters from the church steps. One day she was more drunk than usual and decided to show the churchgoers the 'true face' of another beggar, i.e., to unmask the fraud going on. She went to one of the beggars, called 'Khromaya Maria' (Lame Maria), and tried to tear off her headscarf. She wanted to show everyone that under her scarf Maria's hair was permed. This led to both elderly women fighting, rolling on the ground and tearing each others' hair out. The police then prohibited Zinaida from begging on the church steps. The next few days she hung around near the church, until a priest requested the police to allow her to return. She was allowed to return because begging was her only chance to earn money to survive. This showed the church to be a hierarchical structure where permission to beg is co-ordinated between a number of different instances.

When Valentina told me this story, she found that Zinaida's behaviour had been completely out of place – and this again demonstrated the multifaceted nature of the place. 'What will people think? This is a church! A museum! And she lies around drunk!' Zinaida's 'indecent' appearance and behaviour could discredit the place in all its aspects, both secular and religious.

The papert' of the Kazan Cathedral constitutes a legitimate niche for begging in the very heart of the city. It is an established part of the street-level economy and the public order. Nevertheless, the beggars are in a marginal zone between the church's interior and the world outside. The economic space here is also divided up into formal and informal sectors. The beggars are only permitted to beg for alms on the papert'. This is the legitimate place for informal economic activities. It is regarded as an infringement of the rules if the beggars approach churchgoers inside the church. The church's interior belongs to the formal sector of the church economy where icons, candles and religious texts, among other things, are sold. The church's staff collect donations for the church or for charitable purposes. Despite their marginal position, the papert' contains great economic opportunities for beggars. Zinaida and Valentina never told me what they spend the money on that they collect at the church or have saved. Both rent rooms. Once Zinaida invited me home. She and her partner Alexander, the man who first brought her to Kazan Cathedral, rented two tiny rooms in a house that was already earmarked for demolition, and paid rent on a daily basis. Begging in front of the church allowed them to get by on a day-to-day basis, but not to make any longer term plans. In 2001 I met Zinaida, who told me she intended to buy a small house in a village somewhere. She spoke of great quantities of money that she collected at the church and saved. I found myself unable to believe this story. The beggars tell incredible and contradictory stories. Like Thomas, who conducted field work among young homeless people in Berlin's Zoo Station (Bahnhof Zoo) and also heard a number of detailed, but questionable stories, I regard such stories as a rhetorical means of staging one's own person. Plans and intentions seem only to succeed in narrative self-dramatisations. My informant wanted to portray herself as a person who still had a chance in life. Some months later I learnt that Zinaida had died on the streets. I do not know anything about Valentina's fate. In her case as well I heard contradictory remarks and rumours. A church employee said she had seen Valentina among a group of Russian tourists in Italy.

# Conclusion

In this chapter, I used the example of two urban spaces – the pedestrian underpass under Nevsky Prospekt and the papert' (church steps) of the Kazan Cathedral to describe how 'begging people' shape their practices in accordance with the spaces they occupy. I described begging as a street-level economic activity.

In the pedestrian underpass, which I interpreted as a non-place, a small market has developed encompassing different sectors of the street economy. The police cast an eye over them, but this space in the centre of town, in the centre of the official political public space, constitutes a space of compromise. Compromise spaces function not only as economic niches for poor people but also as places for other social phenomena such as alternative social subcultures or street commerce. Along with other participants in the street-level economy and street art, beggars actively contribute to shaping new meanings and functions for these respective places. This non-place gives beggars the chance of self-expression. They employ numerous props to portray their activity as a sort of work or art. With the emergence of the market, the non-place undergoes a transformation. New social relations, hierarchies and rules pertaining to urban space emerge. We can observe the permanent process to which Augé refers. 'In the concrete reality of today's world, places and spaces, places and non-spaces intertwine and tangle together.... Places and non-places are opposed (or attracted) like the words and notions that enable us to describe them' (Augé 1995: 107).

I regard the space of the Orthodox Church, or, more accurately, the space of the papert', as a legitimate place of begging. Alms giving is an institutionalised, traditional act. The papert' assigns only one role – that of beggar. Such spaces could be termed 'institutional spaces' in contrast to compromise spaces, where individuals shape their role themselves. In the church, people should act as passive, humble and poor objects of charity, but in the role of beggars they enjoy more behavioural options than anywhere else. They can assert themselves as beggars.

The social role of beggars presupposes that the people filling the role always occupy marginal positions in public space. Beggars activate social space through the way they position themselves in physical space. The paradox of beggars is that they use their marginal position to add an economic dimension to public space. Their peculiar economic position creates a hierarchy in marginal spaces, where they find lucrative or less lucrative niches. They compete for the best positions in the marginal spaces and thereby add a new dimension to urban space.

*From the German by Graham Stack.*

## NOTES

1. *Kommunalka* is the everyday name for the Soviet-era phenomenon of communal life. It refers to people lacking any kinship ties who share an apartment. In the Soviet context, this form of living together developed into a specific cultural phenomenon with special rules of communication. See: C. Gdaniec, *Kommunalka und Penthouse. Transformation von Stadt und Stadtgesellschaft im postsowjetischen Moskau*, Münster, 2005; K. Gerasimova, 'Public Spaces in the Communal Apartment', in *Public Spheres in Soviet-type Societies*, eds G. T. Ritterspon, M. Rolf and J. C. Behrends, Berlin, 2003, 165–93.
2. My interview partner regretted that the Petersburg police (Russian: *militsiya*) did not take bribes. She said that in Moscow she used to pay five rubles a day. And that was good, because it allowed her 'to work without being disturbed'.
3. The word papert' denotes church steps or church porch. In architecture, papert' is a raised platform in front of the church door.
4. Once I was given alms, simply because I was talking to beggars and sitting next to them on a bench at the Kazan Cathedral. My outward appearance contrasted greatly to theirs. Nevertheless, a visitor automatically gave me money on leaving the church.
5. The Cathedral's janitor erected this bench specifically for the beggars. He would often borrow a couple of rubles from them 'for a beer' and they asked him to make some benches for them.
6. *Vatnik* is a quilted, padded jacket. It is worn by the inmates of Russian jails and also by roadworkers in cold weather.

## REFERENCES

Augé, M. *Non-Places. Introduction to an Anthropology of Supermodernity*, London, New York, 1995.

Dean, H. 'Introduction', in *Begging Questions. Street Level Economic Activity and Social Policy Failure*, ed H. Dean, Bristol, 1999, 1–11.

Girtler, R. *Methoden der Feldforschung*, Wien, Köln, Weimar, 2001.

Goffman, E. *Behavior in Public Places*, New York, 1963.

Hamm, B. and I. Neumann. *Siedlungs, Umwelt –und Planungssoziologie*, Opladen, 1996.

Low, S. M. and D. Lawrence-Zúñiga. 2003 'Locating Culture', in *The Anthropology of Space and Place. Locating Culture*, eds S. M. Low and D. Lawrence-Zúñiga, Oxford, 2003, 1–47.

Rapoport, A. 'Spatial organization and the built environment', in *Companion Encyclopedia of Anthropology. Humanity, Culture and Social Life*, London and New York, 1994, 460–502.

Thomas, S. *Berliner Szenetreffpunkt Bahnhof Zoo. Alltag junger Menschen auf der Straße*, Wiesbaden, 2005, 50–53.

# ⚛ CONTRIBUTORS ⚛

**Ulia Andreeva,** PhD in Psychology, Ulyanovsk State University, Russia, is vice-chair in Advertising at Ulyanovsk State University and Senior Researcher at the Scientific Research Centre Region (http://www.regioncentre.ru/). Her research interests focus on social and personal psychology and youth studies.

**Svetlana Boltovskaya,** MA in Social and Cultural Anthropology and Slavonic Studies, Albert-Ludwigs-University Freiburg, Germany, is currently completing her PhD thesis in Anthropology on the theme 'Educational Migrants from Sub-Saharan Africa in Moscow and St. Petersburg'. She is also working as a journalist at the independent radio station "Dreyeckland" (http://www.rdl.de) and is an elected member of the Immigrant Council in Freiburg.

**Olga Brednikova,** MA in Sociology, European University at St. Petersburg, is a Research Fellow at the Centre for Independent Social Research, St. Petersburg, Russia, where she has participated in or led numerous research projects (http://www.cisr.ru/about.en.html). She is currently completing her PhD thesis on the theme 'State Borders and the Processes of Re (De-) territorialisation'. Her research interests and publications focus on migration and nation-state borders, women migrants, new reproductive technology and qualitative methodology.

**Megan Dixon,** PhD in Urban and Cultural Geography at the University of Oregon, USA (http://geography.uoregon.edu/). She also has a PhD in Slavic Languages and Literature from the University of Wisconsin-Madison. Her research interests focus on social mixing in urban spaces, landscape change and socio-spatial patterns in post-Soviet Russia. Her research on the Chinese presence in European Russia has been funded by the US National Science Foundation, the US Society of Woman Geographers, and the Tokyo Foundation. She is currently an instructor at The College of Idaho, USA.

**Cordula Gdaniec,** PhD in European Ethnology, Humboldt University Berlin, Germany, MA Human Geography, University of Leeds, UK, is currently an independent researcher and teacher based in Berlin. Her research interests focus on representations in and of the city, consumption cultures, cultural economy of the city, and art and the city, with a special focus on Russia and Eastern Europe (http://www.urbanxposure.org).

**Irina Kosterina**, MA in Cultural Studies, Ulyanovsk State University, Russia, is currently completing her PhD thesis in Sociology of Culture. She is a lecturer and Research Fellow at the Scientific Research Centre Region (http://www.regioncentre.ru/) at Ulyanovsk State University. Her research interests focus on the sociology of youth, gender studies, masculinities and youth cultures. Currently she is also coordinating the Gender Democracy programme at the Moscow office of the Heinrich Böll Foundation.

**Larisa Kosygina**, PhD in Sociology, Novosibirsk State University of Economics and Management, Russia, is currently completing her PhD thesis on the theme 'The Russian migration regime and migrants' experiences: The case of non-Russian nationals from former Soviet republics' at the Centre for Russian and East European Studies, University of Birmingham, UK (http://www.crees.bham.ac.uk/). She has been working as a lecturer at Novosibirsk State University of Economics and Management as well as pursuing various research projects.

**Katja Sarajeva**, BA in Social Anthropology, Stockholm University, Sweden, is currently completing her PhD thesis at the Dept. of Social Anthropology, Stockholm University (http://www.socant.su.se/). Her research interests focus on gay and lesbian studies, dance and visual anthropology.

**Maria Scattone**, MA in Social Anthropology, State University of St. Petersburg, Russia, is an associate member of the Centre for Independent Social Research, St. Petersburg, where she has worked on research teams for numerous projects. She is currently completing her PhD thesis at the Dept. of European Ethnology, Humboldt University Berlin, Germany (http://www.euroethno.hu-berlin.de/). Her research interests focus on poverty and marginal groups, on their economic and spatial practices.

**Olga Tkach**, PhD in Sociology, European University at St. Petersburg, Russia, is a Research Fellow at the Centre for Independent Social Research in St. Petersburg. Her research interests and publications focus on historical sociology, the sociology of everyday life, studies of migration, gender studies and qualitative methodology. She co-edited *Making Bodies, Persons and Families. Normalising Reproductive Technologies in Russia, Switzerland and Germany*, eds. W. de Jong and O. Tkach, Berlin, 2009.

# ⚜ INDEX ⚜